THE IMAGE OF THE ARCHITECT

THE IMAGE OF THE ARCHITECT

Andrew Saint

Yale University Press
New Haven and London
1983

For Ellen
A lapsed but lovable architect

Designed by Caroline Williamson and set in Monophoto Baskerville.

Printed in Great Britain by BAS Printers Limited, Over Wallop, Hampshire.

Library of Congress Cataloging in Publication Data

Saint, Andrew.
    The image of the architect.

    Includes bibliographical references and index.
    1. Architecture—Vocational guidance.   2. Architectural practice.   I. Title.
NA1995.S27 1983   720'.68   82-48909
    ISBN 0-300-03013-4

CONTENTS

LIST OF ILLUSTRATIONS

INTRODUCTION

We are at present in the midst of a widespread transformation of 'architectural history', with its emphasis on aesthetics, design and authorship, into 'building history', which has broader social and economic preoccupations. This book attempts to contribute to the debate on this transition.

The realities of architectural practice, past and present, have often been hidden from those entering upon an architectural career; and the conflict between those realities and the ideals of creativity fostered in the schools is, I believe, something which students of architecture should appreciate, ponder and debate. The idea of this book originated in a course which Robin Middleton invited me to give at the Architectural Association in London in 1978. With his usual liberality, he allowed me any historical topic of my choosing. After some thought, I came to the conclusion that a traditional course on the history of architecture might have charm and enjoy brief popularity among the students, but would have less lasting value. I decided instead to try to discuss the history of the architectural profession over the last two hundred years. My method was to choose special periods of time, episodes, careers or books which I felt contained within them the seeds of the problems which architects had faced or continue to face.

Feeling that the subject was an important one, I decided to make a book out of it, in order to explore the arguments and issues in more depth. The audience which I would particularly like to reach remains the same—thoughtful architects and architectural students. I hope it may also appeal to readers interested in the wider questions of architecture and of history.

In the course of research and writing, the material has changed and expanded out of all recognition. Through the generosity of the British Council, I was fortunate enough to spend the best part of a year in the United States in 1978–9. Much of that time was spent in widening the scope of this book, especially in deepening my acquaintance with the history of the American architectural profession, which with the British profession occupies the lion's share of the following pages. In writing, I have attempted to bring the separate subjects and episodes into better relation with each other. Readers who, for instance, wish to get some coherent impression of the way that the architectural profession evolved in Britain and the United States, can do so by reading Chapters 3, 4 and 7 consecutively. By contrast, Chapters 1 and 5 deal with examples of what might be called the lighter 'literature of architecture' and can, I hope, be read together for entertainment as well as for instruction. But the essays remain to some degree partial, separate and unsystematic 'contributions to the history of a profession'. Since I have made no attempt to be exhaustive, there are obvious and glaring gaps. I have, for example, steered clear of any discussion of architectural education, believing that the nature of architectural teaching at any given time proceeds from the state of the profession, rather than the other way round. There is also no chapter on the nineteenth-century architectural profession in continental Europe, where so much of the ideology and organization of the modern architect evolved.

Many of the chapters are critical pieces of a type not current in recent architectural history, especially in the United States; to some readers they may seem to concentrate upon the shortcomings of the architectural profession and even to cast doubts upon its integrity. To prevent misunderstanding and to absolve myself of the charge of scepticism, arrogance or hostility towards architects in general or any architect in particular, I should perhaps quote some celebrated lines from Marx's *Preface to A Contribution to the Critique of Political Economy* which have had some influence on the standpoint from which this book has been written: 'It is not the consciousness of men that determines their being, but on the contrary it is their social being that determines their consciousness . . . Just as one does not judge an individual by what he thinks about himself, so one cannot judge . . . an epoch of transformation by its consciousness, but, on the contrary, this consciousness must be explained from the contradictions of material life . . .'. The Marxian view of history, in other words, seemed to offer an intelligent framework within which to think about the history of the architectural profession. But the book is too discursive to deserve to be labelled Marxist, whether by admirers or by detractors of that great Victorian thinker.

*   *   *

In pressing this book towards completion, I have had great kindness and help from both individuals and institutions. For the opportunity afforded by the British Council of going to the United States as a Bicentennial Fellow and spending months of general research without rendering full account of my activities, I am especially grateful. My employers, the Greater London Council, kindly released me during this period and took me back on my return, and the staff of the *Survey of London* and the Historic Buildings Division there were good enough to fall in willingly with these arrangements. Later, the Twenty-Seven Foundation made a generous grant towards the cost of gathering the odd assemblage of pictures reproduced in this book. The Architectural Association started things by allowing me to experiment with their students; the Bartlett School of Architecture ended them by allowing me space to finish my writing off there. Readers will soon see that this is a very 'bookish' production, which would have been impossible to write without access to some excellent architectural libraries. Among these the RIBA Library, with its wonderful bibliographical facilities, stands first and foremost; while in the United States I profited also from being given a free run of the Rhode Island School of Design Library and the Brown University Library.

Among individuals, I should first single out Jules Lubbock, who read the whole text, urged me towards greater coherence and suggested many improvements. Likewise,

Robert Thorne read most of the manuscript and made many helpful suggestions. John Bancroft read the penultimate chapter with great care and attention from the point of view of the practising architect. At Yale University Press, John Nicoll has been consistently encouraging and patient in face of tardy progress and persuaded me to make a major revision which was certainly necessary. Mosette Broderick, Dene Leopold and Dick Chafee have helped with American material and saved me from various pitfalls. Mrs Elizabeth Fish, the daughter of H. B. Creswell, has been specially helpful with Chapter 5. Among others who have assisted I am grateful to John Greenacombe, Walter Kilham junior, Richard Haslam, Peter Howell, Lynne Walker and Clive Wainwright. For particular help with photographs I am pleased to thank Dr Kurt Junghanns, Paul R. Baker, Alan Crawford, Godfrey New, and the RIBA Library and Drawings Collection; other suppliers of photographs are gratefully acknowledged in the list of illustrations. Whilst I have made every effort to contact owners of copyright, it has not been possible to do so in every case.

Finally, Ellen Leopold first directed my thoughts along the path they travel in this book, and has consistently given me wise and forbearing advice on this, as on many other subjects.

CHAPTER ONE

The Architect as Hero and Genius

Architectural fictions, or at least those that speak of the conditions of the modern architect's practice, are few and far between. Some novelists who trade in the stresses of middle-class life have found it handy to have an architect as their hero, since architecture carries with it the image of an established life-style, yet suggests a temperament more open to emotional novelty and breadth of sympathy than do the conventional career patterns of lawyer, doctor, accountant or businessman.[1] Rarely however do the architect's professional aspirations and trials come to the surface; more rarely still have they found a ready audience with the public.

Ayn Rand's *The Fountainhead* is the exception. First published in New York in 1943, it has sold over five million copies and still continues in print; a film version, scripted by the author and starring Gary Cooper and Patricia Neal, was released in 1949.[2] It is a lengthy book, philosophical in ambition and rhetorical in style. But its runaway success is not hard to understand, for it deals in heroism: more precisely, with the single-minded life-struggle of a young architect of genius against the architectural and social 'system' of the New York élite in the 1920s and 1930s. We see him pit his personality and powers of design against the strangling conventions of the day—academic classicism, the conservatism of big business, the power of the press—until after any number of hard knocks he emerges spotless, his integrity and will unblemished. The novel, in short, is an unsparing celebration of the architect as hero and genius, and could hardly have sold as it has done without some popular willingness to confirm and indulge Ayn Rand's ideal of the architectural profession.

The main characters of *The Fountainhead* are five. Four are united in upholding a view to which Ayn Rand devoted her life work, namely that altruism and selflessness are hypocritical, humiliating and ultimately self-destructive, while real human virtue resides in individualism and in the proper appreciation and development of the ego, regardless of immediate consequences to others.

Howard Roark, the novel's hero, is naturally the paradigm of this philosophy.

---

1. Howard Roark (Gary Cooper) stands upright and confident before the pure lines of a skyscraper to be built to his design. The pseudo-Corbusian open base and the Miesian matchbox superstructure of this project are reminders that the film of *The Fountainhead*, from which this is taken, appeared in 1949, though the novel was firmly set in inter-war New York.

Trained at the celebrated 'Stanton Institute of Technology', he has already by the start of the book (1922) become an advocate of modernism; indeed for refusing to run in the Beaux-Arts groove of contemporary American architecture he is summarily expelled from the school. His colleague Peter Keating, drawn throughout the book as the obverse of Roark, is meanwhile loaded down with honours. Refusing a scholarship to Paris, Keating settles down with a smart New York architect and designer of confectionery-laden skyscrapers, Guy Francon, and through a series of wiles and manoeuvres rapidly climbs the greasy pole to full partnership. Roark instead acquires an unglamorous position with the bitter and disillusioned Henry Cameron, an architect of genius whose career, after early triumphs, has been wrecked by public indifference.

Soon Roark proceeds to a modest but wholly independent practice of his own, characterized by utter disregard of criticism or compromise. Naturally he encounters a succession of dramatic setbacks and outstanding victories. Among the former are two court appearances. On the first occasion he is sued over a 'Temple' to Humanity, for which at the suggestion of critic Ellsworth Toohey a wealthy client has given him *carte blanche*. The millionaire, returning from a long trip abroad, loathes what he finds: a great, grey horizontal monument in no known style, centred upon the idealized statue of a naked woman. A *cause célèbre* follows and Roark, not for the first time, is nearly driven from practice.

Roark's second trial, several hundred pages later, marks the book's climax. Long jaded by success and worn out by systematic sacrifices of his artistic integrity, Keating comes to Roark beseeching his help in designing Cortlandt Homes, a low-cost federal housing project, since restrictions and economies present him with problems that he cannot solve. As he has done before, Roark agrees to aid Keating – not out of kindness but for the sake of architecture. But foreseeing bureaucratic complexities and frustrations, he stipulates as a condition that no detail shall be altered from the design he makes. Despite Keating's best efforts, Roark's superbly economic and practical conception is inevitably botched by other hands. In retaliation he blows up the buildings when they are complete and ready for occupation, but allows himself to be apprehended standing by the plunger.

Roark's speech in self-defence at his second trial is the novel's peroration. He contrasts the creator with the 'secondhander' and condemns all forms of collectivism of which Cortlandt Homes is a type.

> No work is ever done collectively, by a majority decision. Every creative job is achieved under the guidance of a single individual thought. An architect requires a great many men to erect his building. But he does not ask them to vote on his design. They work together by free agreement and each is free in his proper function. An architect uses steel, glass, concrete, produced by others. But the materials remain just so much steel, glass and concrete until he touches them. What he does with them is his individual product and his individual property. This is the only pattern for proper co-operation among men.
>
> The first right on earth is the right of the ego . . .[3]

Persuaded by Roark's eloquence and courage, the jury moves to acquit our hero who,

2. Howard Roark (Gary Cooper) rejects the desecrating Doric portico and false stone facing proposed as a palliative for his modernism by an influential board of directors. He naturally loses the job. From *The Fountainhead*.

3. Ellsworth Toohey (Robert Douglas) tempts the tycoon Gail Wynand (Raymond Massey) with something very like the Bordman Building, with its 'twenty-two floors and a Gothic spire'. Behind, a side elevation of the tower, or perhaps an alternative stylistic treatment; behind again, a panorama of possibilities, with what looks like the RCA Building to the left. From the film of *The Fountainhead*.

at the end of the story, is discovered erecting the Wynand Building, New York's and the world's tallest skyscraper. As with much else in the book, there is no pretence of verisimilitude about this acquittal. It serves instead as a symbolic gesture on the part of the author in order to confirm the eventual victory of individualism.

The three other chief personalities of *The Fountainhead* are also driven by egoism, if sometimes of a weaker and more faltering type than that espoused by Howard Roark. Of these, the critic Ellsworth Toohey is the most complicated character. Machiavellian or rather Mephistophelean in his operations, Toohey is a manipulator masquerading as a social reformer. He operates through the social élite and has acquired the power of dispensing large architectural jobs to whom and as he pleases. Through his newspaper column, *One Small Voice*, in the New York *Banner*, Toohey at first denounces modern architecture as a faddish indulgence and upholds traditional styles; later he is converted to international modernism, as against the new American tradition of architecture deriving from Henry Cameron. Toohey preaches that architects should be servants of society, not its leaders. He chooses to boost the work of Peter Keating and sedulously ignores that of Howard Roark until the Temple débâcle occurs, when in court he condemns Roark's attitudes and architecture as an insult to humanity. In reality he is not deceived. To Keating, broken after the destruction of Cortlandt Homes, Toohey reveals that his purpose in preaching altruism is to control the souls of weaklings such as him. And in a speech as lengthy and impassioned as Roark's final self-defence, he acknowledges collectivism as the source of all evil, a poison bred in Europe which, whether under its German Nazi or Russian Bolshevik guise, is now infecting even America, golden land of individualism.

Similarly motivated but less eloquent is Gail Wynand, the brutal newspaper tycoon who runs the *Banner*. He is a figure perhaps based on William Randolph Hearst, with touches out of Joseph Patterson, founder of the New York *Daily News*.[4] Wynand feeds poison and placebos to the public through the yellow press, encourages mediocrity, and uses and breaks true talent on a grander scale than Toohey. Yet the soul of this *Uebermensch* remains pure, his taste unsullied. He alone comes to recognize the genius of Howard Roark, employs him when society has repudiated him, and upholds his cause over the dynamiting of Cortlandt Homes, even though this stance comes close to destroying his press empire. Even Wynand, however, has at the last to submit to the pressure of society and bow before the higher integrity of Roark.

Finally, *The Fountainhead* has a heroine: Dominique Francon, icy intellectual beauty and daughter of architect Guy Francon. Though introduced chiefly to provide a love-interest, Dominique offers greater depth of character than the men. Emotionally violent and self-destructive, she approximates, Ayn Rand once confessed, to 'myself in a bad mood'.[5] Dominique, like Toohey, writes a column for the *Banner* called *Your House*, which she converts from vapid hints on interior decoration into a polemical forum for architectural criticism. Dispassionately, she involves herself with Keating. But retiring one summer to her father's country estate she for the first time encounters Roark, who has been forced temporarily out of architecture and is working incognito in the Francon family quarry nearby. Stirred by the silent virility of this unknown workman, she asks him to repair a fireplace in her bedroom where he proceeds, in an act condoned by the author, to rape her. Later, when Roark has re-established his

4. Howard Roark, on the point of closing his office for lack of work and recognition, contemplates another unbuilt masterpiece without false sentimentality, before committing it to the flames. From *The Fountainhead*.

practice, they meet again and their aggressive sexual relationship recommences. She writes violent denunciations of his buildings in her column and then presents herself for his use at nights; words hardly pass between them. Over the business of the Temple, she testifies ambiguously in court and then in self-punishment cuts herself off from Roark and marries Keating. After divorce, she contracts a surprisingly happy union with Wynand, based on their mutual egoism. But because of Wynand's support for Roark she cannot forget or avoid him. Having acted as his accomplice in the destruction of Cortlandt Homes, she marries him in the happy ending.

What relevance has this improbable tale to the realities of architecture or the architectural profession?

*   *   *

Ayn Rand's repeated statements, the stilted speeches allotted to the protagonists, and the bearing of her subsequent work, notably the monumental and much-acclaimed novel *Atlas Shrugged*, show that she chose architecture only as a battleground. Here she could parade before a broad audience the opposing forces of individualism and collectivism or, as she has since put it, she could defend capitalism against the assaults of the Judaeo-Christian ethic.[6]

Yet the choice of ground is telling and apposite. In the two short centuries since architecture has become a well-defined profession of its own, its identity has afforded endless controversy. Is it an art practised by and for the sake of individuals, or a commercial enterprise geared to the needs of the market and the generation of profit, or a communal undertaking dedicated to the service of society? Most enquirers rash enough to essay a serious answer to these questions have ended in admitting compromise—each or some of these ideas have a place in the best architecture. Architecture, if it is to go beyond the drawing board, is divided from the disciplines with which it is most often compared, the other 'arts', by the need to compromise, by the insistent demands of what is real and what is practical. Before these obligations all transcendent principles of 'truth' in architecture will always fall down. A compromise of ideals lies at the heart of the matter, to the chagrin of the pure in soul.

Nevertheless down the centuries one strain of architectural ideology has been heard much louder than others. That is the strain of artistic individualism, which ascribes both merit in particular buildings and general progress in architecture according to a personal conception, usually of style, embodied in buildings and developed from architect to architect over the course of history. According to this ancient theory (first applied to art by the disciples of Plato), a building is significant or insignificant in so far as it incorporates an idea or ideas conceived by its individual designer, and the history of architecture becomes the web of such significant ideas, worked out in special buildings.

This understanding of architecture, long prevalent, shows only limited signs of receding today. It has been and goes on being popular because it appeals to the interests and intellectual traditions of the two most articulate groups who concern themselves with the matter—architects and critics of architecture. An individualized view of architecture attracts architects because it enables them to see themselves not only as top dogs in the construction process but also as creators and romantics, heirs to a tradition that offers them a chance of fame and remembrance from posterity. Critics, if not architects *manqués*, are characteristically scholars brought up in the study of the humanities, and so bring to architecture from the other arts a tradition of honouring artistic expression as pre-eminent. They make of architecture, in fact, an analogue with poetry or music, and ascribe exclusive or primary virtue to its original creator.

From this standpoint *The Fountainhead* is an illuminating curiosity. For by applying this theory of creative individualism to architecture in its extremest, least compromised form, implications which rarely surface in the accepted canons of architectural criticism are unearthed. Ayn Rand scarcely concerns herself, as do critics, with the purely artistic trappings of architecture or speaks of Roark's buildings as works of art. Architecture, though in special danger from the muddles and compromises of 'altruism', to her merely epitomizes a hundred pursuits in which the individual will has in this century been increasingly frustrated by collectivism, to the detriment of society. The battle for individualism in her mind is a political one.

*　　*　　*

Like her novels, Ayn Rand's life has been an extreme statement of the individualistic point of view.[7] Born in St Petersburg in 1905, she witnessed the Russian Revolution only to be disenchanted when her father's business was confiscated. After a spell in the Crimea under White Army rule, she returned to study history and philosophy at the University of Petrograd, but left Russia for the United States in 1925. She soon made for Hollywood, where after hanging about in hope for some time she encountered Cecil B. De Mille and acquired some junior writing jobs on screenplays. Though her first assault on collectivism was a novel, *We The Living* (1936), she did not confine herself to literature. In the presidential campaign of 1940 she worked against Roosevelt who, she believed, was luring America into collectivism. *The Fountainhead*, begun in about 1937 but not published till 1943, brought fame. Following its success Ayn Rand became prominent in the post-war ideological battles of Hollywood. Asserting that communists were corrupting film scripts with their propaganda she joined the Motion Picture Alliance for the Preservation of American Ideals, and in 1947 she testified on communist infiltration in the film industry before the House Committee on Un-American Activities. From the 1950s she propagandized from New York and, following *Atlas Shrugged*, the completest fictional statement of her philosophy, she organized a movement called 'Objectivism'. In due course splits occurred within this movement, and though Ayn Rand continued to uphold her ideals as forcefully as ever, her influence had much diminished by the time of her death in March 1982.

The intellectual ancestry of Ayn Rand's views is not obscure. Her admired authors—the great Greek tragedians and thinkers, Nietzsche, Herbert Spencer—were common philosophical heroes in the last decades of the nineteenth century and the early years of this one. Among novelists she was drawn young to Victor Hugo, in whom she found events and men portrayed not as they were but as they ought to be. The characters of *The Fountainhead*, the author herself has said in the foreword to a recent reprinting, derive from just such a theory of Aristotelian idealism.

So to architecture Ayn Rand brought an entrenched personal philosophy, untrammelled by any deep knowledge of the workings or history of the profession. Besides the sordid commercial reality of contemporary practice she consciously set a highly romanticized ideal of the architect. But it would be wrong to ascribe either picture wholly to the fertility of her imagination. She undertook much research for *The Fountainhead*. A note at the front of the book salutes 'the great profession of architecture and its heroes' but also acknowledges their technical assistance. Ayn Rand read widely about architecture, familiarized herself with the professional issues, incidents and personalities of the day, and even when she began work on the book worked briefly as a typist in the office of the gifted Ely Jacques Kahn. A leading practitioner in New York between the wars, Kahn (1884–1972) was known along with Raymond Hood and Ralph Walker as one of the 'three little Napoleons of architecture', each having to his credit a set of the smart, stacked-up skyscrapers that proliferated in the boom years of

5. Ely Jacques Kahn, one of the ablest designers of the stacked-up skyscrapers of 1920s New York City, and briefly the employer of Ayn Rand. A cartoon of 1931 by Tony Sarg.

6. Project for a skyscraper by E. J. Kahn of Buchman and Kahn, *c.* 1928. A fantasy in the authentic spirit of Howard Roark.

the 1920s.[8] Kahn was a moderate modernist; his background was in the Beaux Arts, but he specialized in ornamental *jazz-moderne* detailing of some sophistication. Genial and past his best work when Ayn Rand came to him, Kahn would have been well stocked with anecdotes about architectural personalities and politics of the period.

As a result *The Fountainhead* at times approximates to a *roman à clef* about the American architectural profession of the 1920s and 1930s. From the start the architectural detail is knowingly, even wittily managed. The first building presented to the reader is the Stanton Institute of Technology, where Roark and Keating receive their training. Crowning a hill site over the town 'like a medieval fortress, with a Gothic cathedral grafted to its belly',[9] it sounds for all the world like a study from the fanciful pen of Bertram Goodhue. Soon we reach New York (whose skyscrapers Ayn Rand had admired before ever she saw them) and encounter Guy Francon's Frink National Bank Building, a squeezed-up 'wedding cake' of the type popular early in the century: 'for a long time it had been considered the best building of the city, because no other structure could boast a single Classical item which it did not possess'.[10] Other tall towers drift by in the narrative, like the Bordman Building, 'twenty-two floors and a Gothic spire,'[11] or Peter Keating's *chef d'oeuvre*, the Cosmo-Slotnick Building, a movie-mogul's office block won in competition after secret help from Roark: 'a Renaissance palace made of rubber and stretched to the height of forty stories'.[12]

Praise is reserved for the works of Howard Roark, whose career naturally begins with houses. The Heller House, his first commission, conforms to the tenets of horizontality and openness advocated by architects of what is now termed the Prairie School. A little later comes the Whitford Sanborn House,

of plain field stone, with great windows and many terraces. [It] stood in the gardens over the river, as spacious as the spread of water, as open as the gardens, and one had to follow its lines attentively to find the exact steps by which it was tied to the sweep of the gardens, so gradual was the rise of the terraces, the approach to and the full reality of the walls.[13]

(This business ends in tears as Mrs Sanborn alters details, a practice which is of course anathema to Roark.) In his New York works—the Enright Apartment House, the Aquitania Hotel, the Cord Building, the Stoddard Temple—Roark sweeps away traditional elaboration, even refusing one corporate commission for which the style has been prescribed. But being no fan of the inhumane European *Modernismus* to which Ellsworth Toohey turns in the 1930s, he lavishes a modicum of refreshing detail on his every masterpiece.

E. J. Kahn himself seems to have been spared in *The Fountainhead*, but in the person and practice of Guy Francon there are some shrewd hits at contemporary methods in New York, where specialization within the large private architectural firm had

7. The idiosyncratic house designed in 1930 by Raymond Hood at Ossining, N.Y., for Captain Joseph Patterson, eccentric proprietor of the *Daily News* and partial model for Gail Wynand in *The Fountainhead*. Patterson insisted that the house could be camouflaged in case of war.

perhaps gone further than anywhere else in the world. When Peter Keating first comes
to work for him, the meticulously dressed Francon is in partnership for the sake of
contacts with a 'withered aristocrat', Lucius Heyer. He spends most of his time in
convivial pursuits in order to secure jobs, which are routinely designed by the head
draughtsman, Claude Stengel. Keating soon worms his way into Francon's confidence,
learns his methods, displaces Stengel and then Heyer, and so arrives at full partnership
after winning the Cosmo-Slotnick competition.

Though Francon may stand for no precise architect on the New York scene, his
Beaux-Arts background, wealth, snobbery, perhaps even his cynicism, place him close
to the flamboyant Whitney Warren (of Grand Central Station), Cass Gilbert (of the
Woolworth Building) or James Gamble Rogers (of Yale University).[14] The lesser
architects whom Ayn Rand satirizes are recognizably representative characters. A
chorus of these pygmies appears at regular points along the plot, each inveighing
against Roark and his works and putting forward his own petty viewpoint. There is
Gordon L. Prescott, ever ready with some obscure transcendental *bon mot* to push his
stripped half-modern, half-classic vocabulary of form. Prescott becomes the leading
force of the architectural establishment, runs a clique started by Toohey called the
'Council of American Builders', and intervenes along with the crude, blaspheming Gus
Webb to alter the Cortlandt Homes project. A second figure, Ralston Holcombe, is
president of the Architects' Guild of America, Ayn Rand's equivalent of the American
Institute of Architects. His name appears on the *Social Register*, but like many a real-life
American architect he has married business money. Holcombe specializes in
memorials and state capitols, and avers that the Renaissance style is universally
appropriate. Yet another architect, Jon Erik Snyte, is an eclectic and like Francon
relies on his staff, different members of whom are dubbed 'Classic', 'Gothic',
'Renaissance' and 'Miscellaneous'. Roark, who serves under Snyte for a short term,
becomes Mr 'Modernistic'.[15]

Some architectural events in the narrative are lifted straight from life. One minor
incident that probably came from E. J. Kahn is the Arts Ball at which Keating,
Francon, Holcombe, Prescott and the rest dress up in cardboard models of their own
most famous buildings.

Peter Keating was the star of the evening. He looked wonderful as the Cosmo-
Slotnick Building. An exact papier-mâché replica of his famous structure covered
him from head to knees; one could not see his face, but his bright eyes peered from
behind the windows of the top floor, and the crowning pyramid of the roof rose
over his head; the colonnade hit him somewhere about the diaphragm, and he
wagged a finger through the portals of the great entrance door. His legs were free
to move with his usual elegance, in faultless dress trousers and patent-leather
pumps.

Guy Francon was very impressive as the Frink National Bank Building,
although the structure looked a little squatter than in the original, in order to
allow for Francon's stomach; the Hadrian torch over his head had a real electric
bulb lit by a miniature battery. Ralston Holcombe was magnificent as a state
capitol, and Gordon L. Prescott was very masculine as a grain elevator. Eugene

8. The Beaux-Arts Ball at the Hotel Astor, New York, 23 January 1931. Scene from the pageant 'The Skyline of New York' with architects modelling their own creations. From left to right: A. Stewart Walker as the Fuller Building (Walker and Gillette, 1929); Leonard Schultze as the Waldorf Astoria (Schultze and Weaver, 1930–1); Ely Jacques Kahn as the Squibb Building (Buchman and Kahn, 1929–30); William Van Alen as the Chrysler Building (1928–30); Ralph Walker as No. 1 Wall Street (Vorhees, Gmelin and Walker, 1931–2); D. Everett Waid, unrecognizable as the Metropolitan Life North Building (H. W. Corbett and D. E. Waid, 1931–3); Joseph H. Freedlander as the Museum of the City of New York (1931–2). This was the undoubted model for a similar scene in *The Fountainhead*.

Pettingill waddled about on his skinny, ancient legs, small and bent, an imposing Park Avenue hotel, with horn-rimmed spectacles peering from under the majestic tower. Two wits engaged in a duel, butting each other in the belly with famous spires, great landmarks of the city that greet the ships approaching from across the ocean. Everybody had lots of fun.[16]

This idea comes directly from a real Beaux-Arts Ball of 1931 at which Kahn and others had masqueraded in just such a manner.[17] The 'March of the Centuries Exposition', held in 'a western city' in 1936, is another parallel, derived from the Chicago World's Fair of 1933. In *The Fountainhead* Roark declines to join the seven other architects chosen on the grounds that 'one can't collaborate on one's own job';[18] his offer to do the whole thing is refused, so Keating, Prescott, Holcombe and assorted incompetents are left with the task, and the show naturally flops. A similar sequence of events had occurred before the 1933 fair, when Raymond Hood, Harvey Wiley Corbett and others in charge were rebuffed by a single, overweening architect who suggested his own alternative—Frank Lloyd Wright.[19]

*   *   *

Perhaps because Wright's personality and philosophy lie so close to the heart of *The Fountainhead*, Ayn Rand has chosen to deny any direct connection between them. Nevertheless facts speak for themselves. By the late 1930s Wright had recovered from his two long decades of disaster and comparative oblivion. During the years that the book was taking shape he was constantly appearing in print. *An Autobiography*, packed with suggestive incidents, appeared in 1932; it was followed by a stream of lectures, visionary plans and pronouncements and, in 1941, by the first readily available selection of his writings.[20] After the novel's success Ayn Rand continued to be preoccupied with Frank Lloyd Wright. Soon after buying a house near Hollywood designed by the one-time Wright admirer Richard Neutra, she met the great man himself, who predictably admired *The Fountainhead*, pronouncing: 'Your thesis is the great one. Especially at this time.'[21] In 1945 she visited Wright at Taliesin East and he designed a three-storey house for her, but nothing ever came of it. Perhaps their temperaments were uncomfortably close.

The book's own evidence is, if anything, more compelling. Henry Cameron, Roark's single architectural mentor, clearly represents Wright's hero and *Liebermeister* Louis Sullivan. Like Sullivan in his later years, Cameron is irascible, obsessive, egotistic, poverty-stricken, on the bottle, but unbowed by failure. Sullivan's decline was attributed exclusively by Wright, forgetting the depression of the 1890s, to his master's awkward personality and to the surge of classicism following the Chicago World's Fair of 1893; so is Cameron's. Cameron, like Sullivan, is visited by Roark–Wright shortly before his death. Ten years later comes grudging recognition of Cameron's stature and partial recantation from Ellsworth Toohey who writes, as might an avant-garde critic of the 1930s have done speaking of Sullivan:

> Premonitory echoes of the new grandeur can be found in some of his work. But like all pioneers he was still bound by the inherited prejudices of the past, by the sentimentality of the middle class from which he came. He succumbed to the superstition of beauty and ornament, even though the ornament was of his own devising . . .[22]

Perhaps closest of all, the tense interview at which Roark seeks employment with Cameron and the fierce, comradely spirit with which they work together mirror Wright's romantic portrayal of his early days with Sullivan in *An Autobiography*.

Howard Roark's houses, it has been said, are long, low and closely bound to the soil,

---

9. Frank Lloyd Wright drinks in the drama of the prairie, *c.* 1936.

resembling the Prairie homes of Wright and his school, or perhaps more precisely the 'Usonian' houses to which Wright had progressed by the 1930s. The 'Monadnock Valley scheme', a private colony deep in the countryside designed by Roark for the supposedly neglected middle classes, has more than a whiff of Wright's Broadacre City; it consists of naturally-set houses fashioned from plain slabs of stone and sheets of glass like a hundred mini-variations of Falling Water, Wright's much publicized rural retreat for the millionaire Edgar Kaufmann. The Unity Temple in Oak Park, to which Wright devoted several pages of his autobiography, seems to have supplied some of the philosophy behind Roark's Stoddard Temple. Another project perhaps 'ghosted' from the master's *oeuvre* is Roark's second job, a simple roadside filling station which becomes a concrete-and-glass 'study in circles';[23] Wright had sketched such a station, albeit more angular, in 1928. More significant than any particularities of resemblance are the materials and feeling of Roark's work: modern and functional, but natural and humane. One almost searches for the telltale epithet 'organic' to confirm that the values of Howard Roark's architecture are fully Wrightian.

By the late 1930s Frank Lloyd Wright's eccentric personal philosophy, no less than his buildings, had been loudly promulgated before the American public. The similarities with Ayn Rand's views need hardly be laboured. There are matters on which they would have differed violently: contemporary Russia, for instance, which Wright at the time was disposed to admire. But on the substantive questions of personal belief, in their admiration for individualism and enterprise as the pristine American virtues, in their contempt for the state, for mass culture, and for compromise and in their propensity for hero-worship, architect and author are in uncanny agreement. The origins of their thinking, too, lie in the same authors. It was *Notre Dame de Paris* by Hugo, Ayn Rand's favourite novelist, that first posed to the youthful Wright the question of architectural style.[24] A little later, reading Goethe's *Wilhelm Meister*, 'action and more action was his urge'.[25] Later again under Sullivan's guidance, Wright took home the Synthetic Philosophy of Herbert Spencer, whose ideas first kindled ambition in Gail Wynand, Roark's *alter ego* in *The Fountainhead*.[26] The intellectual foundations of Roark and Wright are at all essential points one and the same. Together they point to the primacy of a single, much admired stereotype: the creative individual manifesting his will in action.

*   *   *

The career of Frank Lloyd Wright sums up an era of individualism in the history of architecture. Yet it runs in plain contradiction to the chief forces acting upon the profession during his lifetime, which saw the role of the individualistic designer being gradually whittled away. Partnerships, with interlocking tasks each crucial for the completion of a job, proliferated; the public sector of architectural practice grew; and the complexity and technicality of all stages of building increased vastly, entailing participation not just from engineers but from financial and legal experts to whom 'creativity' could barely be ascribed.

In Chicago, Wright was exceptionally well placed to witness the early development of some of these patterns, and he was shrewd enough to grasp their implications. As an assistant under Adler and Sullivan, one of the world's first great commercial partnerships, and as a participant in several of the classic early high-rise office buildings, he understood the turbulent, challenging conditions of contemporary practice. Yet gradually he turned his back on them—not out of any political or social motive but for the sake of art. It is illuminating to chart the progress of this flight from reality in Wright's thought, if only to suggest how the ideal of architectural heroism may against all the odds come to captivate the mind of a practising architect.

Wright's strong natural individualism was reinforced at a critical point in his development by the rhapsodical ideas of Louis Sullivan. Hardly less important, however, was the economic downturn of the years during which he began his independent career, for this channelled his talents at first almost exclusively into domestic architecture. In this sphere, where artistic licence still had a comparatively free rein, he was able to nurture theories which later he propounded in an extremer, more pugnacious form.

Wright's earliest invocations of the individual ideal were intelligently qualified. After all, he knew something of Ruskin's and Morris's notion of collaborative virtue in artistic undertakings, he stood to the fore in Chicago's burgeoning arts-and-crafts movement, and he had seen more than most young architects of his age of the need for co-operation on large jobs. In his first well-known lecture, an address of 1900 on 'The Architect', he confessed that the professional position as it then existed in Chicago deeply troubled him. Distinguishing the true professional from the businessman as one whose concern should be with quality rather than profit, Wright lamented architecture's decline from ancient ideals to the status of a 'commodity'. But though he defined the true architect in terms of art, he was at this stage far from conceding *carte blanche* to architectural individualism.

> Another feature of his [the architect's] plight is that not wholly respecting himself, (how can he?) he is apt to be a hypersensitive individual, and like other unfortunates who depend upon prominence of personality to get in the way of the 'choosers' he is interested in pretty much everything as long as he counts one and at that No. 1; none of his bloom or lustre is to be rubbed off by contact. So, concerted effort in matters touching the welfare of his profession, is rare among him . . .
>
> There are intelligent architects who argue that only the selfish few give value to art, the high lights only give value to the pattern of the fabric; but I believe it is because of warp and woof, undertone and motive, that he has any value as a 'high light', and that that type of individualism is one of the superstitions he must shed before he really comes to his own.[27]

Fourteen years after this speech Wright published his second article *In the Cause of Architecture*, a personal utterance in self-defence and repudiation of alleged imitators. In the intervening years he had become internationally famous, then notorious, and a certain paranoia—rarely absent subsequently—had begun to infect his statements. He had also matured an architectural philosophy, notably in the preface to his *Ausgeführte Bauten und Entwürfe* of 1910. Here he claimed that America could never acquire a worthy architecture until it laid hold of its natural traditions, which were vital for 'organic' development. Casting about for a tradition on which to build, he found it (following Sullivan) in the American ideal of democratic individualism, particularly as manifested in the business communities of the west and mid-west—in other words of course, Wright's own clients. This, his German-speaking admirers read, was the spirit that informed his buildings.[28]

Now, *In the Cause of Architecture II* held up 'individuality undefiled' as Wright's watchword before the home public. It got stronger and more strident as years went by. But in the context of the 1914 article some of the snags were already painfully evident. Since he denied that an individual's style could ever be worthily imitated, Wright felt obliged to arrogate to himself all credit for the 'new school' of architecture and to minimize the contributions of friends and helpers. How far this is from the truth, recent scholars like H. Allen Brooks have shown.[29] Possibly Wright himself did not yet wholly believe it, but insisted on such repudiation merely to maintain his ideal. More honestly, he admitted that he could not see how a school could develop from his ideas, although he ardently hoped for one growing from the spirit, not the letter, of his achievement.

> There are enough types and forms in my work to characterize the work of an architect, but certainly not enough to characterize an architecture. Nothing to my mind could be worse imposition than to have some individual, even temporarily, deliberately fix the outward forms of his concept of beauty upon the future of a free people or even of a growing city. A tentative, advantageous forecast of probable future utilitarian development goes far enough in this direction. Any individual willing to undertake more would thereby only prove his unfitness for the task, assuming the task possible or desirable. A socialist might shut out the sunlight from a free and developing people with his shadow, in this way. An artist is too true an individualist to suffer such an imposition, much less perpetrate it; his problems are quite other.[30]

In so many words Wright here prophesied his oft-remarked failure to produce a school.

Wright was never able to get himself off this hook. From here on his writings, always stirring, became more heavily sentimental. Though his fame spread and his buildings proliferated, his theories and example accorded less and less with the condition of the typical architect in modern America and became at times insultingly dictatorial. Confident in the correctness of his judgment to the last, Wright paid his individualism the final, ludicrous compliment of consistency in Broadacre City, his Utopian vision of the decentralized town of the future. Here the supreme authority of government rests with the architect, otherwise Wright himself.

Wright took pains to make sure that nobody should suppose that this was just a theoretical position. He took his power over his customers solemnly, brooking no misinterpretation of the matter. Excoriating the slavishness of past American architects in a lecture of 1931, he approved a sharply contrasting stance:

> A few held out, all honor to them. A tale told of Louis Sullivan has the lady come in and ask for a colonial house—'Madam' said he, 'you will take what we give you.'[31]

A joke, perhaps, and a common enough one in architectural circles; but the point

10. Frank Lloyd Wright being lionized outside the Architectural Association, London, 1950.

occurs too often in Wright to be misunderstood. Here for instance from *An Autobiography* (the passage was expunged from the later editions) is Wright's version of a conversation in which, according to Raymond Hood, Wright had said a client would '*have* to take' what he offered if it was the 'right thing'. The difference hardly seems to matter:

Ex [pert, i.e. Hood]: 'All right, then, how do you get your houses built? By telling the owner what he's got to do? Or do you hypnotize him?'

W: 'Yes, I hypnotize him. There is nothing so hypnotic as the truth. I show him the truth about the thing he wants to do as I have prepared myself to show it to him. And he will see it. If you know, yourself, what should be done and get a scheme founded on sensible fact, the client will see it and take it, I have found.'

Ex: 'But suppose he *wouldn't* take it?'
W: 'But, by God, Ray, he *would* take it.'[32]

A last word on Wright may be left with Raymond Hood's friend and sometime colleague, Ralph Walker. 'Wright does not have a social sense,' remarked Walker. 'His buildings are designed on the principle "Treat the client rough".'[33]

*   *   *

To understand the nature of the architectural individualist, it is worth turning back once more from Wright to Howard Roark. A first serious note in *The Fountainhead* is struck when Peter Keating asks Roark whether to spend four years at the Ecole des Beaux Arts, or go straight to Guy Francon's office. 'Never ask people,' replies Roark. 'Not about your work. Don't you know what you want?'[34] Complete self-containment, even selfishness, is Roark's ideal. Later, he refuses a client who wants a house modelled on a colonial design, arguing that that would be a monument 'Not to your own life or your own achievement. To other people. To their supremacy over you. You're not challenging that supremacy. You're immortalizing it.'[35] Later again, Roark confesses that building is a mixture of 'holy sacrament, Indian torture and sexual ecstasy'.[36] The purpose of this struggle? Originality. The wretched Keating is obliged to acknowledge his inadequacy and parasitism in such terms. 'In the whole of my life I haven't added a new door-knob to what men have done before me. I have taken that which was not mine and given nothing in return.'[37] Roark is indifferent to Keating's plight, for his view of human relations is simple: 'I don't think a man can hurt another, not in any important way. Neither hurt him nor help him.'[38]

No architect, not even Frank Lloyd Wright, aspired in reality to the individualism, almost solipsism, which motivates Howard Roark. Yet the greatest praise has traditionally been kept for architects who came closest in logic to his position, even when their temperamental and practical shortcomings have been made known. To reply that these are the architects who have always done the best work merely presupposes a standard for work measured by purely aesthetic ideals. One must look deeper into the history of architecture and set truth against the traditions of aesthetic criticism and propaganda in order to take a deeper hold on the subject.

CHAPTER TWO

Myth and the Mediaeval Architect

As I wandered about thy grave, noble Erwin, seeking the stone that should tell me 'In the year of Our Lord Thirteen Hundred and Eighteen and on the sixteenth day of the Kalends of February, died Master Erwin, Governor of the Fabric of the Minster of Strasbourg', neither could I find it, nor could any of thy countrymen show it me, that I might pour out my veneration upon the sacred spot; then was I dismayed to the depths of my being, and my heart, younger, warmer, rasher and purer than today, pledged to thy memory a monument of marble or of limestone, as might lie in my power if I should succeed to the peaceful enjoyment of my inheritance.

What need hast thou of a monument? Thou hast raised to thyself the most glorious one! And though the ants that scrabble around it trouble not about thy name, thou hast a fate like to the master-builder's who piled the mountainpeaks up into the clouds!

To few was it granted to conceive in their souls Babel-thoughts, complete, gigantic, wholly lovely down to the finest part, like the trees of God; to fewer still, to light upon thousands of willing hands, to dig out stony foundations, to conjure towering structures thereupon, and then in dying to say to their sons: 'I am with you always in the works of my spirit—carry on that which I have begun to its consummation, high in the clouds!'

What need hast thou of a monument? And from me! When the rabble utters sacred names, it is superstition and profanation. Before thy Colossus, those of trivial taste will ever shrink and swoon; while pure, true souls will know thee without an interpreter.

Therefore, excellent sire, before I again venture my mended bark upon the ocean, destined to death more likely than to fame or fortune; see—here—in this grove where the names of my beloved ones are for ever green, I carve thine upon a beech slender and soaring like thy tower. And I hang up by its four corners this kerchief filled with gifts, not unlike the cloth let down from the heavens to the holy apostle full of beasts clean and unclean; filled too with flowers, buds, leaves, dried grey grass and moss, and mushrooms shot up overnight; all that I coldly garnered as I strayed through these unmeaning tracts, botanizing to while away time; these I dedicate to thee, in honour of decay.[1]

So starts the most famous essay ever written upon architecture, Goethe's paean to Strasbourg Cathedral, *Von deutscher Baukunst*—'on German architecture', written in 1772. Goethe then was twenty-three and knew little about buildings save what he had got from books. He had travelled hardly at all from his native Frankfurt. He had studied at Leipzig, he had visited Dresden, but he had never seen a Gothic monument of the first order before reaching Strasbourg in 1770. Towering with its solitary spire above the little houses, the minster smote him with immediate awe, yet puzzled him.[2]

Still, being studious as well as impetuous, the young Goethe soon set about trying to understand the nature of Gothic. He consulted the Abbé Laugier's recent *Essay on Architecture*, the first rationalist classic of architectural criticism, which some of the cleverest passages in *Von deutscher Baukunst* aim to refute or qualify. He studied the façade of the cathedral and traced its detail with the intensity that dominated his every pursuit. Perhaps too he looked around the cathedral archives, saw something of the great cache of mediaeval architectural drawings that remain among Strasbourg's most priceless possessions, and learnt all he could of the history of the fabric. Probably he noted the inscription attached to one of the chapels stating that Master Erwin built it in 1316. What he for some reason failed to find (lamenting the fact in his essay) was Erwin's epitaph of 1318, well-recorded in Goethe's time, extant today but seemingly then hidden away. This describes Erwin as 'Gubernator Fabrice Argnt', or master of the fabric of Strasbourg Cathedral.[3]

That was enough to allow any eighteenth-century *savant* to claim the obscure Erwin von Steinbach as architect of the unfinished cathedral. But Goethe went further. In his thoughts Erwin became superhuman, unapproachable, inspired—in brief, a romantic genius. And Gothic (or 'German' architecture as the young nationalist liked to call it) became the rude, natural and 'creative' style which alone could give reins to a freedom and fancy such as Erwin's.

The source of these strange and wonderful ideas has long been known.[4] Germany of the 1760s and 1770s was a staging post in the history of ideas. Concepts, many of them deriving from attempts by English literary critics to fit the baffling phenomenon of Shakespeare to classic canons of taste, found a ready audience among German intellectuals. Early in the century the pious philosopher Shaftesbury had talked of God-given inspiration and natural genius as admirable moral qualities. But soon these terms acquired almost exclusively aesthetic application. From 1750 onwards, a flood of literary pamphlets appeared on the subject. Only one of these is still remembered, the *Conjectures on Original Composition* of the aged poet and clergyman Edward Young (1759). A resounding proclamation of the superiority of natural genius in letters, the essay was fast translated into German and fell into the hands of the juvenile Herder. Soon enough Herder nailed his colours to the mast; with his *Fragmente über die neuere deutsche Literatur* (1767) was born the epoch of *Sturm und Drang*. A few years older than Goethe, Herder was in Strasbourg with him and for a time influenced him deeply. But Goethe soon outgrew him. When *Von deutscher Baukunst*, perhaps at first a speech for a set occasion, was republished along with some literary essays in Herder's *Blätter von deutscher Art und Kunst*, Goethe obviously intended it as the architectural contribution to the new theory of artistic creation. Herder, more doubtful and evidently no enthusiast

11. The grave that Goethe missed. The tombstone of Master Erwin (d. 1318), *gubernator fabrice ecclie Argnt*, 'master of the fabric of the cathedral of Strasbourg'. A further fragmentary inscription now in the cathedral museum records work by Erwin on one of the chapels in 1316.

12. Strasbourg Cathedral from the south-west, rising out of a sea of ancient houses. This view, taken before the First World War, shows a scene little changed since the time of Goethe's sojourn there in 1770–2.

for Gothic cathedrals, appended a cold, classicizing essay by another author to redress the architectural balance.[5]

That this first and boldest attempt to apply the concept of genius to architecture met with scepticism from the start is hardly surprising. For in essentials Goethe's essay was wildly wrongheaded. A controversial theory of creativity could not be purloined from poetry and allotted to architecture without profounder adjustments than Goethe was willing to make. Indeed Young, despite his fervour for 'originality', expressly denied that architecture might be the object of spontaneous creation. 'A *Genius*', he said, 'differs from a *good Understanding*, as a Magician from a good Architect; *That* raises his structure by means invisible; *This* by the skilful use of common tools.'[6]

Young's train of thought is obvious. Perseverance, compromise and revision are essential for building, and inspiration counts for little without execution. All this makes architecture quite unlike the arts which preoccupied him. Goethe tried to sidestep this problem by invoking the Gothic; Erwin von Steinbach could be both magician and architect because he worked intuitively, individually and spontaneously, a method alien to pedantic classicism but essential to the savage naturalism of Gothic. Erwin alone conceived Strasbourg in his pure and primitive soul, argued Goethe, 'complete, gigantic, wholly lovely down to the finest part, like the trees of God'. His 'thousands of willing hands' were mere tools to carry out his bidding and complete the conception after his death.

Alas, the facts fail to match up to this thrilling idea. Strasbourg is the work not of Erwin von Steinbach alone but of many architects. Erwin came on the scene in 1284 after the nave was built. His chief work, say recent scholars, was to build the great rose window and revamp the west front to fit the proportions of the nave. With the tower and spire extravagantly admired by Goethe, Erwin had nothing to do; these are works of the fifteenth century by Ulrich von Ensingen and Johann Hültz.[7] More generally, the claim that Gothic design was spontaneous has long been discredited, and the parallel idea that it was individualistic needs at the very least delicate qualification.

To fault an intellect like Goethe's in rhapsodical flight would just be pedantic were his misconceptions not so instructive. They say less about the sensibilities of Erwin and his age than about the preoccupations of the *Sturm und Drang* epoch. In this, as in so much, *Von deutscher Baukunst* was a pioneer. From this time on, mediaeval architecture and the mediaeval architect became the proverbial mirror in which each culture caught an idealized glimpse of its own aspirations. A century ago this myth-making was at its zenith. One party concluded that the great abbeys and cathedrals were designed and built by pious, monkish craftsmen. Then came another school, insisting on the collective, anonymous nature of mediaeval building; no such thing as an architect existed, some said, since building was an exercise involving the instincts, hearts and hands of the whole community. Flawed and programmatic these two theories may be, but they are not devoid of truth. In their place we think we have a more balanced and informed view of mediaeval architects and their creation. We are probably right in the main; yet the scholarship which has given this to us has spawned a third myth, one which takes us back in full circle to Goethe. Mediaeval architects, one may sometimes read today, acted, thought and felt little differently from their present-day counterparts, and at their highest achieved just that pinnacle of lonely genius ascribed so long ago to Erwin von Steinbach.

Let us take a closer look in turn at each of these three myths.

*   *   *

Allan Cunningham was a minor Scots poet of the school that flourished in the wake of Burns.[8] On account of his modest background Cunningham was obliged (like the famous 'Ettrick Shepherd' James Hogg) to ply a trade, in his case masonry. Arriving in London in 1810, he worked as a mason now and again and was for a time in the employ of the rascally statuary J. G. Bubb. Cunningham perhaps knew Nash, for reputedly he was one of the few defenders of Nash's Buckingham Palace at the time of its bitterest unpopularity.[9] Soon however he became the faithful assistant and amanuensis of a more distinguished sculptor, Francis Chantrey.

This friendship was probably what impelled Cunningham to embark on his *Lives of the Most Eminent British Painters, Sculptors and Architects* (1829–33). Vivid and lucid if for the most part unoriginal in research or sentiment, these biographical sketches deserve to be better remembered. Those on sculpture and architecture, of which he had personal knowledge, are the most colourful. Of British architects he chose to notice eight, seven of them classicists: Jones, Wren, Vanbrugh, Gibbs, Kent, Burlington, and Chambers. Prefacing these stands a solitary Goth: William of Wykeham, Bishop of Winchester—and architect.

13. William of Wykeham, Bishop of
Winchester. An engraving by W. C.
Edwards made from a painting at
Winchester College for Allan
Cunningham's *Lives of the Most Eminent
British Painters, Sculptors and Architects*. It
shows the fourteenth-century architect–
prelate as he was envisaged in the early
nineteenth century.

Before Architecture became a defined science, and had schools, professors, and
disciples, a class of men existed in England, who, trained to other studies, and
living in the daily discharge of devout duties, planned and reared edifices with a
mathematical skill, a knowledge of effect, and a sense of elegance and usefulness
which regular practitioners have never surpassed. The architects to whom I allude,
were divines of the Roman Church . . .[10]

So starts Cunningham's essay on Wykeham. With the aid of royal favour, he tells his
reader, Wykeham designed and supervised many great buildings of the fourteenth
century: Windsor Castle, Queenborough Castle, St Martin-le-Grand in London, the
nave of Winchester Cathedral and of course his own foundations of Winchester College
and New College, Oxford. That Wykeham was a *bona fide* architect Cunningham never
pauses to doubt: 'Under whose auspices he attained his knowledge in architecture has
not been told, nor have we any notice of any of his designs before his twenty-third
year.'[11]

   In summing up Cunningham reveals a romantic (if Protestant) partisanship for
Gothic, calling Wykeham

one of a band of consummate architects whose genius adorned our land with those
cathedrals which are yet unrivalled for beauty and splendour in any country . . .
The architecture in which Wykeham excelled, and the religion which he so
ardently loved, were doomed to sink in this land together. Against the latter,
knowledge and reason and Scripture were directed; against the former, classic
caprice and the pedantry of learning preached a crusade; and where one only
merited success, both succeeded.[12]

This concept of the architect–priest was not a new one, nor confined to Wykeham. The general thesis with which Cunningham begins may be found embryonically in many a monk-loving antiquary of the eighteenth century. Reading in some mediaeval chronicle that a monk or priest 'built', 'erected' or 'made' something, such *literati* assumed that he really did the work himself. Sometimes indeed the texts truly suggested this interpretation. On the strength of an ambiguous reference the sub-prior Alan of Walsingham is still sometimes credited with designing the crossing tower of Ely Cathedral.[13]

But in Georgian England few scholars felt the need to put the thesis forward with precision, since nothing then seemed more natural than that a prosperous and influential divine should devise the plan of a building, at least in general outline. For his information on Wykeham, Cunningham depended much on a scrupulous biography of 1759 by Robert Lowth. That author too believed that Wykeham 'designed' buildings, noting for instance that the problems he overcame at Queenborough 'only served to display more evidently the skill and abilities of the Architect'. Yet without sense of contradiction Lowth could name William of Wynford (to whom the glory for Wykeham's building works is nowadays categorically ascribed) as 'Architect' for the bishop's recasting of the nave at Winchester Cathedral.[14] For Lowth there was no problem: Wykeham by virtue of his education would generally design, appoint, discriminate and pay, while Wynford would execute and supervise. Beset seventy years later by the ideal of romantic creativity on one side and by a new, aggressive professionalism among architects on the other, Cunningham betrays a novel anxiety about apportioning historic responsibility for design.

The same transition occurs in successive editions of another vital source for Cunningham, Horace Walpole's *Anecdotes of Painting*. This hotchpotch of a book, concocted by Walpole in 1762 from unfinished notes of the antiquary George Vertue, was never meant to be systematic. Yet the chapter on the 'State of Architecture to the End of the Reign of Henry VIII' proved a starting point for a serious enquiry into the history of Gothic architecture in Britain. Walpole himself cheerfully left open the question of how much monks did or did not design. The disappearance of the names of those who designed the great English churches while the names of the founders survive, he attributed to the policy of monkish historians 'to celebrate bigotry and pass over the arts'. But, drawing perhaps on his own experience as an architectural patron, he added:

> As all the other arts were confined to cloysters, so undoubtedly was architecture too; and when we read that such a bishop or such an abbot built such and such an edifice, I am persuaded that they often gave the plans as well as furnished the necessary funds; but as those chroniclers scarce ever specify when this was or was not the case, we must not at this distance of time pretend to conjecture what prelates were or were not capable of directing their own foundations.[15]

This chapter was revised for the 1828 edition of the *Anecdotes* by the scholarly James Dallaway, who qualified many of Walpole's lazy generalities on the strength of his own researches into mediaeval architects. Dallaway was among the first to try putting the relationship between clerical and secular architects in the middle ages into chronological perspective, pronouncing in 1806: 'In the earlier ages, at least, they [the artisans] are not to be considered as the inventors, but as the executors of the plans which were proposed to them by ecclesiasticks, the only men of science at that time. The freemasons were blessed by the pope, and were first encouraged in England by Henry III, where they were constantly employed till the close of Gothick architecture.'[16] So such ambiguities as Lowth's account of Wykeham and Wynford plainly troubled Dallaway and constrained him in the revised *Anecdotes* to document the evidence in favour of Wykeham as practical architect. He concluded: 'The munificent prelate's claim to the science and practice of architecture rests upon an undisputed tradition; and that plans or 'Vidimus' were drawn out by ecclesiastics for the master mason to work by, appears to be certain, from remaining MSS.'[17]

Dallaway's final conclusions on the matter of ecclesiastical and masonic architects appear in *A Series of Discourses upon Architecture in England* (1833), where after 'strict scrutiny' he reduces ecclesiastical designers to a handful, of whom Wykeham is one. But the topic was now passing beyond mere scholarship. As the Gothic Revival merged with the rekindling of religious enthusiasm, the concept of the monkish or priestly architect quickly attracted adherents. Such a book as Carlyle's *Past and Present* (1843), contrasting the order of the ancient cloister with the hurly burly of modern life, predisposed even Protestants to esteem the mediaeval clergy. Even so discriminating, austere and conservative a classicist as C. R. Cockerell came to trust unshakeably in William of Wykeham's skills as a designer. Wykeham's work at Winchester Cathedral he dubbed 'the epitome of his professional career as a consummate architect and engineer'; Wynford, by contrast, became in his judgment just the 'executive architect, wholly confined to the care and advancement of the new work'. Cockerell added of Wykeham: 'It is not too much to conclude that, as a professional architect, twice Lord High Chancellor, respected for his integrity and his taste by all the governments he lived under, himself a rich patron and adept practitioner, he advised upon if not designed every work of magnitude executed during his life.'[18] In his enthusiasm for the architect–bishop, Cockerell even sent his son to Winchester College and, on account of the Houses of Parliament, dubbed Charles Barry 'the modern Wykeham'.

If these were the reactions of Protestants, what might not be the enthusiasm of Catholic revivalists? Pugin, for once, seems oddly mute on this score. That he believed in monkish mediaeval architects the whimsical title page to *Contrasts* and frontispiece to the *True Principles* declare. He also extolled Wykeham and Elias of Dereham, the latter a favourite as 'rector' and possible designer of Pugin's beloved Salisbury Cathedral.[19] But Pugin did not trouble to dogmatize as to the methods and personalities of mediaeval architecture. That task was left to his one-time correspondent and ally in the Catholic cause, Charles, Comte de Montalembert.

Not quite deservedly, Montalembert has been the main butt for those modern scholars who have laboured to bury the legend of the monastic architect.[20] Half Scots and half emigré French aristocrat by parentage, he was born and brought up near London by a doting grandfather, in an aura of lonely, romantic precocity not unlike that which beset his close contemporary, the young Ruskin. Restored to France and the Catholic traditions of his father's family, Montalembert was drawn to the 'Christian' political idealism of Chateaubriand and his disciples, particularly Alexis-François

14. The mediaeval architect at work in his study: the frontispiece to the second, posthumous volume of the elder Pugin's *Examples of Gothic Architecture* (1836), drawn by the younger Pugin in 1834, engraved by Talbot Bury, and published by Thomas Walker and Benjamin Ferrey, all fervent mediaevalists in the Pugin circle. 'This composition represents an Artist of the fifteenth century,' explains Pugin, 'seated in his study, amidst his books and drawings, making an architectural design.' The garb of this 'Artist' is priestly, yet in the cupboard are displayed earlier books by the Pugins.

Rio.[21] In the early 1830s Rio was the first to popularize both in France and in England the idea, German in origin, that there could be a specifically Christian interpretation of art. Architecture did not much interest Rio, but it did concern his lifelong friend Montalembert. He was among those who influenced public opinion in the 1830s to end the maltreatment of the great French cathedrals and begin the official work of restoration.[22] At the same time he evolved the 'Christian' theory that those who built the cathedrals were not only priests but also especially holy.

This sentimental idea began to take shape in Montalembert's head when, in a mood of romantic solitude, he came in 1833 upon the shrine of St Elizabeth at Marburg Cathedral and there and then resolved to write her life.[23] Concerning architecture, his *Life of St Elizabeth* (1836) says merely that the design of the great cathedrals of the thirteenth century was 'traced out by the hands of men of the most sublime genius— men whose names have not been handed down to us, for their love towards God and their brethren in Christ, has left no room in their hearts for the love of earthly glory.'[24]

Montalembert intended to expand this theme in a similar life of St Bernard, which would parenthetically explore, in the detail suggested by Rio's work on painting, the links between piety and mediaeval architecture up to the end of the twelfth century. But his concentration was broken by a series of rash excursions into the turbulent arena of French politics. In 1847 he got so far as publishing a fragment of the project entitled *Art and the Monks*, perhaps written several years earlier. This article painted a picture of the early mediaeval architect as pious and priestly. It also contained the following passage, later to become notorious:

> When we say that the innumerable monastic churches scattered over the whole face of Europe were built by the monks, this assertion must be taken in its literal sense. They were, in fact, not only the architects but also the masons of their buildings; after having drawn up their plans . . . they worked them out with their own hands, in general, without the help of outside workmen. They chanted psalms as they worked, and laid down their tools only to go to the altar or the choir.[25]

Then the revolution of 1848 intervened. For three years Montalembert was enmeshed again in the political web, until Napoleon III's coup of 1851 forced him to retire. He now decided to shelve the life of St Bernard and set about a longer history of the early monastic orders. The result was the enormous *Monks of the West*, still unfinished when Montalembert died in 1870. To this an editor added in 1877 sections of what Montalembert had in his latter life discarded, including in unrevised form the article on art and the monks. This was the chapter, published perhaps forty years after its conception, that earned Montalembert the ridicule of later mediaevalists.[26]

Wild though his generalizations unquestionably are, they are not entirely absurd, for Montalembert was concerned almost exclusively with the earlier middle ages. *The Monks of the West* treats mainly of the 'dark ages'; St Bernard was a figure of the twelfth century, and St Elizabeth of the thirteenth. Montalembert never got beyond this, indeed rarely beyond about 1150. And for this earlier period there was something to be said for his view that the monks preserved art and civilization not just passively, by dint of copying old works or commissioning new ones, but actively, sometimes indeed by being craftsmen, painters, builders or architects.

15. The mediaeval architect at work in his study: another rendering of the same subject by the younger Pugin, from the frontispiece to his *True Principles* (1841). This gentleman seems not to be a priest, but the appurtenances of his chamber leave the reader in no doubt as to his faith. In the margin are the names of some of those whom Pugin took to be distinguished English mediaeval architects: William of Wykeham, Thomas Chillenden, William Bolton, William Waynflete, Reginald Poore, William Orchard, Thomas of Canterbury, Alan of Walsingham and John Islip.

On the whole it has not been hard to refute Montalembert. He was after all writing with political intent, for the glory of Catholicism; he was not an especially thorough researcher, allowing work to be 'devilled' for him, so that mistakes in *The Monks of the West* are not hard to spot. On the strength of such errors G. G. Coulton, his most dogged detractor, concluded that the book was not serious, citing in support Montalembert's distress when his own daughter took the veil.[27]

Yet neither Coulton nor his disciple R. E. Swartwout, who devoted a monograph to the subject, ever disposed of the monastic craftsman quite satisfactorily.[28] Conceding that monks very occasionally did build and design themselves, they dismissed these as exceptional cases. At Gloucester Cathedral, for instance, poverty was the spur that impelled the monks to help finish the nave vault—and an embarrassing botch they made of it. A school of artist–monks that flourished at St Albans at much the same time was, says Coulton, unique to England.[29] All this is fair comment; from, say, 1150 laymen were preponderantly the authors of Gothic building and Gothic art. But for the earlier period of which Montalembert chiefly speaks the roles of priest and layman are harder to disentangle. Guilds of lay craftsmen, in so far as they existed in the later mediaeval sense, were not so strong, so monks did sometimes assume a practical function in planning and erecting buildings which in later days of prosperity they tended to relinquish. One such undoubted architect was the monk Eginhard, who designed a chapel for Charlemagne at Aachen.[30] In sum, for the Gothic period the monkish architect was a myth, but for the earlier period he was not so mythical at all.

In France, just such a conclusion had been reached as early as the 1840s, not perhaps out of careful scholarship but from political enmity to Montalembert and his party. For there the Gothic past had become part of the long political tussle between church and state. Since the revolution, the state had owned the cathedrals and abbeys of France and from the 1830s began to undertake their restoration, to the disquiet of Montalembert and the church party. Catholics and Loyalists insisted that Gothic was a child of the church which should now be returned to its parent. Against them were ranged the secularists and reformers, of whom Viollet-le-Duc was the most famous among architects. Wanting the state to continue in control of the churches, they in their turn advanced all the evidence they could find to show that Gothic was the creation of the laity. Hence was born the idea, first expressed by Daniel Ramée in 1843 and then popularized by Viollet-le-Duc,[31] that Gothic style grew in the twelfth century from the Romanesque just as the lay people wrested control of the building arts from the priesthood. Though not wholly accepted by mediaevalists today, it is a view that still commands respect.[32]

The progress of serious Gothic scholarship certainly tended to confirm Ramée and Viollet-le-Duc by turning up the names of more and more Gothic lay architects. The publication of Villard de Honnecourt's sketchbook in 1858 may have been a turning point.[33] In England, the erudite Wyatt Papworth gave a paper in 1860 which gently demolished William of Wykeham's claims to architectural skill, elevated Wynford in his stead and concluded frankly: 'The Master Masons were generally the Architects during the Mediaeval Period in England.'[34] There was some resistance to Papworth's conclusions. Although the anticipated 'execration of some four hundred Wykehamists' failed to materialize, the bishop's reputation was not easy to dismantle. A new biography of Wykeham perpetuated the old interpretation as late as 1887, while on the strength of his supposed contribution to art he was even allotted a statue on the front of the Victoria and Albert Museum (1906).[35] But few architects believed in him any longer. Edward Prior in 1905 classified him as 'the most accomplished and famous of the drill sergeants who got the masons into line', in other words as 'the official who was between the ecclesiastic and the mason'.[36] Even among Catholic architects the claims of the laity for the authorship of Gothic were accepted, for in 1899 J. F. Bentley could take a young colleague and co-religionist to task thus:

I don't think William of Wykeham had anything more to do with the architecture with which his name has become associated than had the bishop of the day of Charles II with the building of St Paul's. In my opinion he was a great patron of Architecture, and nothing more . . . When you can give some proof that a bishop of the past was an Architect, well, then I shall accept it as an exceptional instance, and you know that such an exception would prove my rule.[37]

One or two revivalists of the old type stuck obstinately but unspecifically to their guns. Ralph Adams Cram in America, blending Montalembert and Morris, still spoke in 1907 of styles developed by abbots and priors 'percolating down' through the masons to every class of society so as to achieve 'perfect unity of impulse expressed through infinite variety of personal genius and inspiration'.[38] By then, few felt that this meant much more than that Cram admired Gothic architecture extravagantly.

Yet just as the ecclesiastical myth was laid, a secular one replaced it. If in France it was a triumph of a sort of radicalism and a blow against the clerical party to uphold the lay craftsman of Gothic, in England too mediaeval architecture came to have its political significance. With the recrudescence of Catholicism it became a task for the Protestant intellectual to reinterpret the middle ages if they were to continue to be admired. From this theological need, allied to new social stirrings in British politics of the 1840s and 1850s, arose one of the most potent theories in the recent history of architecture—the myth of the architect as handworker.

*   *   *

In 1848 Europe was shaken to the core by uprisings. In alarmed reaction, a wave of 'Christian Socialist' reform swept Britain. Clubs and associations for the working classes were founded and in 1854 a group of reformers, led by F. D. Maurice and F. J. Furnivall, set up a Working Men's College in London. Just before the opening a grand public meeting was convened. Furnivall recalls: 'As our visitors came up the stairs, each received a copy of Mr. Ruskin's eloquent and noble chapter on the Nature of Gothic Architecture, *and herein of the Function of the Workman in Art*, which he and his publishers kindly allowed me to reprint.'[39] The chapter thus distributed was to become the most famous part of *The Stones of Venice*, just published. Here it is often said, Ruskin's deepest beliefs about the creation of mediaeval architecture were formulated. To judge the truth of this, and to understand what this bizarre pamphlet was doing at the meeting, we must look at the context of Ruskin's architectural criticism.

Ruskin's mature writings on architecture were not many. Most of the important works belong to the period immediately after 1848; in 1849 appeared *The Seven Lamps of*

Architecture, in 1851–3 *The Stones of Venice* and in 1854 the *Lectures on Architecture*. Later comes a scatter of brilliant but increasingly bitter harangues, and then silence, excepting some unambitious accounts of old Italian buildings in the 1870s and a piece of 1884 on Amiens.

In the *Seven Lamps* Ruskin was just starting to stumble into a first, crude political awareness. Europe's troubles disturbed him but the only medicine he could prescribe— in one word, 'work'—was commonplace and jejune. Yet with a quirky, intuitive leap he linked this remedy to the subject of his study in the book's peroration.

> I know too well the undue importance which the study that every man follows must assume in his own eyes, to trust my own impressions of the dignity of that of Architecture; and yet I think I cannot be utterly mistaken in regarding it as at least useful in the sense of a National employment. I am confirmed in this impression by what I see passing among the states of Europe at this instant. All the horror, distress, and tumult which oppress the foreign nations, are traceable, among the other secondary causes through which God is working out His will upon them, to the simple one of their not having enough to do . . . There is a vast quantity of idle energy among European nations at this time, which ought to go into handicrafts; there are multitudes of idle semi-gentlemen who ought to be shoemakers and carpenters; but since they will not be these so long as they can help it, the business of the philanthropist is to find them some other employment than disturbing governments . . .
>
> We have just spent, for instance, a hundred and fifty millions, with which we have paid men for digging ground from one place and depositing it in another. We have formed a large class of men, the railway navvies, especially reckless, unmanageable, and dangerous. We have maintained besides (let us state the benefits as fairly as possible) a number of ironfounders in an unhealthy and painful employment; we have developed (this is at least good) a very large amount of mechanical ingenuity; and we have, in fine, attained the power of going fast from one place to another. Meantime we have had no mental interest or concern ourselves in the operations we have set on foot, but have been left to the usual vanities and cares of our existence. Suppose, on the other hand, that we had employed the same sums in building beautiful houses and churches. We should have maintained the same number of men, not in driving wheelbarrows, but in a distinctly technical, if not intellectual employment; and those who were more intelligent among them would have been especially happy in that employment, as having room in it for the development of their fancy, and being directed by it to that observation of beauty which, associated with the pursuit of natural science, at present forms the enjoyment of many of the more intelligent manufacturing operatives . . .
>
> I could pursue this subject willingly, but I have some strange notions about it which it is perhaps wiser not loosely to set down.[40]

Thus far nothing is said about the past, only about the present. So it is too in another and better-known passage of the *Seven Lamps* in which Ruskin set forth a novel criterion for architectural criticism:

I believe that the right question to ask, respecting all ornament, is simply this: Was it done with enjoyment—was the carver happy while he was about it? It may be the hardest work possible, and the harder because so much pleasure was taken in it; but it must have been happy too, or it will not be living.[41]

Unquestionably Ruskin meant here to suggest that the greatness of Gothic sprang ultimately from the spiritual contentment of its builders. The concept of mediaeval contentment was not new. But Ruskin had given it a twist by blending two sources, Protestant and Catholic. In Carlyle he read that the old monks found inner peace by pursuing useful and communal activities; from propagandists like Rio and Lord Lindsay he learnt that faith alone brings happiness to life and quality to art. Now he was combining these two dogmas to make a theory of architecture.

The 'strange notions' at which Ruskin hinted at the end of the *Seven Lamps* he worked out in *The Stones of Venice*, especially in *The Nature of Gothic* (to give that chapter its original short title). This essay enriches the criterion he had proposed in 1849 in two ways. Firstly, in attempting to define Gothic quality Ruskin ascribed to the middle ages as fact what he had previously only set out for the future as ideal. The value of Gothic detail, he argued, flowed from the 'liberty' and 'thoughtfulness' of the mediaeval craftsman. Secondly, Ruskin was starting to grasp political problems more maturely; social discontent originated, he now realized, in the relation of opposing classes. Handwork on the mediaeval model would cement such relations:

We are always in these days trying to separate the two [handwork and brainwork]; we want one man to be always thinking, and another to be always working, and we call one a gentleman, and the other an operative; whereas the workman ought often to be thinking, and the thinker often to be working ... In each several profession, no master should be too proud to do its hardest work. The painter should grind his own colours; the architect work in the mason's yard with the men; the master-manufacturer be himself a more skilful operative than any man in his mills; and the distinction between one man and another be only in experience and skill, and the authority and wealth which these must naturally and justly obtain.[42]

Utopian though these sentiments are, they were enough to impel F. J. Furnivall to reprint this chapter for his meeting of 1854; they even sustained Ruskin himself along with his friends Ford Madox Brown and Edward Burne-Jones in teaching drawing at the Working Men's College during its earliest years, until towards the end of the decade the impetus of Christian-Socialist reform began to slacken.[43]

In all this there is hardly the germ of a historical thesis about the mediaeval architect. By his own confession Ruskin saw the past in the light of present needs. Looking back in 1877, he offered this interpretation for *The Stones of Venice*:

The chief purpose with which ... I undertook my task of the history of Venetian architecture, was to show the dependence of its beauty on the happiness and fancy of the workman, and to show also that no architect could claim the title to authority of *magister* unless he himself wrought at the head of his men, Captain of manual skill, as the best knight is Captain of armies. But the modern system of superintendence from a higher social position renders good work impossible; for with double fatality, it places at the head of operations men unacquainted with the handling of the chisel, and sure to think the mechanical regularity meritorious (which a true artist hates as a musician does a grinding organ); and makes it the interest of the superintendent to employ rather numbers of men educated in a common routine—so as to be directed with little trouble, yet whose collective labour will involve larger profit—than the few whose skill could be trusted, but whose genius would demand sympathy, and claim thoughtful guidance, regarding not the quantity of their work, but its excellence.[44]

Here and there Ruskin did throw in occasional historical justification for these views. One point he never tired of emphasizing. The great architect of the past, he claimed, had always been a great painter or sculptor as well—and he would adduce Phidias, Giotto, or Michelangelo. With special relish he would cite the story of Giotto's appointment to build the campanile of Florence Cathedral 'because nobody in the whole world could be found who was more highly skilled in these and many other arts'.[45] On this basis he mercilessly advised Victorian architects to study painting and sculpture if they hoped ever to achieve anything.[46] That the good old architects had enjoyed 'universal' talents not only strengthened his contempt for modern professional demarcations but also supported his most outlandish theory—that building only became architecture when painting and sculpture were added to grace a structurally adequate skeleton.

Ruskin himself never believed in the deliberate anonymity of Gothic architects and craftsmen. That was an element of the monkish interpretation of Montalembert and his party, curiously transferred by some of Ruskin's followers to fit their own views. In art and society alike Ruskin believed in an élite, past and present; but he thought that art fails when this élite develops into a class set apart with its own rules and styles. The subjects of his later lectures are often particular painters and sculptors, sometimes even architects (Niccolò Pisano is one such treated with an almost reckless individualism).[47] When he had a good work of scholarship by his side, Ruskin could very occasionally be persuaded to attend to the master craftsmen who created those decorative finishings of the Gothic to which he was always drawn. One such case comes in *The Bible of Amiens*, where he celebrates the *menuisiers* who carved the flamboyant stalls in the cathedral there.[48]

Nevertheless, considering how much he wrote about Gothic art, Ruskin is astoundingly vague about the men who put up the mediaeval churches and their fittings. The best that can be found is a letter of 1854, significantly answering a query from his friend Furnivall of the Working Men's College. 'The cathedrals were built by companies of men who travelled about, popularly known as "Logeurs du Bon Dieu". They had a Master of Works, whose name might, or might not, be of celebrity. He would sketch, plan, and give each inferior workman his bit to do, as he liked best. I will bring you a book, which has something about it, on Wednesday . . .'[49] Here at last is a hint of deeper historical understanding about Gothic architecture. Though differing in emphasis from Ruskin's own theories it does not contradict them; and Ruskin, never at heart a historian, did not trouble to reconcile the two.

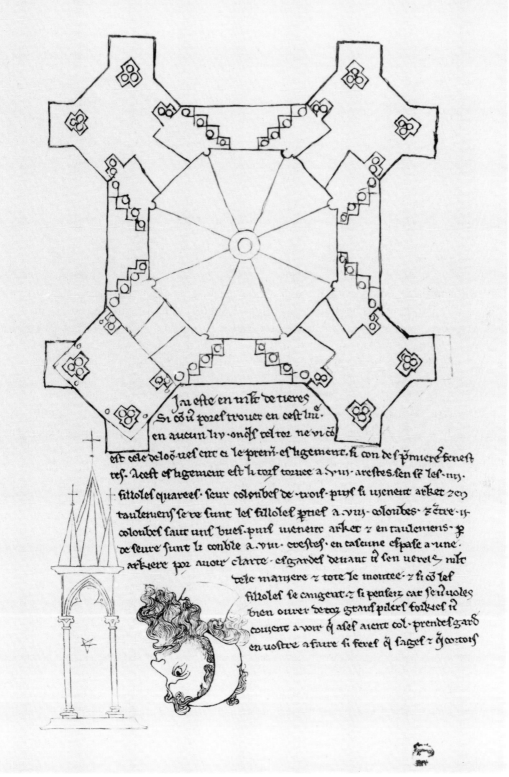

16. *J'ai este en mult de tieres si com vos pores trover en cest livre*, writes Villard de Honnecourt on this page of his sketchbook: 'I have been in many countries, as you may see by this book.' This plate shows the plan of a tower at Laon Cathedral, with a detail of a turret. Elsewhere he speaks of a working journey to Hungary, evidence of the itinerant habits of thirteenth-century Gothic architects.

The tradition of the 'Travelling Bodies of Freemasons' was an old one, still just about intellectually respectable when Ruskin wrote to Furnivall. The odds are strong that the book he recommended was Thomas Hope's *Historical Essay on Architecture* (1835) on which he often relied.[50] Hope himself depended ultimately upon Wren, or strictly upon an excerpt from the section on Gothic attributed to Wren in his grandson's *Parentalia*.

The *Italians* (among which were yet some *Greek* Refugees) and with them *French*, *Germans*, and *Flemings*, joined into a Fraternity of Architects, procuring Papal Bulls for their encouragement, and particular Privileges; they stiled themselves Freemasons, and ranged from one Nation to another, as they found Churches to be built (for very many in those ages were every where in Building, through Piety or Emulation). Their Government was regular, and where they fixed near the Building in Hand, they made a Camp of Huts. A Surveyor govern'd in chief; every tenth Man was called a Warden, and overlooked each nine: the Gentlemen of the Neighbourhood, either out of Charity or Commutation of Pennance, gave the Materials and Carriages. Those who have seen the exact Accounts in Records of the Charge of the Fabricks of our Cathedrals near four hundred Years old, cannot but have a great esteem for their Oeconomy, and admire how soon they erected such lofty Structures.[51]

Such stories of travelling bands and papal bulls eventually collapsed under the scrutiny of scholars like Wyatt Papworth, who demolished them in a pioneering paper of 1861 on the mediaeval masons. But at the same time Papworth noted how far other masonic traditions do embody truths about mediaeval building organization.[52] Like Dallaway before him, Papworth acknowledged the masons to be the real authors of mature Gothic design and was interested in the many manuscript 'legends' and 'constitutions' (or 'old charges') that survive for masons in Britain. Some of these go back to about 1400 and, it is now agreed, include some practical rules observed by mediaeval masons. More controversially, many boast an elaborate 'pedigree' for the masonic guilds and lodges, whose privileges are variously referred back to King Athelstan in England, Charles Martel in France and even in some cases to Noah and King David.[53]

Not himself a mason, Papworth examined these documents with some scepticism and refused to be too much influenced by them in determining the date at which masonic guilds were formed in England. On other evidence he decided that the correct date was surprisingly late, round about 1375, partly because of the stronger power of artisans following the Black Death and their consequent ability to defy the 'statutes at large' of the period, which were aimed precisely at preventing combinations and strikes.[54] Later writers have tended to confirm Papworth's findings. Masons were late to organize, argue Douglas Knoop and E. P. Jones, because the relative rarity of stone buildings made them characteristically itinerant and weak compared to more settled tradesmen. The scale and cost of their operations meant that they worked mostly for wealthy taskmasters some of whom (notably the king) exercised the right of 'impressing' their workforce.[55]

By the time that Papworth wrote, some of the 'old charges' had been published as part of the strong scholarly current in nineteenth-century British freemasonry. By now freemasonry had shaken off its previous reputation for radicalism, occultism and atheism and was attracting the new professional classes including architects and scholars. Such men were concerned to provide an authentic account of masonic tradition. This stimulated a vigorous debate from about 1870 among freemasons about the mediaeval past. Some Victorian freemasons certainly clung to the 'pedigrees' as proof of the antiquity of their traditions, but others were more sceptical; one writer spoke of them in 1892 as 'a pretended history fabricated by learned men, with the object of acquiring a greater influence over working masons under their care and survey'.[56] At its best, as in Robert Freke Gould's *History of Freemasonry* (1883) and in a number of papers published in the transactions of the Lodge 'Quatuor Coronati', this debate represented the first really mature discussion in English of the identity and methods of mediaeval architects.

So by 1880, thanks to Papworth and the freemasons, much more was known than when Ruskin wrote in the 1850s about the contribution that mediaeval masons and their organization made to Gothic architecture. Meanwhile historians concentrating on other spheres of mediaeval urban life had uncovered the ubiquity and power of the craft guilds. So persuasive indeed did the idea of the guilds become as the explanation for both greatness and beauty in the mediaeval city, that so far as building at least was concerned the late date which Papworth had allotted to the founding of masonic guilds in England seems to have been quickly forgotten.

This background helps to explain how Ruskin's essentially intuitive theories were developed by his great disciple William Morris. What Morris specifically brought to interpreting the mediaeval craftsman were the tools of economic history. After about 1855 Ruskin too had taken an interest in economic questions. But when he wrote his best work on architecture he was still in the thrall of simplistic moral and religious explanations for the achievements of Gothic culture. He had certainly not read what little mediaeval economic history was available. Morris in this respect was luckier and more diligent. Maturing politically in the early 1880s, he wished to reconcile his new-found commitment to socialism for Britain's future with his long-time love for its Gothic past. So he set himself a crash course in modern mediaeval history of the 'evolutionary' school: Stubbs, Freeman, Green, the radical Thorold Rogers, and, above all, the available portions of Marx's *Capital*.[57] Morris (not uniquely) admitted to finding the historical sections of *Capital* more illuminating than the pure economics, but to his credit persevered with both. By analysing the late middle ages, Marx sought to trace what he believed to be a necessary and progressive transition of society from a feudal to a capitalist economic basis. Morris accepted this view and agreed that the change was inevitable. But so strong were his instinctive attachments to the middle ages that he cared much more than Marx about the subjective aspect of this transition; he wanted, following Ruskin, to understand the spirit of the craftworker, first in the middle ages and then under capitalism. If he could explain this difference, Morris felt, he could unlock the secret of Gothic architecture. And perceiving on the one hand the virtues of mediaeval art and on the other the evils of modern capitalist production, he was led to believe that conditions of work and livelihood in precapitalist mediaeval society were very much better than under early capitalism.

In this he was generally supported by the 'evolutionary' historians. Thorold Rogers, for instance, a pioneer in the study of mediaeval work and wages, always extolled the prosperity of the fourteenth-century working man while playing down factors like the Black Death.[58] By its nature this subject remains controversial, even insoluble; some historians still believe that the working man's condition in Britain crumbled after 1350 and took many centuries to recover, while others discern a much more chequered pattern. All that matters here is that William Morris was able respectably to draw the conclusions he wanted about the mediaeval craftsman from the sources available to him in the 1880s.

Armed with this reading, Morris proceeded in a series of lectures of 1884–9 mightily to reinforce Ruskin's interpretation of the mediaeval architect and craftsman. Gothic developed in the twelfth and thirteenth centuries, he argued, not just because laymen wrested control of building from priests and monks but because powerful crafts guilds arose in the towns. These were productive enough to restrain old feudal landlords and democratic enough to outgrow the aristocratic town 'guilds'. For Morris the crafts guild was the crucial source of virtue in mediaeval art because it fostered combination, looked after its members and forbade accumulation of capital. Since there was no division of labour its members were equal and free collaborators skilled in every aspect of their trade; after his exhaustive training, every apprentice became a master.[59] The only restraint was the hand of tradition. Under these auspices,

> the craftsmen of the middle ages were all artists, and art or the creation of beauty was a habit to them which they could not forego if they would; and hence happened that which I have said was necessary to a real style of beautiful architecture, that all building was beautiful; which beauty if we now want we have at least to pay extra for, if indeed we get it by paying extra which is doubtful: it was once a free gift like the air of heaven; it is now a marketable article, and like all other marketable articles is much adulterated.[60]

All this, Morris incautiously believed, applied to every sphere of Gothic workmanship. Without distinguishing between different guilds or making a special study of the building crafts he saw the cathedrals as the consummation of the system. Ignoring altogether any conscious element of religion, he attributed their construction to

> the strong desire for the production of beauty . . . They are the outcome of corporate and social feeling, the work not of individual but collective genius . . . If they had been coaxed out of the people by the bribes of the rich or the tyranny of the powerful . . . they would have lacked the life which we all consciously or unconsciously feel which they possess and the love with which we have surrounded that life.[61]

Continuing, Morris by no means denies that the design of such churches may have originated with one man but explains why he finds this irrelevant to the spirit in which they were erected.

> Take now some one great work of collective or popular art, and in some such way as follows I think it will have been done: the hope and desire for it moving in

people's minds stir up some mastermind to plan it; but he is not puffed up with individual pride by finding himself ready for this creation; for he knows well that he could not even have thought of it without the help of those who have gone before him, and that it must remain a mere unsubstantial dream without the help of his fellows alive now and to live hereafter: it is the thoughts and hopes of men passed away from the world which, alive within his brain, make his plan take form; and all the details of that plan are guided, will he or will he not, by what we call tradition, which is the hoarded skill of man handed down from generation to generation. But, as he belongs to the past and is a part of it, so also he belongs to the present and the future: his plan must be carried out by other men living and to live, who share his thoughts, his memories of bygone times, and the guidance of tradition: through these men he must work, men it may be of lesser talent than himself; that is as it may be and matters not, but at any rate men of divers aptitudes, one doing this work, one that, but all harmoniously and intelligently: in which work each knows that his success or failure will exalt or mar the whole; so that each man feels responsible for the whole; of which there is no part unimportant, nor any office degrading: every pair of hands is moved by a mind which is in concert with other minds, but freely, and in such a way that no individual intelligence is crushed or wasted: and in such work, while the work grows the workers' minds grow also: they work not like ants or live machines, or slaves to a machine—but like men.[62]

What happened to destroy this great tradition? Here Morris follows Marx, but with an added accent of pessimism. The towns grew too big; the old feudal masters to save their interests fomented war and nationalism; the crafts guilds themselves became less democratic and took on journeymen who never rose to be masters. Hence arose in the fifteenth century the division of labour on which capitalism is based. In the building industry, always conservative, this change from craftsmanship to divided labour was not fully accomplished until the eighteenth century, which is why buildings up to that time are still of some value. Even in the 1880s, Morris adds shrewdly, building is too backward to have become fully industrialized, though 'the division of labour system has eaten deep from the architect to the hod-man'.[63]

When Morris gave these lectures he was a socialist. One clue to the sincerity of that socialism is the diligence with which he applied Marxist criteria to his understanding of the mediaeval past. But this was little appreciated by his colleagues in the arts, even those favourable to his hopes for the future of the crafts. Consequently, although his general beliefs about Gothic architects and craftsmen were accepted among his followers in the Arts and Crafts Movement, the economic framework was quickly forgotten, with results ultimately disastrous for the coherence of the whole theory. In such hands the theory retrogresses into something Ruskinian and becomes again merely eccentric, if always challenging.

Edward Schroder Prior is the best example of such an author. One of the ablest of the architect-scholars who fuelled so much of the ideology of the Arts and Crafts Movement, Prior was as doggedly individual in his books as in his buildings. *A History of Gothic Art in England*, published in 1900 but partly written in 1894, may lay claim to being the first sustained history by an arts-and-crafts man of the fabled golden age of architecture. Lethaby had in 1894 produced a remarkable treatise on Santa Sophia, but with characteristic hesitation and care hid his opinions behind the veil of evidence. Bolder and less ambiguous, Prior yet aimed at objectivity. He repudiates in his opening chapter both the 'Christian' school of Gothic interpretation and the 'Ruskinite' literature (including Morris), to uphold either of which 'the evidences of history as to morality and social progress have had generally to be doctored'. Art cannot be juxtaposed with ethics, says Prior; Gothic architecture must be studied for its own value.[64]

Yet Prior's own explanation for the power of Gothic relies on the old Ruskinian cycle, positing successive periods in art of ascent, achievement and decline; he merely strips the cycle of its moral attributes and reclothes it in the garb of collective anonymity. In the early period of mediaeval art, 'there may have been individual skill, but its excellences were more of a traditional than a personal stamp; the aesthetic qualities had their power from collectiveness, dominating the moral and intellectual, and extinguishing individuality.' Then comes sudden progress:

> The circle of experimenters has become immensely widened; instead of art being the province of a sect, the whole people combines in the pursuit of beauty, and becomes endowed with the faculties of artists. Instead of slow traditional skill handed on from father craftsman to son, or from master to pupil, every member of the community instructs his neighbour in artistic effort, and gains a step from him himself . . . The passion for the beautiful controls every sphere of life and feeling.

Eventually this charmed unity is broken:

> The first symptom of the decline is the birth of artistic individuality; the segregation of the artist from the community at large; the making of art a personal rather than a collective ambition. In the Gothic art of France, as elsewhere, the appearance in the thirteenth century of distinct names of architects and sculptors seems to herald the loss of the finest feeling, and the coming of a less natural and instinctive production in its place.[65]

The analysis of decline is striking, if only because by Prior's time it was decidedly old-fashioned to belittle Perpendicular. In so doing he placed himself squarely with Ruskin and an earlier school. Another passage theorizes more precisely on what occurred from the fourteenth century:

> By this time, a building caste, distinct from the nation, had not only developed itself but separated into many dexterities: each craft had now become a mystery, that sought protection for its secrets in a guild, and so immediately had interests of its own outside the common fund. Its skill increased thereby, but its expression of beauty was narrower.

The Black Death and the French Wars

> combined to raise the status of the craftsman and so promoted the decline of his art, by the specializing of his individuality . . . His individuality could no longer be

pressed, but had to be begged so that its importance could make its own terms. In fact, the conditions with which we are familiar in regard to our painters and sculptors—which modern notions have picked out of the ruck of labourers, to call them 'artists', were in existence in the fifteenth century for the whole body of craftsmen. Every trade that ministered to the bright-coloured, art-endowed life of the fifteenth century, had the honour and emoluments which we reserve mostly for the professors of easel-painting. But Art, which had been the matter of course of environment, though a widespread, had now become a privileged article, sold for the honour and enrichment of its producer.[66]

Exact though this argument is, it rests upon taste, nor scholarship. For even if its historical accuracy is allowed, what has Prior to say to those who simply prefer the art of the fifteenth century to that of the thirteenth? Little, except to insist that a richer experience may be derived from the pure mediaeval church of the earlier period. That is confirmed in Prior's later book, *The Cathedral Builders in England* (1905). There he gropes once more for what is special about our experience of mediaeval building, and why 'no lover of art goes a mile out of his way to look at restorations and new Gothic churches'.[67] He cannot accept that either mere picturesqueness or some secret method of proportion and contour can explain 'that mysterious hold, which the great mediaeval works, as if they were natural objects, have upon us'.[68] So he is thrown back on a half-mystical notion, that it is the spontaneous effect of life upon life. An object of communal growth and accretion, in other words, is supposed like nature itself to speak inevitably to the human spirit in a way that a work of individualistic art never can. (The idea accords well with Sullivan's obsession at just this period with the 'organic' quality of good architecture.) To reinforce his views, Prior recapitulates his tale of decline from anonymous collaboration to individual competitiveness, summing up with the most extreme statement of this school of thought:

The conclusion is that the power of designing art in mediaeval times was common property, not merely very usual, but what could be demanded of any workman, and was existent in the masses of the people. Beauty was the attribute to be expected of all the work of craft. Every building was a 'fair' building, every mason 'cunning', every painter 'incomparable', every sculptor a 'master': that is to say they all knew their crafts, and that was all that was wanted. The idea of a man being an artist and therefore lifted by a special faculty above the rank of mankind, as a teacher, a prophet, and what not, all this belongs to another age than that which produces the great arts of life, such as was Gothic art. In the middle ages artists, architects, sculptors, painters, were just folk generally, and the credit of their art must not be attributed to extraordinary personalities, but to the life history of the race.[69]

So wild and 'biological' a thesis about the makers of mediaeval architecture could be refuted only by the dry facts. In so doing nobody had a greater share than Prior's close friend and Morris's disciple W. R. Lethaby. A baffling figure, Lethaby used scrupulous caution and scholarship in everything he wrote and so sometimes failed to make himself clear. Though at some personal sacrifice he practically gave up architecture to become a teacher and writer, it is hard to say what precisely he gave the many architects, designers and scholars who fell under his charismatic influence.

As ardently as Ruskin, Morris or Prior, Lethaby believed that collective endeavour was the great inspiration of Gothic society and architecture. He had faith, too, that with pertinacity and sense the mediaeval example might become the pattern for modern artistic development. But he was never blind to the historic importance of individual Gothic architects. Indeed, the love of Gothic seems simply to have drawn Lethaby to find out more about the men responsible for it. He soon discovered when investigating French Gothic that the anonymity of the old craftsmen had been much exaggerated by those who had never troubled to look. In *Mediaeval Art* (1904) he says: 'The impression that the Cathedrals cannot be assigned to particular builders, and that mediaeval masons were little honoured in their day, is curiously far from the truth. Masonry, including sculpture, was the representative art of the age, and the captains of masonry received most honourable public recognition.'[70]

Lethaby's later books on Gothic art centre almost obsessively upon rescuing the master craftsman from oblivion. *Westminster Abbey and the King's Craftsmen* (1906), the fruits of his fullest research into these matters, he characterized not as an account of the building but as an attempt to give human interest to what might appear 'an otherwise abstract art'.[71] By disinterring Gothic designers like Henry de Reyns, John of Gloucester, Robert of Beverley, William de Ramsey and Henry Yevele, he trod out a path which later scholars have eagerly followed. At all costs, Lethaby felt, these great men must come to life. Recounting a racy story of how William de Ramsey (reputedly the originator of Perpendicular) abducted a man and forced him to marry his daughter, he comments: 'This bold way of dealing with affairs seems to fill out our conception of what a mediaeval craftsman should be.'[72]

Yet Lethaby never quite reconciled himself to the idea of the mediaeval 'architect'. Quotation-marks creep around that term in many places in his text, and he sharply dismissed the claims of Wykeham, Dereham and other amateurs to any skill in design. However eminent individual masons and carpenters might be, to Lethaby as to Ruskin their worth depended on their toiling with their hands as well as their heads.

In 1909 Arthur Kingsley Porter cited extracts from two sermons which seemed to contradict this:

Master-masons, with a rod and gloves in their hands, say to others 'cut it for me in this way' and labour not themselves, yet take higher pay.

In those great buildings, there is commonly one chief master who commands only by word of mouth, who seldom or never lays his hand to the job and yet takes higher pay than the rest.[73]

Such texts helped to shatter what was left of solidity among the old Ruskinian interpreters. But though Lethaby must certainly have known them he cannot have felt the need to alter his position. As late as 1926, in perhaps his finest essay on mediaeval architecture, he continued to insist that since architecture and building are inseparable the very concept of 'design' as a separate process is mistaken. Yet he also approvingly quoted Mâle:

The art of the Middle Ages was collective, but it was more intensely incarnated in some men; crowds do not create but individuals.[74]

To the end, the Lethabitic ambiguity persists.

*   *   *

From Lethaby it is a short step to John Harvey, the foremost living British scholar on the mediaeval architect and his work. Indefatigable in his zeal for Gothic, trenchant in scorn for the misapprehensions and bigotries of past interpreters, patient, clear, insistent but not repetitive, Harvey is Lethaby's spiritual heir. Over forty years he has fathered a stream of learned articles and readable books which centre upon a single, challenging proposition: that the mediaeval architect can and should be identified as precisely as his modern counterpart, and that once identified he should be honoured for his great gift to civilization.

To this quest Harvey's own background is relevant. His father William Harvey was an architect of some modest reputation who imbued the son with his own knowledge and love of Gothic. William's father George practised architecture too; so the traditions of the trade were strong in the family.[75] John Harvey himself became a pupil of Herbert Baker, one of those architects who having been brought up on the ethos of the Arts and Crafts Movement reacted against its puritanical moralism without rejecting its architectural method. Baker's generation cordially detested Ruskinism as the hidden element that explained the tastelessness of Victorian architecture. But they still loved mediaeval buildings and styles. Many went on building in modern Gothic, while a few reinforced the long tradition of British architect–scholars of the Gothic—a line stretching all the way back to Wren. Rather younger, John Harvey virtually gave up practice in the 1930s to become perhaps that tradition's last and certainly its most learned representative.

> It is a fantastic misconception of the facts of artistic creation to suggest that the mediaeval cathedrals, the mural paintings, the poems, and the songs and dances are the work of the community acting as a whole.
>
> For every great work of art, for every work possessed of a unity of conception, we must posit a personal creator, a single human artist in whose imagination the form appeared before it was wrought with hands. That the names of these persons may be lost does not alter the facts . . .[76]

With these words from Harvey's *Gothic England* (1947) we have passed beyond the qualified individualism of Lethaby and are back almost in the world of *Von deutscher Baukunst* and the legendary Erwin. The lay artists and architects who created the Gothic cathedrals, says Harvey, were of eminent stature. Ignorance alone has blinded us to the esteem in which such creators were held:

> So far as social conditions can be paralleled in modern times, the status of the mediaeval architect seems to have been analogous to that of his present-day counterpart. He was to be found at the tables of important clients, doubtless an interesting guest, but found himself more at home among the merchant citizens and well-to-do yeomanry.[77]

Much of Harvey's work has been devoted to proving this. In *Henry Yevele* (1944), a great fourteenth-century designer is rescued from oblivion and presented not only as crucial to the development of Perpendicular but as a prosperous and well-known personality. *English Mediaeval Architects* (1954) documents everything that is to be known of the obscurest masons and carpenters who it is thought designed anything. *The Mediaeval Architect* (1972) epitomizes Harvey's conclusions on that difficult subject, and *The Mediaeval Craftsman* (1975) gives them broader social context.

By their substance and accuracy these powerful books have hugely advanced mediaeval studies. No future lover of Gothic can entertain the dilettantisms of a Wren, a Walpole or a Ruskin about the identity or methods of the great fourteenth- and fifteenth-century church-builders. Yet as to Harvey's broader achievement there remain a doubt and an ambiguity of precisely the kind we found in Lethaby.

Harvey candidly idealizes the late middle ages in northern Europe, especially Britain. For him, English art of the early fifteenth century may be ranked 'not second even to the Athens of Pericles in supreme beauty.'[78] Every facet of the nation's culture and social life lived up to the same lofty standard of civilization: 'The leaders of mediaeval action sought an all-pervading unity; unlike either Confucius or Goethe, they were able not merely to discover the principle, but to go far in introducing it in their daily life, and that of the whole people.'[79] This is hardly so different from the ideas of Ruskin and Morris (perhaps also of Pater). Harvey's political interpretation of this elusive 'unity' certainly differs from that of his predecessors. Where Morris values democracy and secular combination among guild members, Harvey speaks of the craftsman's independence, emphasizes the pre-eminence of royal patronage, and believes (with Taine) that the greatest periods of art can occur only under 'strong and well-rooted government by an individual of exquisite taste'. *Gothic England* even ends with the eccentric cry: 'Where can we find again such a King Richard?'[80] But the more important thing is that Harvey, like others before him, locates ultimate virtue in the life of the people.

What then are we to make of the great individual creators like Yevele? How did they partake of the mysterious communal ideal? Evidently by collaboration and interaction. Yet Harvey insists that at least in original conception the great mediaeval buildings are the products of a single mind. And this thought dominates, sometimes even warps, his researches.

Harvey's preference for individualism affects his judgment of work even when more than one mediaeval 'professional' is involved. When for instance Villard de Honnecourt speaks in his thirteenth-century textbook of a plan worked out in discussion (*inter se disputando*) with another master, Pierre de Corbie, Harvey tells us this is 'the rare exception'.[81] Yet in the whole book that is the only architectural composition actually claimed by Villard. Sometimes Harvey has to admit defeat as in the case of King's College Chapel, Cambridge, where great pains have failed to disentangle the respective roles of Robert Westerley, Reginald Ely, a host of minor masons and the learned patron, Henry VI himself.[82] But he still believes that the designing role is separable in principle and must be assigned to a master craftsman.

Often it seems oddly pedantic not to allow experienced amateurs some major and regular part in the evolution of the appearance of Gothic buildings. Harvey concedes

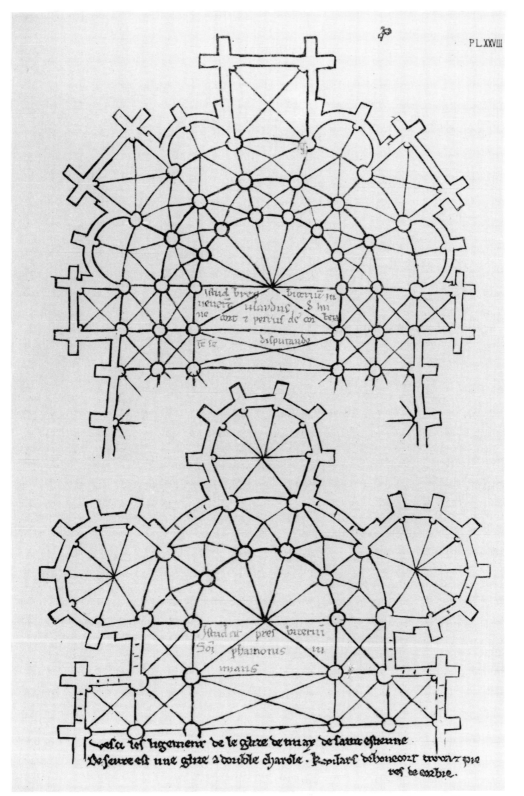

17. Plans of the east ends of two French Gothic churches, from the sketchbook of Villard de Honnecourt. The upper one is inscribed: *istud bresbiterium invenerunt ulardus d'hunecort & petrus de corbeia inter se disputando*; 'this presbytery was designed by Villard de Honnecourt and Peter de Corbie in mutual discussion'. An equivalent inscription in French is given at the base. This is the only drawing in the whole sketchbook claimed as a 'design'. The lower plan shows the east end of the church of St Stephen at Meaux.

as much for music. By his own admission Henry V, a king, and John Dunstable, a canon, could compose; yet Wykeham and his fellow-clerics are sedulously excluded from *English Mediaeval Architects*. By this criterion Abbot Suger, who on the orthodox view gave the critical spur to French Gothic, would be excluded from the ranks of great creators because he was not the actual executant of St Denis.[83]

Harvey allows that there are attested cases of clerical involvement in design in the twelfth and thirteenth centuries but assigns all the examples that he possibly can to craftsmen who took orders after their apprenticeship was complete. He is certainly consistent in prizing the English architecture of the later Gothic period, un-questionably designed and built by lay craftsmen, above the earlier work in which monasticism seems still to have found some expression. But, eager to push back the claims of lay dominance in building to as early a date as possible, he stretches evidence to the limit.[84] He construes as meaningful and continuous the ancient privileges 'after the English fashion' assumed by the Strasbourg lodge of masons in 1275. He takes seriously the tradition of effective masonic organization back to the time of Charles Martel in the eighth century. And to underpin his belief in congresses of masons held regularly at regional and occasionally at international level he boldly links practices from fifteenth-century Germany with very moderate hints from earlier English documents. All this is ingenious but far from conclusive. So long were the middle ages, that we should rather expect change than continuity between the institutions of the twelfth century and those of the fifteenth.

The same chronological rider applies to Harvey's remarks on the status of the mediaeval architect. His comfortably-circumstanced architect, sitting at the king's table in honour or at ease in the company of wealthy yeomen, undoubtedly existed from the prosperous era of Chaucer onwards, when art in northern Europe was gaining as much in social esteem as in Italy, and when prosperous craftsmen began to own quarries or run contracting businesses (in contravention of previous guild ideals). But they hardly belong to earlier epochs. G. G. Coulton has shown that before the fourteenth century the status and pay of masons were moderate, and that occasional mason serfs existed (one as late as 1475). So little prized were practitioners of the arts by churchmen that when Dante celebrated Giotto and Cimabue he was sneered at by one preacher for mentioning 'men of unknown repute and inferior art'.[85] Harvey insists that the old distinction between the pure and the mechanical arts, common in late mediaeval rhetoric and argument, was just literary and not mirrored in the real world. If so, it is odd that apologists for art in the fifteenth century should have leapt to challenge it. Even in the fourteenth century the lot of the skilled artisan was often humiliating. 'No F.R.I.B.A. is likely to be paid fifty shillings for dancing on a table before the king, as befel Jack of St Albans in the time of Edward II,' comments Swartwout.[86] Jack was a painter royal; ordinary masons were far less favoured and were always vulnerable to the royal licence for impressment.[87]

This brief critique of Harvey's work is no attempt to undermine a scholar's well-founded reputation. It is included rather to remind us that depth and niceness of scholarship, in which our century can generally pride itself, in themselves offer no guarantee that the architectural past will be interpreted with objectivity. Ever since Walpole and Goethe, the masterpieces of mediaeval architecture have provided a fruitful means for architects, scholars and philosophers to unburden themselves. In so doing they have revealed as much about themselves, their preoccupations (not always architectural) and their culture as about the subject. Goethe sought in Gothic an inspirational theory of creativity that could embrace all those arts wherein 'nature' seemed to play a part. Walpole found in Wykeham the patron-cum-dilettante which he himself embodied. Dallaway, Cunningham and Cockerell scanned the mediaeval past for the type of professional architect emergent in their own age. Montalembert and his fellow Catholics found in the same period a rallying cry for restoring the church's lost glory in France, while Viollet-le-Duc and his school saw proof in Gothic that the population had once emancipated itself from the chains of religion, and justification for their having done so again. Ruskin, starting from political disturbances in Europe but soon broadening his concerns to the drudgery and divisiveness of industrialized toil, dreamt of old ways of working as a panacea for his own times. Morris took this on at a period of overt social strife and linked it to a contemporary theory of class and production, while in Prior it assumed the more sinister note of social Darwinism.

And so one might go on; modern scholars, especially those committed to the 'glory' of the middle ages, are scarcely likely to be exempt. Harvey's work is too recent for its tendencies to be categorized with accuracy. But in once again championing individualism against the bogey of collectivism, he falls within a current of contemporary political concern which has much affected scholarship. In the work of the Cambridge Group for the History of Population and in books like Alan Macfarlane's *The Origins of English Individualism* (1978), the whole nineteenth-century account of the 'anonymous' or 'peasant' middle ages found in Marx, Weber and Tawney is challenged with equal vigour. Harvey's reaction is doubtless the more emotive because of the natural tendency of all architect–historians to uphold their own calling.

*   *   *

We need not scoff at any of the myths embodied in these divergent interpretations of the Gothic architect. For, just as each derives from particular preoccupations, so each corrects and augments the received picture and adds to our imaginative understanding of the middle ages. If they are contradictory and arbitrary, that is because they grapple with a time for which sources are elusive or poor and where the terms on which the modern argument is most usually conducted, those of the creative imagination, are nowhere more than half recognized. Nor should we be, as so much history is today, discouraged by lack of objectivity from using our own contemporary experience to make some small progress in comprehending mediaeval architecture.

Let us return briefly to the mediaeval mason, in whom especially Harvey and others discern the equivalent to the architect of today. Was there anything in his conditions of work that made great architecture, individual or collective, a probability? He endured long hours, irregular or itinerant work, disease and social disturbance leading to the pattern of fluctuating demand still so familiar in construction. The liberty of the lower craftsman was negligible, that of his master probably until the fifteenth century as greatly circumscribed by his client as today. In bad times he was lucky if he had a small piece of land to work. The skill and ability acquired through apprenticeships and the guild system are not enough to explain the special qualities of Gothic architecture. Coulton was able to show of mediaeval output 'how small a fraction was artistic except in the sense in which we apply the word to an honest deal table or chair'.[88] There were shopwork and standard details, as the least discerning visitor to parish churches can see. Originality was sometimes frowned upon as a danger to the interests of the trade; as late as 1456, well within the age of individualism, a Silesian mason was boycotted for introducing novelties.

Yet mysteriously inspiring buildings did arise throughout the later middle ages. If not by the piety of the priest, the will of the workman, the natural endowment of the architect or the purity of social organization, then how?

The organization of mediaeval building depended upon separate, skilled specialisms, of whose intricate collaboration the Gothic cathedrals are the consummate representation. To admit so much is not to be a Ruskinian. For Ruskin and his followers—no less than Montalembert and his—tried to plumb this mystery by concentrating on the craftsman's state of mind, which they took to be simple and in some ultimate sense devotional. Harvey by contrast has pointed out the sophistication of mediaeval building skills, but generally seeks the origins of this in the individual.

The pattern of our great industries today (including, increasingly, architecture and construction) is also that of shared specialisms. The key to that is not singleness of purpose but simply good organization, through the interaction of management, skills and labour. For Gothic architecture it is the element of organization and management that has been lost in past interpretations, causing, for instance, Prior to deride Wykeham as a mere official or 'drill sergeant'. In this sphere the tendency of the most powerful and imaginative scholars to look always to architecture's sister arts for analogy has much to answer for. As a result we have been searching incessantly for the creative and spiritual figure, whether individual or collective, when it might have been shrewder to know how building committees functioned, how finance was arranged, how labour was kept at least reasonably content, how priest, mason, carpenter and the rest reconciled their respective interests. We do not, after all, often ask ourselves who designed the Rolls-Royce, or a jumbo jet, or even for that matter most great modern works of engineering. The complexity of the answers, we know, would only demonstrate the unhelpfulness of the original question.

Of course, to some these industrial analogies will always be profane.[89] Certainly they cannot account for the awe which the Gothic cathedrals evoke. But for such people a preciser mediaeval scholarship can offer little, since what is dear to them is their experience of the building however conceived—whether as sublime, picturesque or purely devotional. This experience may be governed or guided or misguided by one of the great interpretations of the mediaeval past. But who is to say that they should be deprived of the poetry of their particular myth if it bolsters their enjoyment? Probably no interpretation lacking in poetry would have power to hold them.

I end therefore with two stories of the kind that it is now unfashionable to take seriously

18. The Prentice Pillar at Rosslyn Chapel, Roslyn, Scotland. Among romantic antiquarians it was a symbol of the mystery of mediaeval creativity.

but which embody some truth, albeit in mythical form about the designers and craftsmen of the Gothic. The first is the tale of the 'Prentice Pillar' at the intricate fifteenth-century chapel of Rosslyn, a building held in special veneration by early romantic mediaevalists. It is told not just of Rosslyn, however, and so has the virtue of universality.[90] In his search for consummate art, the master mason travels to Rome to study an original column as a model for one in the chapel. During his absence his apprentice, inspired by love or a dream (versions differ) builds the pillar to perfection. Returning, the master finds himself surpassed and slays the youth with his mallet. Traditionally, carvings at Rosslyn Chapel show the protagonists: the prentice has a cut over his eye, the master mason frowns, and between them the young man's mother weeps. Here are linked some of the great qualities of the Gothic, good and bad: the value set above all economic sense in striving for the ideal and attaining perfection in the work; and the bondage and tyranny of apprenticeship, of covertly doing better work than the master and getting worse than no credit.

The second story is a poem, Thomas Hardy's *The Abbey Mason*.[91] Hardy was trained as an architect and had some small practice before he turned to fiction. He was a Goth, and like others of his age struggled with the great mystery of mediaeval creativity. *The Abbey Mason* answers the question with a story about the origins of Perpendicular at Gloucester Cathedral. The anonymous master-mason and his fellows are recasting the old Norman abbey. He has reached the transept but can go no further, since no forms of tracery known to him will fit the existing spaces. In despair he visits the open-air tracing floor early one cold and rainy morning, when to his joy he observes the raindrops streaming down

> in small white threads
> From the upper segments to the heads
> Of arcs below, uniting them
> Each by a stalactitic stem.

Thus is born the Perpendicular style (in which the mullions carry through to meet the head of the arch). For a while the Gloucester mason becomes famous. But he knows that the invention is not his own and feels obliged to give all the credit to Abbot Wygmore, his patron. Time passes; mason and abbot die alike, and a later abbot enquires how the new style arose. A single 'decrepit sage' can be found to recollect the ambiguities of the strange old story,

> And how the master lost renown,
> And wore in death no artist's crown.

The abbot replies:

> Nay; art can but transmute;
> Invention is not absolute;
> Things fail to spring from nought at call,
> And art-beginnings most of all.
> He did but what all artists do
> Wait upon Nature for his cue.

CHAPTER THREE

The Architect as Professional: Britain in the Nineteenth Century

Much was amiss with architects in Britain between about 1820 and 1860. A well-known and graphic instance of this is the celebrated Seth Pecksniff, who has earned an enduring notoriety unique among architects, real as well as imaginary.[1]

Mr Pecksniff's calling makes a brief enough showing in *Martin Chuzzlewit*. 'A resident near Salisbury, ostensibly an architect and land surveyor, who receives Martin Chuzzlewit as a pupil': so Dickens describes Pecksniff in the cast of characters. His profession acts as a device to get the book's hero into the world, while his office system serves to introduce poor, put-upon Tom Pinch, 'an unpretentious but high-souled man, assistant to Mr Pecksniff'.

Yet Pecksniff, Pecksniff's office and Pecksniff's domestic arrangements rank among Dickens's sharpest satires on the early Victorian hypocrisy of fact—the narrow, smug, grinding and prosaic outlook that constantly deformed ambition in early industrial society. For Dickens, architecture was as sound a canvas as any other on which to splash the dark colours of social heartlessness. And Pecksniff offers not a few clues to the true 'state of the profession' in Dickens's day, at a time (1844) when Britain alone could boast a substantial, organized body of architects.

Early in the novel, Dickens initiates his readers into the mysteries of Mr Pecksniff's profession:

The brazen plate upon the door (which being Mr Pecksniff's, could not lie) bore this inscription, 'PECKSNIFF, ARCHITECT', to which Mr Pecksniff, on his cards of business, added, 'AND LAND SURVEYOR'. In one sense, and only one, he may be said to have been a Land Surveyor on a pretty large scale, as an extensive prospect lay stretched out before the windows of his house. Of his architectural doings, nothing was clearly known, except that he had never designed or built anything; but it was generally understood that his knowledge of the science was almost awful in its profundity.

Mr Pecksniff's professional engagements, indeed, were almost, if not entirely confined to the reception of pupils; for the collection of rents, with which pursuit he occasionally varied and relieved his graver toils, can hardly be said to be a strictly architectural employment. His genius lay in ensnaring parents and guardians, and of pocketing premiums. A young gentleman's premium being paid,

and the young gentleman come to Mr Pecksniff's house, Mr Pecksniff borrowed his
case of mathematical instruments (if silver-mounted or otherwise valuable);
entreated him, from that moment, to consider himself one of the family;
complimented him highly on his parents or guardians, as the case might be; and
turned him loose in a spacious room on the two-pair front; where, in the company
of certain drawing-boards, parallel rulers, very stiff-legged compasses, and two, or
perhaps three, other young gentlemen, he improved himself for three or five years,
according to his articles, in making elevations of Salisbury Cathedral from every
possible point of sight; and in constructing in the air a vast quantity of Castles,
Houses of Parliament, and other Public Buildings. Perhaps in no place in the
world were so many gorgeous edifices of this class erected as under Mr Pecksniff's
auspices; and if but one twentieth part of the churches which were built in that
front room, with one or other of the Miss Pecksniffs at the altar in the act of
marrying the architect, could only be made available by the parliamentary com-
missioners, no more churches could be wanted for at least five centuries.[2]

This passage skilfully pinpoints the two most burning issues of the architectural
profession from Dickens's time down to our own: the status of the architect, and the
education of his pupils. Firstly, as to Pecksniff's activities there is equivocation. Is he an
architect, a surveyor, a rent collector, or none of these things but just a lodging house
keeper? Secondly, what of his pupils? They are 'young gentlemen', they lodge *en famille*
as in the ancient manner of apprentices, yet they are sorely imposed upon by their
master. According to Pecksniff's customary advertisement, a pupil under his aegis 'will
avail himself of the eligible opportunity which now offers, for uniting the advantages of
the best practical architectural education, with the comforts of a home, and the
constant association with some who (however humble their sphere, and limited their
capacity) are not unmindful of their moral responsibilities.'[3] The reality, successive
pupils find, is otherwise. In the 'memorable two-pair front' they are left to fritter their
capacities away on 'Salisbury Cathedral from the north. From the south. From the
east. From the west. From the south-east. From the nor'-west. A bridge. An almshouse.
A jail. A church. A powder-magazine. A wine-cellar. A portico. A summerhouse. An
ice-house. Plans, elevations, sections, every kind of thing.'[4]

As for Pecksniff himself, the book unfolds to expose him as a humbug. A single incident
reveals his lack of the least professional probity or talent. Soon after Martin Chuzzlewit
arrives as a pupil, Pecksniff goes away. He is prodigal with suggestions on how Martin
may employ himself during this absence.

'Suppose you were to give me your idea of a monument to a Lord Mayor of
London; or a tomb for a sheriff; or your notion of a cow-house to be erected in a
nobleman's park . . . A pump,' said Mr Pecksniff, 'is very chaste practice. I have
found that a lamp-post is calculated to refine the mind and give it a classical
tendency. An ornamental turnpike has a remarkable effect upon the imagination.
What do you say to beginning with an ornamental turnpike?'[5]

Rejecting these hints, Martin tries his hand at a competition for a grammar school.
Later, having quarrelled with Pecksniff and departed for America, he forgets all about

19. 'Meekness of Mr. Pecksniff and his charming daughters.' The celebrated vignette from *Martin Chuzzlewit* by Phiz (Hablot K. Browne) of the Pecksniffs at home. The architect is surrounded by his family and a choice selection of his designs, prominently signed. Behind him, his poor assistant Tom Pinch; before him, portrait by Spiller, bust by Spoker, the latter surmounting volumes by Vitruvius and Palladio.

this. But on return from his adventures, he is astonished to witness by chance the laying of the foundations of just such a school, built to his designs but credited of course wholly to Pecksniff.

*   *   *

Dickens was not greatly interested in architecture. The conditions of Pecksniff's office could therefore be dismissed as caricature, were they not corroborated by the reminiscences of several architects who underwent pupillage in this period.

The experiences of the lively George Wightwick are a good example. Wightwick, though by no means wealthy, was certainly a 'young gentleman' when in 1818 he submitted to articles for a normal five-year term with the London surveyor–architect Edward Lapidge. Of these five years he recalled in his memoirs:

> No instructions, not even as to the course of my artist-study, were ever given; while the miscellaneous and unsystematized character of the mere office business left me uninformed as to the introductory knowledge necessary to its full apprehension. I expected to find a tutor: I found only an employer . . . I found, in short, that I had paid my premium for the opportunity of self-instruction—for the advantage of the 'run of the office'—for the privilege of serving my master and picking up such information as might lie in my way.[6]

Not long after finishing his articles, Wightwick spent a period working under the ageing Sir John Soane. Though difficult and eccentric, Soane took the dignity and educational responsibilities of the architect very seriously, and his office had as high a reputation as any. Yet Wightwick seems not to have learned much from the old man, nor did this post avail him when he took the plunge and set up in practice. With an advance from a friend, he furnished a ground-floor room in the Adelphi, put up a brass plate, got out a book of travel drawings to attract clients, sat, and waited. In the preface to his book, the scrupulous Wightwick avowed it to be 'a card, a notice, an advertisement,' excusing himself 'that so completely are the advance-posts in the profession occupied, that young aspirants have no resource left, but to make themselves known by a patrician species of puffing.'[7] The fruits of this tactic disappointed him. A few people bought the book; he was prevailed upon to design a porch free of charge for one house, then failed to secure payment for a survey he made of another. Meanwhile, obeying the friendly maxim 'if you cannot obtain it, *make* work', Wightwick kept busy by concocting ideal designs and entering competitions, which he never won because he adhered to the financial limits prescribed instead of enticing clients with meretricious ornament.

After a year, Wightwick gave up the struggle: 'I had done all I could to be-Pecksniff those who might call upon me; but the callers were few indeed, and, with equal certainty, none were be-Pecksniffed.'[8] He retreated to Plymouth. There in a few years he amassed a successful practice. Then he fell foul of architectural fashion and retired prematurely, at the age of 49.

Other instances of the lottery of English architectural practice and the miseries of the pupillage system at this period could be given. On the hardships of training, Frank

20. 'Martin is much gratified by an imposing ceremony.' Another illustration of architectural hypocrisy from *Martin Chuzzlewit*. The local Member of Parliament, who is 'returned upon the Gentlemanly Interest', performs a 'little sleight-of-hand' with the silver trowel as he lays the foundation stone of an important grammar school before the assembled mayor and corporation. Pecksniff looks on with smug satisfaction; in reality, the design was unwittingly 'ghosted' by Martin Chuzzlewit when working in Pecksniff's office.

Jenkins's *Architect and Patron* (1961) cites two further cases: the grinding 'social system' under Mr and Mrs Augustus Pugin, brilliantly sketched by Benjamin Ferrey in his biography of the younger Pugin, and the dispiriting introduction to architecture suffered by the young Gilbert Scott under James Edmeston.[9] To these might be added the history of C. J. Mathews, whose brief and indifferent career as an architect encompassed pupillage under the elder Pugin, a period under Nash, one or two more or less abortive jobs of his own, and a few dismal months as a district surveyor in the East End of London, at Cutthroat Lane, Bow. Mathews was wise enough to give up the unequal struggle and return to the theatre, his first love, where he became one of the most celebrated comedians of the Victorian stage.[10]

Yet all these architects eventually succeeded in some way or another, acquiring the leisure and literacy to pen their memoirs. Only one document plumbs the depths of architectural practice, the autobiography of Thomas Wayland Fletcher (1833–1901), East End pub architect very un-*extraordinaire*.[11]

Fletcher's parents were a London schoolmaster–tutor and a millinery manageress. When he was fifteen, they advertised for any architect who might want a pupil. He was articled for £20 (which his father could ill afford) to Campin and Clements: 'Mr Campin conducted a patent agency. Mr Clements was only a draughtsman but certainly a very good one. He was however no designer and knew little or nothing about construction.'[12] There being no architectural work to speak of, Fletcher just copied plates from *The Builder*. The partnership soon dissolved; he went with Clements, who took a back room in Soho and made ends meet by drawing for the building press.

At the end of his articles, Fletcher had never worked on anything that was actually built. He now advertised for a job as an 'improver without salary' and was taken on by John Burges Watson, a genial architect with a modicum of quite interesting work. Watson nicknamed his new assistant Bentinck and poured into his ears 'all sorts of smutty stories. Our offices in which we used respectively to work were separated by a small lobby and I used sometimes to quietly close the two doors. He would then call "open the door Bentinck", this I knew was the preface to a fresh edition of smut.'[13] From Watson, Fletcher moved on to a Mr Humber, 'a most unprincipled man in debt everywhere and I had the greatest difficulty in getting my money from him and when I left he owed me a considerable sum . . . Mr Humber left his designing entirely to me, the elevations specially.'[14] After experiences not much better with other architects, Fletcher took to drink, from which he was saved by religious conversion. He then went into partnership, became surveyor to two small building societies and enjoyed some very modest success. It does not seem to have made him happy. Of his twenty-one-year partnership he had this to recall:

> Our practice was a general one and in addition . . . we had numerous surveys, valuations, assessments, quantities, disputed accounts, levelling and surveying all of which with the exception of the levelling I had to do, my reptile of a partner taking no responsibility, hampering me with his little priggish mind in every way and thereby ruining our business. The reason why he did the levelling was he would not let me use the level which was his.[15]

* * *

Of the frustrations encountered by these architects at the commencement of their careers, poor training and lack of opportunity were the most immediate and galling. But these obstacles derived from the more basic misunderstandings about the nature of architectural practice. Scott, for instance, a self-confessed 'romantic youth' whose love of architecture had been fed on mediaeval churches, was pained when he found himself 'condemned to indulge his taste by building houses at Hackney in the debased style of 1827';[16] others were not so lucky as to assist in any designing at all. The question is: how did these illusions arise?

For about a century from 1660, English architects (in the simple sense of those who designed buildings) tended to belong to one of two classes. There were the talented amateurs with architectural proclivities, whether literary or mathematical, like Pratt, Wren, Vanbrugh or Burlington; and there were the higher building craftsmen, generally masons or carpenters by background, who had amassed a reputation for design: Hawksmoor, John James, Ware and Flitcroft are examples of this type. The latter class, as a glance at Howard Colvin's *Biographical Dictionary of British Architects* shows, was much more numerous, especially in provincial centres. They were the 'profession' proper, whose expertise was essential to the amateurs. Today we wilfully call them architects because we are preoccupied by their skills in design, but in reality they were also superior surveyors, builders, measurers, house agents, carpenters, masons, suppliers of materials and so on. The amateurs shaped only a small fraction of what was built: churches and public works, where dignity of appearance or symbolic requirement called for a level of scholarship hard to find among building tradesmen, and of course houses and other pleasure-buildings for themselves and their friends. The craftsmen designed and built everything else, notably the small urban family house which until the end of the eighteenth century satisfied most domestic and commercial needs, and also many larger works into the bargain.

After about 1750 this balance broke up. Economic growth meant more and bigger buildings, fashioned from varying materials and equipped with a new range of services. The skills needed to erect these buildings were too diverse and technical for the old habits of work to deal with. So, by a long process recognizable in outline but blurred in detail, the practical craftsmen became master builders and the amateurs professional architects. In this sense, early full-time architects like Chambers and Soane were among the first specialists in the construction industry. They stand at the head of a vast diversification and fragmentation in building organization which has gathered pace from that day to this.

Of course, the architectural profession of the nineteenth century was heir to more than the amateur tradition of design alone. Well into the Victorian period, many architects emerged almost imperceptibly from the building trades, having at least a family background in the craft skills. This exercised a strong, steadying influence upon an as yet unstable profession. And at least till 1850 there were still too few large buildings erected to keep a whole profession afloat upon design alone. Architects of the new specialized type therefore remained few in number and economically insignificant. The bread and butter of very many Victorian architectural practices— and not just poor ones—still consisted of tasks today allotted to other professions: arranging leases, assessing rents, measuring property, taking out quantities and so forth. To be either an estate surveyor to an extensive landlord or a district surveyor supervising local building standards was devoutly to be desired as a steady source of income for an architect in an otherwise hotly competitive field.

Yet as fast as they could afford to do so, architects shed their less congenial tasks. Why they did so is not hard to comprehend. Design was a literate and highly esteemed skill; it allowed close contact with the client rather than continual haggling with tenants and artisans, and it brought chances of enhanced status, even perhaps of fame. If one could rely on this for a living and prosper, so much the better. There was no lack of practical men able and willing to take over the more laborious part of the business.

Nevertheless these early professional architects required some guidelines for their conduct. Here it was that the tradition of the independent scholarly gentleman–designer, heir to the values of Alberti and Wren, shaped architectural ideology. Their best promise of respect, security and status lay in sticking to commissioned buildings, avoiding speculation, and striving to act as impartial agents midway between client and builder. This difficult balancing-act became the classic ideal of the nineteenth-century profession. The young Soane gave prophetic formulation to it in 1788:

> The business of the architect is to make the designs and estimates, to direct the works, and to measure and value the different parts; he is the intermediate agent between the employer, whose honour and interest he is to study, and the mechanic, whose rights he is to defend. His situation implies great trust; he is responsible for the mistakes, negligences, and ignorances of those he employs; and above all, he is to take care that the workmen's bills do not exceed his own estimates. If these are the duties of an architect, with what propriety can his situation, and that of the builder, or the contractor, be united?[17]

Soane's question shows that an alternative means of achieving architectural independence was familiar to him. This was for architects to move into the traditional field of the urban building tradesmen as their ally and co-ordinator, by promoting speculative development. On the whole this occurred rarely in the early eighteenth century; the first true trials of this method coincided with the London building boom of 1763 onwards, when (among other schemes) the brothers Adam undertook the Adelphi, James Paine laid out Salisbury Street off the Strand and Henry Holland (a little later) set about the development of Hans Town. The pattern was familiar enough by 1774 for a carpenter, Thomas Skaife, to bemoan

> the present mode of architects engrossing the whole business into their own hands, which seems to be the general plan, if some stop is not immediately taken to prevent it . . . The capital architects and surveyors that have adopted the plan of finding all the materials, and only allowing even principal masters a sort of prices like task-masters for executing the work, do this through a knowledge of the exorbitant advantages that arise from work at the original customary prices.[18]

The most celebrated early speculating architect was John Nash.[19] Nash's tempestuous London career proclaims his conviction that the Adams and Holland were as much models for the modern architect as the soberer Chambers, Soane or Smirke. Architects, he evidently felt, should promote rather than serve or arbitrate;

21. Sir John Soane (1753–1837). Engraving by J. Thomson of the famous portrait by Sir Thomas Lawrence now in the Soane Museum. The great consolidator of British architectural professionalism is shown at the height of his powers and influence.

22. John Nash (1752–1835). A hitherto un-published sketch of Soane's wily and unorthodox rival, made by Edwin Landseer in about 1830.

only thus would the chaos and petty scale of building-trades development be broken. Nevertheless Nash himself had perhaps more responsibility than anyone else for the eventual triumph of Soane's philosophy and the failure of his own. His own 'harum scarum' roguishness and buoyancy, his hand-to-mouth methods of management, the hurried, hamfisted detail of his wonderful schemes and their ingenious but sometimes slipshod structural qualities, all contributed to a profound distrust of his example in leading architectural circles. After Nash's disgrace in 1830, the ideal of the architect as developer was slowly suppressed and remained in disrepute in Britain for more than a century.

But the ultimate reasons for the decline of the architect–developer from this time onwards were economic: the rise in competition against him of the modern master builder. Backed by ever more accessible capital, fortified by better and more advantageous means of organizing contracting, gaining also from the withering of the old apprenticeship system in the building industry under the employment pressures of early industrialism, the master builder encompassing all trades soon reduced the threat of the architect–developer to a minor and occasional one.[20]

Once the professional builder had taken hold of housing in the three decades after 1820, the significance of architectural endeavour in this field, historically never very great, shrank. Few independent architects again became large prime movers in the process, in the way that the Adam brothers, Holland and Nash had aspired to be. That is not to say that architects were not as much involved in housing as before; in fact they were probably more so. In smart districts they were often called in to make elevations as a selling point for the builder or to enforce conformity on behalf of the proprietor. And in London at least, wherever the facts can be ascertained, a great deal of Victorian speculative development appears to have been designed in detail by architects working in subordinate positions within or close to building concerns.[21] The largest London builders like Thomas Cubitt, William Cubitt and Company, C. J. Freake and William Willett ran capable architectural offices through which some distinctive personalities passed. It is not accidental that such architects have received scant attention. The Victorian profession, having failed to conquer this field, set its face against admitting that speculation and architecture had anything in common. Yet if one scratches the surface of any ordinary architectural career, involvement in at least some small amount of speculative work may usually be found.

To make matters worse for architects, the new professional builders began encroaching on their territory by offering even the grandest clients what would now be called 'design and build' services without any speculative element. Osborne House, built directly for Victoria and Albert in 1845–50 by Thomas Cubitt from designs produced in his drawing office, is the classic example. Such a palace, erected without an independent architect of the type championed by Soane, made the spectre of his redundancy painfully close. Nor was he beset only by builders. All the skills within the construction industry were being shaken up, and several parties laid claim to areas which the architect had thought within his sphere at least of superintendence— engineers, surveyors, cabinetmakers and even house agents. The old-fashioned cabinetmaker, for instance, was gradually going middle-class and turning into the Victorian interior decorator, who would blithely refit and extend houses without consciousness of inferiority or limitation. Engineering in particular captured the public imagination, and ended any claim to monopoly that architects might have tried to maintain over specialized types of construction. While there was nothing architectural which the staff of a great engineer like Brunel could not handle competently, few architects could boast of half his constructional capacities.

*   *   *

Such depredations upon what was keenly felt to be architectural territory were the underlying causes of the frustrations experienced by budding architects as dissimilar as Wightwick, Scott, Fletcher and the fictional Martin Chuzzlewit. Their masters were not so much Pecksniffian hypocrites and abusers of their trust as persons in whom the Soanean vision of a gentlemanly *camaraderie*, creating works of art and commanding inferiors, clashed with the daily realities of drudgery, impotence and insecurity. This is a time-honoured situation for young architects. But it was worse for early Victorian ones, because the profession had expanded to meet the demand for new types of building in an entirely unregulated way, while the station which architects were to occupy within the growing, fragmenting building industry was still obscure.

Such depredations also played a decisive part in the founding of the Institute of British Architects (1834), dedicated to securing 'uniformity and respectability of practice in the profession'.[23] In other words, the founders were obliged to begin by holding their ground and defining what they thought was the architect's patch. By excluding surveyors, measurers, and those with interests in the building trades, they confirmed Soane as their ideological mentor. The first years of the 'Institute' proved candidly dull and masonic. 'Respectability', in the form of a royal charter, was secured in 1837. The few members (159 in 1840) were caught up not with the stylistic ferment in English architecture but with professional self-defence—not a rewarding or imaginative task. It did not take long to discover that the only broad line of defence within the Soanean formulation, the only element in architecture to which some other professional group did not have a prior or better claim, was 'art'. Yet ironically, those most concerned with professional dignity and exclusiveness were in practice those least taken up with matters of art, and vice versa. The infant RIBA was replete with Pecksniffs, when what was wanted was a Pugin.

Nevertheless from this period onwards the concept of the 'art-architect' made steady progress. Already latent in the amateur ideal of the architect, the term seems first to have come into conscious use during the pamphlet war of 1834–7 over the competition for the new Houses of Parliament. The chaos of architectural competitions at this time, with cries of 'foul play' regularly arising afterwards from unsuccessful entrants, had contributed not a little to the low repute of the profession. One parliamentarian even went so far as to pronounce: 'All the public buildings of the last half century have been behind the average architectural talent of the day, manifestly because the employment has been consigned to *Professional Men*.'[24] As for the new Parliament building itself, its unprecedented scale and complication had within ten years engulfed two architects, two heating engineers, the foremost early quantity surveyor and several contractors. This in itself showed that there was bound to be further professional division of labour in the future. From about now, those at the privileged end of the profession like C. R. Cockerell started speaking of distilling the Soanean ideal still further by employing 'the Art Architect to design, and the practical architect [lower case, of course] to carry out and superintend'.[25]

This programme is enlarged upon in a little book which, better than any other, expresses the contradictions in architectural ideology of the period, Robert Kerr's *The Newleafe Discourses* (1846).[26] Kerr, later a founding father of the Architectural Association, author of *The Gentleman's House* and a stalwart pillar of the RIBA, was just twenty-three at the time: pugnacious, prolix, but touched with an enthusiasm and levity signally missing from his subsequent productions. Written in a halting sub-Carlylean style akin to early issues of *Punch*, *The Newleafe Discourses* consist of overlapping, rambling dialogues on the policies of the 'Institute' and the general state of British architecture. Newleafe, acting for the most part as Kerr's mouthpiece, is dominant. He ridicules both the impractical artist–dreamer who supposes himself the only true architect, and the great Alderman Beefeater, the architect–tradesman, yet he pronounces that each is needful in his way. He believes in the independent professional architect whose interests the RIBA is committed to defend, he condemns the encroachment of outsiders upon architecture, and he insists that anything 'artistic' must be within the architect's domain. Yet at the same time he recognizes that much of the hubbub has been 'got up'.

> Horrible carpenters, monsters in the form of masons, malignant—very malignant bricklayers, shameless decorators,—an overpowering host of barbarous Vandals,— sweep dire destruction through our lovely Italy and devastate with ruthless hand the plains where Art was wont to hold sweet empire!
> And all this because such a carpenter 'drew the plan' of such a house; or because such a house was built without superintendence, in order 'to save the expense of an Architect.'
> ART did you say? Why, all this magniloquence and fluency of indignation, this vehemence of lamentation and complaint, my very mournful friend, have very little indeed to do with *Art*; so little that I think your fears, if they refer to Art alone, are pretty nearly groundless and imaginary. If you will but wipe your tears away and compose yourself for a moment's serene consideration perhaps you may find that it is merely the 'business' which is despoiled and preyed upon, the 'business' whose flocks and herds the fierce barbarians have borne away, the 'business' the invasion of whose realm you thus so bitterly bewail. And even if then your tears burst forth anew, we shall have at least this consolation, that you have a clearer notion of the object of your woe, that you weep for the 'business' and not for the ART.[27]

For the future Newleafe, just like Cockerell, recommends an

> improved division of labour . . . whereby the real Architect might be relieved from the inspection of sewers and cesspools and wells, and the shoring up of old houses, and the rating of dilapidations, and the ventilation of foul cellars, and the fitting up of stables, and the curing of smoky chimneys, and the exclusion of rats, and all such like 'Architecture'; and entrusted with the design of much of the decoration which is at present confided to the painter, upholsterer, cabinet-maker.[28]

*   *   *

The kind of division here suggested was increasingly carried into effect after 1850 in the smarter architectural practices, for whom the great private wealth of the age afforded plenty of artistic opportunities. The best of these architects also kept abreast of the technical side of building, and their broader practices and educational advantages even sometimes allowed them to be technical innovators. But in growing numbers they were now able to make a living out of art and style, in other words to become 'art–architects'. More recruits to the profession now came from the middle classes, even from the universities; more, notably those with some private means, were able to sustain themselves as gentlemen, limiting their practices to what they felt befitted the true dignity of an architect. These changes gave rise to increasing animosity between the old-fashioned 'professional architect', accustomed to sweat for his bread, and the new-fangled 'art–architect'. An example of this may be found in the unpublished memoirs of W. W. Pocock (1813–99), a prosperous London architect of limited artistic ability whose career combined commercial work and chapel-building with some well-judged speculative development. Contrarily his son, Maurice Pocock (1854–1921), was possessed with the spirit of art and disdained his father's methods when taken into partnership in 1875:

> He did not act fairly, but left me to do much of the work he ought to have either done himself, or found clerks to do. So again, it had always been the practice in my office, to make up the builders' accounts at the end of the job, without calling in the aid of a surveyor. This the most irksome part of an Architect's duties he would not undertake, so I was obliged to consent to his employing a Surveyor whom consequently he ought to have paid as doing his work. This he so pertinaceously refused to do, that I did not think it worthwhile to hazard a quarrel. Yet he was so high minded as to refuse to adopt as his own, designs that had principally emanated from myself. It was thus obviously useless for me to keep alive my business for his sake, so I let it die out.[29]

This widening rift between 'art' and 'professionalism' was a feature in some degree peculiar to Britain, and it had large consequences for British architecture. Between about 1850 and 1875, the glamour of the Gothic Revival and the crusading spirit of the associated church-building movement drew the first conscious generation of art–architects into strenuous public attitudes for which the RIBA and the early architectural magazines were useful outlets. Scott, Street, Burges and their peers all engaged in frequent debate on their creed and published their designs in order to promulgate the gospel of Gothic. But after about 1875, domestic architecture re-established its pre-eminent status in Britain. Country-house architects with high-class practices had, in general, less need for publicity and no strong ideological axe to grind. For many of them, the curiosity of the architectural magazines and institutions intruded upon their personal relations with their clients.

This sentiment was an old one. It had been especially strong in the highly organized office of Robert Smirke, among whose pupils were C. R. Cockerell and William Burn. Burn became the leading country-house architect of the 1840s and 1850s, first in Scotland and then in England too. He and his disciple David Bryce would not publish designs because they saw it as an ungentlemanly betrayal of trust; nor did they see why their plans should be pilfered from them by less able architects. For these reasons they had truck with neither the RIBA nor its early rivals and reformers. Though Burn in 1840 reluctantly joined the budding Institute of Architects in Scotland, he found it handy to leave a year later when Bryce was refused membership. This influential resignation wrecked the IAS and unintentionally reinforced the RIBA.[30]

Burn's sentiments, as much 'professional' as 'artistic' in nature, passed intact to the next generation of leading domestic architects, George Devey, Philip Webb and Burn's own pupils Eden Nesfield and Norman Shaw. Of this group, only Shaw was not wholeheartedly averse to publicity and he, like the others, was thoroughly opposed to the RIBA, which he suspected of trying to foist an unartistic orthodoxy upon the profession. It was Shaw, the most public figure of the four, who initiated the campaign that led to the one significant manifesto of the late Victorian art-architects and one of the rare British books to conduct a reasoned argument on a matter of architecural principle, *Architecture a Profession or an Art* (1892).[31]

A summary of the circumstances surrounding this much-discussed book may perhaps suffice. It appeared at the climax of an argument about 'registration', in other words about restricting entry to the architectural profession by means of examination. The final outcome of the campaign of professional self-defence ushered in by the RIBA in the 1830s, the idea of registration followed on from the mushrooming of voluntary courses at places like the Architectural Association which were beginning to supplement the lonely office-only training undergone by Martin Chuzzlewit's contemporaries. Voluntary courses led in their turn to examinations run by the RIBA; and soon enough examiners and candidates alike naturally began to clamour that these tests should mean something tangible. The speed of progression had been extraordinary. In 1840 there was precious little architectural education at all. Yet by 1880 there was already a lobby for registration. No wonder the question stirred up bitterness.

Registration split its proponents and opponents alike into two groups of uneasy allies. Among its supporters, the older members of the RIBA, men like W. H. White, Macvicar Anderson and Robert Kerr (who had long abandoned his youthful rebelliousness) cast themselves as the profession's rulers and judges. Few of them cherished artistic ambitions any longer; all enjoyed large practices and a growing amount of consultancy work in the shape of assessorships, arbitrations and court cases. Kerr even wrote what must be the first textbook to guide wayfarers along this now-much-trampled path, *The Consulting Architect* (1886). Generally these people wanted registration under the RIBA's control, but they were not in a hurry to get it. The younger enthusiasts for registration were different. They simply wanted to see their qualifications recognized, and they suspected the Institute of dragging its feet. In 1884 they set up the Society of Architects, a ginger group which had the first registration bills introduced in Parliament in the late 1880s. Though these failed, they forced the RIBA to adopt registration as its official policy in 1890.

The opposition group consisted of more interesting men with less conventional yet fundamentally muddled ideas. On one side stood the older generation, notably the editors of *Architecture a Profession or an Art*, T. G. Jackson and Norman Shaw; they were gentleman art–architects, heirs to the ideals of Soane, and they opposed registration on the simple yet eccentric grounds that art and professionalism were incompatible. On the other side were the younger men of the Arts and Crafts Movement, centred upon Lethaby. They correctly perceived registration as a symptom of the further fragmentation of the building industry, and wished to redress this by giving embodiment to some of the profounder, non-stylistic ideas about architecture and architects expressed by Ruskin and popularized by William Morris. From Ruskin's precept that the worth of architecture proceeded from the quality of labour expended upon it, they drew practical lessons about the value of craftsmanship, the use of

23. Cover of the Architectural Association Soirée Programme, 1882. The 'Sweet Stuff Man', thinly disguising the features of Horace Jones, then President of the RIBA, lures eager architectural pupils from the schools and universities, through the AA, and thence by means of the new voluntary examination into the crowded portals of No. 9 Conduit Street, at that time the home of the 'Institute'. Meanwhile some shady dealing goes on at the back door.

materials and the organization of building work. But their difficulty was that they had no means (and, really, no idea) of altering the structure of the industry, which every day was diminishing the independence of the craftsman and the shared responsibilities which lay at the base of arts-and-crafts philosophy. From Pugin's time, English architects had been adjured to attend more to decoration, finishings and craftsmanship. In response, many of them promoted or supported particular crafts firms (and thus no doubt encouraged the demand for crafts products in certain circles). But this involvement further compromised the craftsman's already dwindling autonomy. In the most prestigious circumstances, architects had by 1890 become the dictators and the artisans practically their servants; the more 'artistic' a building was, the more control there was likely to be. The various experimental buildings of the Arts and Crafts Movement, however adventurous in form, tended to confirm this and in due course to draw most of these men back to the more reassuring idea of architectural direction over building and the crafts. Only in this less radical guise—to the effect that architects should command a revitalized crafts process—did Ruskin's theories communicate themselves to the Deutscher Werkbund and so gain the status of orthodoxy. In this shape, they posed no threat to the professional ethic but rather reinforced it.

*   *   *

Architecture a Profession or an Art was a historic document, but its critique was too shallow, its standpoint (from the highest echelon of architectural practice) too restricted to have much bearing on events. Though registration in Britain was delayed for forty years, that was for other reasons. A parliamentary bill put up by the Society of Architects in 1895 nearly succeeded. But the RIBA opposed this and other measures because as yet it did not control the profession. Only a quarter of British architects were members of the 'Institute' in 1911. Once this figure rose to half in the 1920s the RIBA soon took up the cudgels in earnest, achieving registration in 1931. The profession of surveying has a similar history; registration of surveyors was also held up in the 1890s because of their institute's inability to control the profession.[32] The 'art' question in fact was a red herring. That was one reason why in the first decade of this century, the RIBA was able to entice back most of the opponents of registration without further spilling of blood.

Yet in a fundamental sense, the 'art' question was a very important red herring which continues to this day to be drawn across the path of architectural politics in Britain. To recapitulate: the idea of art in building as the special province of the architect became more conscious and widespread between about 1820 and 1850, as a means of professional self-defence during a period of adjustment and change in the building industry. In the second half of the century, things became easier: the industry settled down, areas of professional responsibility became better defined, and architects found it easier to make a living.

The temptation for architects at the top of the tree, for those emanating from offices which had already shed the more menial tasks, was to attribute this new-found security to art and the propaganda for art. The true reasons are, as usual, more complicated. Economic growth, the diffusion of wealth, and the increase in population of the cities, were of course the underlying factors, but there were at least two more specific developments which particularly benefited architects.

The first was the explosion in the number and complexity of building types from 1840 onwards. Hotels, libraries, railway stations, gaols, hospitals, pubs, schools, offices, town halls, factories, markets, fire stations, middle-class and working-class flats, department stores: few of these had existed previously as purpose-built buildings in any quantity, and all required experience to design efficiently. During the later Victorian period, the first private architectural practices began to specialize outside the realm of churches and country houses; the Saxon Snells enjoyed a national reputation for their hospitals, C. J. Phipps and Frank Matcham for their theatres, Rowland Plumbe for his artisans' housing. The first full-time municipal architects' departments also ceased at this period merely to regulate the projects of others and began building special buildings themselves. In London, the City Corporation's architects J. B. Bunning and Horace Jones designed such important technical works as the Caledonian, Smithfield,

24. An Edwardian architect curries favour with his clients. Joseph D. Wood was a very obscure pub architect in the Birmingham district. This curious drawing, half cartoon and half advertisement, depicts the brewers of Birmingham, 'their architects, and allied traders', looking on complacently as H. H. Asquith attempts to curb the drink trade with his Licensing Bill of 1909, but succeeds in injuring only himself. As the caption shows, this particular architect makes no pretensions to professional independence.

Leadenhall and Billingsgate Markets; while the Architect's Department of the Metropolitan Board of Works and its successor the London County Council erected a proliferating series of handsome and always individual building types, starting with fire stations (1867), then adding public housing (1893), tramway buildings (1902) and other works as municipal intervention became a favoured tool of policy.[33]

The other great boon to the security of the profession lay in the growth of building regulations. Always tiresome to conform to, and the pride of ingenious architects to evade, bye-laws also require literacy to understand and interpret. As a whole, architects had long been more literate than others in their industry; indeed they managed in the nineteenth century gradually to monopolize the district surveyorships set up to administer the early London building acts.[34] They were therefore well placed to tussle with the increasing complexity of Victorian building law, on behalf both of clients, who naturally lacked the requisite knowledge, and of builders, who often lacked the literacy. This ability to cope with paperwork and to negotiate between client, contractor and the new building bureaucracy, helped re-establish the architect as the natural 'intermediate agent' (to use Soane's phrase) on any job of complexity. At the same time building services were also becoming more complicated and causing further fragmentation of trades. The regular subcontracting of heating, lighting, drainage and ventilation made the existence of an off-site co-ordinator separate from the main builder more necessary than ever before.

Economic and technical reasons, therefore, were really what made later Victorian architects securer and better esteemed. Yet this hardly made itself aware to those who upheld art as the over-riding architectural value. And since these were the people who set the tone of ideological debate within the profession, the deeper issues were obscured. *Architecture a Profession or an Art*, for instance, entirely slurs over the question of how the public may be protected from 'bad architecture', a matter on which the registrationists (naively, no doubt) hoped for much from the new examinations. Later, a great reorganization of architectural education in the Edwardian decade set schools of architecture in Britain upon a proper footing at last. Yet the topics most attended to were general education, style, and the formal process of design; management, building technique and 'professional practice' were largely brushed aside as tiresome matters. The profounder courses pioneered a little earlier by Lethaby at the Central School of Arts and Crafts and by Owen Fleming at the Architectural Association, which tried to draw together the skills within the world of building, soon withered away with little to show for them.

The repercussions of this situation were profound. At the turn of the century the ideal of art coupled with the security of opportunity brought British architecture, as practised by the favoured few, to an international reputation and originality it has never known before or since. But the professional legacy of this era was not so happy, as a few examples to conclude this chapter may show.

*   *   *

First of all, efficiency, whether in management, economy, planning or technology, was rarely highly rated by the British architectural élite in the first half of this century. Inseparable from the idea of architecture as art, from Pugin to Lutyens, was a humane, comfortable belief in small offices, intimate client-relations, and delegation of the mundaner tasks alone. These precepts were conducive to a happy office and a more or less pleasurable working life. But such things could look different from the outside. Harry Hems, a carver, provides a rare glimpse of the contrasting working methods of the church architect G. E. Street, one of the progenitors of the Arts and Crafts Movement, with his more successful rival, Sir Gilbert Scott (whom superior architects at the turn of the century were apt to despise):

> In the zenith of his fame, I recollect at his unobtrusive offices in Spring Gardens, S.W., he [Scott] had a staff of no less than thirty-six assistants, and these, taken as a whole, probably represented the very best Gothic men in the country. And the system that prevailed in those offices was simply marvellous. Contractors were never kept waiting by the hour, as was and is sometimes the case in minor architects' offices; details and everything else were always ready to the minute.

25. Charles Canning Winmill on a sketching trip in Norfolk, 1890. A close friend and disciple of Philip Webb, Winmill became the most impressive designer in the radical London County Council's Architect's Department of the period 1893–1914. Because of his official position as a salaried architect, his talents were virtually unknown to a wider world.

On this point Sir Gilbert offered striking contrast to the late Mr. George E. Street. Many a time I saw the latter in that upstairs office of his in Cavendish Place, W., standing at his desk knocking off large detail drawings—and beautiful drawings too—at the rate of a dozen and more an hour, but in spite of that and all his wonderful energy and ability, Mr. Street was always behind. The most vexatious delays were constantly occurring "all over the shop" on Mr. Street's jobs, because the foreman or clerk of works in charge was "waiting for details". Mr. Street, as a rule, large as was his practice, drew all details with his own hand in pencil. Sir Gilbert aimed at nothing of the sort, but he had at his command splendid specialists who did what he wanted, and who, always in complete touch with their work, had everything ready as it was required.[35]

That the Streets of the profession were admired above the Scotts in part explains why, as late as 1962, the RIBA found a disproportionate number of British architects inefficient, in however amiable a manner.

Secondly, since artistry was equated with individualism, the natural and healthy

26. Young men of the Fire Brigade Section of the London County Council's Architect's Department, c. 1902. Rear (left to right): A. J. Peyto, H. S. Jardine, J. R. Vining, H. F. Ponton. Middle: F. C. Wylde, A. M. C. Young, P. Nobbs, W. B. Y. Draper. Front: B. C. E. Bayley, D. S. Cullen. Most of these architects were appointed as 'temporary' assistants on a weekly salary and received no public recognition, let alone encouragement from the RIBA. Yet their responsibilities were considerable and their work was frequently impressive. The only architect in this group who became well known in later life was Percy Nobbs, who emigrated to Canada and made a name for himself there.

development of collaborative architecture during this century was constantly being stifled. This was especially so for the growing municipal and other 'public' practices. From its earliest days, the RIBA had committed itself to sustaining the independent 'principal' in private practice, and therefore was of little help during the last century to the office assistant or the municipal employee. This situation persisted far too long into the present century, in part because of an equal prejudice against public practices from the artists of the profession. Such instances as the London County Council's early housing projects and fire stations were enough to show that architecture could be anonymous, economic and collaborative yet also highly artistic and idealistic; they were in fact perhaps the most consciously rational application to modern conditions of the Arts and Crafts theory of architecture cited earlier. Yet because of the tradition of official anonymity surrounding these works, their remarkable creators (men like Owen Fleming, C. C.Winmill and R. Minton Taylor) received as little recognition from the upholders of art as from the world of the RIBA and seem in the long term to have grown disillusioned.[36] In fact municipal and other public architects took an increasing share of building work and did much of it very well. Yet their claims for professional attention went largely unheeded until after 1945—a situation detrimental to their morale, their chances of recruitment and, eventually, to the quality of their work.

A final example of how a too great reverence for the artistic side of architecture distorted matters may be found in the history of British town planning.[37] Town planning as a conscious concept came to maturity late in Britain, in the first years of this century. This late flowering of planning is sometimes represented as the triumph of art over petty-minded commercialism, of the broad Beaux-Arts vision over the blinkered empiricism of the previous age. Against this, it is worth pointing out that many planning schemes of major importance were carried out in Britain between 1850 and 1900. Few of these were controlled by architects, or at least by architects of standing. In part this was because of the weakness of the profession, to which this chapter has so many times alluded; but in part also it was because architects of this period were prone to see their buildings as finite and indivisible works of art, not as organic schemes to be carried out in stages over time. Architects therefore restricted themselves in the planning field not only because of professional pressures but also because of the ideology of the artistic masterpiece; this was particularly so between 1870 and 1900, when individualism of architectural style ran rampant in Britain. Then, in response to growing social and legislative interest in town planning, architects took up the question. Many, to judge from statements made at this period, thought it no hard thing for architects to come belatedly into the complicated matter of city planning and take it over, *de haut en bas*. Some profounder thinkers, notably Raymond Unwin, avoided these easy ideas, but the simplifications of Beaux-Arts formalism allured many others, and were to persist through the modernist plans of the 1930s and inflict much damage in the post-war world. In this way the 'lines-on-the-map' approach to town planning, now so much discredited, owes a good deal to art as well as to barbarism.

The reader who is interested in following these threads further will find some of them picked up in Chapters 5 and 7.

CHAPTER FOUR

The Architect as Businessman: the United States in the Nineteenth Century

The American architectural profession commenced more rudely and therefore found its feet more gradually than its counterpart in Britain. In one way it still lags behind. Architects in the United States, that is to say persons licensed by state law to use that name, have been slow to acquire more than a fraction of the design and execution of buildings. Continuously reliable or comparable statistics on this matter do not seem to exist, but those estimates that are available support each other. Immediately before the First World War, one writer claimed, almost 90 per cent of buildings in the U.S. were erected without architects. Later, a survey of 1925–9 suggested that nearly 13 per cent of all work was supervised by an architect, while at about this time 80 per cent of all dwellings (which then represented over half the value of all national construction) were put up without the direct involvement of an architect.[1] Since then, the increased complexity of construction has favoured the architect. By some contemporary estimates he is now responsible in value terms for a fifth to a quarter of all construction.

The chief beneficiary of this situation has been the American builder. To his superior adaptability, his transformation from simple carpenter, mason or 'housewright' into the modern realty and construction corporation or package house-builder, belongs much of the credit for his having retained his customers in the face of economic vicissitudes.

One may hazard some guesses as to why this should have been. Having so vitally needed them for her early development, the United States has always put a premium on the most practical skills, sometimes (as in Thoreau) raising them to the level of ideology. So to many an American there is nothing superior about the status and skills of an architect as opposed to a builder. Early American architects felt this disdain deeply. 'Had I in England, executed what I have here,' lamented Benjamin Latrobe of Philadelphia in 1804, 'I should now be able to sit down quietly and enjoy *otium cum dignitate* . . . Here I am the only successful Architect and Engineer. I have had to break the ice for my successors, and what was more difficult to destroy the prejudices the villainous Quacks in whose hands the public works have hitherto been, had raised against me.'[2] Later in the century, such pressures were still there. One of the best-known of nineteenth-century Chicago architects, Peter B. Wight, virtually gave up architectural practice for the role of fireproofing contractor and structural expert after 1880, when his reputation as a designer was long established.[3]

More substantively, differences of organization within the construction industry proceeding from divergent patterns of urban development have made the American builder more flexible than, for instance, his British counterpart. During the last century, contractors 'in gross' who handled as much of the work as possible themselves achieved a remarkable dominance in British urban building. But in the United States this was by no means the only pattern. Even in the most advanced American cities, a tradition of 'separate contracts' long flourished. Here is how the system operated in Boston in 1874.

Then a city house demanded the drawing of from ten to twenty different contracts, a separate one being made for each trade employed. The architect had to correlate the working of all these trades, and it required much tact and firmness to settle the incessant questions of responsibility arising under these conditions . . . Mr. O. W. Norcross was one of the earliest of our local builders to take general contracts. The advantages of the system were so obvious that the practice spread rapidly, and the earlier methods soon became obsolete.[4]

However redundant separate contracts had become in turn-of-the-century Boston, they still prevailed elsewhere in the U.S. Within living memory, architects supervised a greater dollar value of construction without general contractors than with them, the bulk of such work being in the smaller cities.[5] Rudolph Schindler, for instance, was not exceptional among modern west coast domestic architects in personally directing nearly all his buildings under a system of separate contracts.[6]

At the larger end of the scale, the great urban contractors learned much earlier than in Europe how to specialize in management. Starrett Brothers, one of a handful of New York firms able to undertake skyscrapers, and chief contractors for the Empire State Building, found it efficient and profitable to subcontract as much work as possible and operate principally as managers. Hegeman-Harris, another mammoth concern of the interwar years, actually became construction managers alone. Yet at the same time many of the big contractors (e.g. O. W. Norcross, the George A. Fuller Company, the Thompson-Starrett Company, Starrett Brothers, and Todd, Robertson and Todd) had a profound impact on the design of what they built and employed capable architectural staff. Three of the famous five Starrett brothers, who did much to shape the urban construction industry in the early years of this century, trained under Daniel Burnham as architects; while Wallace K. Harrison, of the great New York architectural firm of Harrison and Abramowitz, began his career under Norcross.[7]

If architects in the United States failed to capture more than a small corner of the market in construction, it was not for want of trying. More consistently and consciously than in Europe, the early American profession behaved as an interest group striving for an ever larger share in building on grounds of superior efficiency, safety, appearance and economy. The particular stratagems employed by its pioneers in face of their particular difficulties make up the narrative of the rest of this chapter.

Newly independent America had no well-defined class structure, no broad category of educated patrons to whom the aspiring artisan could appeal for help in education or, that once achieved, offer his professional services. Society was relatively fluid, as yet careless of permanence. If ample opportunity existed for planning and construction, most building was basic, especially in virgin territory. In the longer-settled districts there were limited openings for the gifted amateur of European type, for Peter Harrison in Newport or Thomas Jefferson in Virginia. But nearly all building was still in the hands of the traditional tradesmen.

The first changes naturally took place in the great settled east coast cities. It is worth tracing the pattern as it emerges in two of them, Boston and New York.

*   *   *

Charles Bulfinch (1763–1844) was by universal acknowledgment Boston's first true architect. His disciple Asher Benjamin, 'housewright', architect and prolific author of builders' manuals, put the matter thus in 1823:

> The time has been, within my own recollection, when New England did not contain a single professed architect. The first individual who laid claim to that character was Charles Bulfinch, Esq., of this city; to whose classical taste we are indebted for many fine buildings . . . The construction of the Franklin Street houses, of which that gentleman was the Architect, gave the first impulse to good taste; and Architecture, in this part of the country, has advanced with accelerated progress ever since.[8]

Prosperous, well-educated and fortified by a visit to Europe in 1785–6 where he absorbed the latest contemporary architecture, Bulfinch might have remained an amateur architect had he not come to grief financially over the houses here referred to by Benjamin, the famous 'Tontine Crescent' in Franklin Street, a speculative venture of 1793–6. The disaster obliged him to hire himself out generally as an architect and to take an administrative post working for the city of Boston. Hence Bulfinch developed a large practice. It was run (so far as is known) without much formal office help, yet included buildings as big as the Massachusetts State House (1795–8).

Bulfinch's name is linked particularly with the Beacon Hill district of Boston. He was one of the original 'Mount Vernon Proprietors' who acquired a large speculative 'take' on Beacon Hill in 1795. He sold out in 1797, not out of any 'professional' embarrassment at having an interest in the development (such ethical scruples troubled only a later generation of architects) but because of pressures over Tontine Crescent. So his practical contribution to Beacon Hill and its environs was mostly confined to design, ranging from conspicuous detached villas and town houses for the 'proprietors' and their friends to obscure commissions for humble speculators building a handful of row houses.[9]

The renown of Bulfinch as Boston's early architect and the continued popularity of the district he helped to create have led, since his death, to a familiar sequence; at first buildings are fancifully, lavishly and somewhat arbitrarily ascribed, then modern scholarship arrives to sort the wheat from the chaff. Not surprisingly the sorting has left Bulfinch with an impressive but quantitatively diminished *oeuvre*. Most houses on Beacon Hill were largely designed and built by 'housewrights' (a term peculiar to New England): in other words by carpenters, still at this time (1805–30) the most skilled and

27. An early view of the first American architectural school, that at the Massachusetts Institute of Technology, then simply housed in the Rogers Building, Boylston Street, Boston.

organized of building tradesmen, by masons, bricklayers, plasterers and even by upholsterers. Among important working developers of the district were Asher Benjamin, Joseph Lincoln and Hezekiah Stoddard, all normally called 'housewrights'; Moses Grant, 'upholder'; and Grant's son-in-law Cornelius Coolidge, variously referred to as architect, builder, real estate broker or simply 'agent'. Such vagueness of nomenclature reflects the professional mobility of the time. But plainly most of Beacon Hill was built by skilled tradesmen who as yet needed no more than an outside draughtsman or two to assist them. Once these men had got the hang of the traditional 'row' house-type that Bulfinch brought to Boston and Benjamin then published in his manuals, they could adapt and alter it to their hearts' content without recourse to a wholly new design. As for labour, they relied on the time-honoured practice of bartering their own skills for those of others; they worked on the houses of fellow craftsmen in return for help on their own, so reducing the need for liquid assets.[10]

As Boston grew richer and more self-conscious and its buildings bigger and costlier, so the number of architects rose. In 1818 a local directory listed three. In 1830 there were a mere eight as against 574 housewrights but by 1846 (when the term housewright had been dropped) there were twenty-one as compared with 272 carpenters and builders. Many of these, or indeed of the seventy-three architects listed for 1867, still dabbled in development.[11] In the South End, the next smart area to be built up after Beacon Hill, several entrepreneurs were architects. One such was Nathaniel J. Bradlee, who designed much speculative housing in the South End during the 1850s.[12]

But once the city's increase allowed an independent full-time architect to make his way by charging a percentage commission, an animus quickly became felt against the architect–developer or architect–contractor. In Boston's third great residential district, the Back Bay (developed from 1857 onwards), speculating architects like Bradlee yielded pride of place to organized 'professional' firms charging fees.[13] With this change came increasing self-consciousness. In 1860 the new firm of William R. Ware and Henry Van Brunt brought to Boston the latest in architectural ideology from New York, where their mentor Richard Morris Hunt and others were representing architecture as a respectable and dignified calling, distinguishable from trade. Five years later, Boston found itself host to the nation's first permanent seat of architectural education, the Massachusetts Institute of Technology's School of Architecture, headed by Ware. In 1867, the year that teaching began at MIT, the locals started the Boston Society of Architects, in emulation of New York's American Institute of Architects founded ten years previously. Several among its prime movers, of whom Bradlee was one, had until recently had plenty to do with contracting or speculative buildings; but they now forswore these pursuits, nominally out of love for architecture.[14] Very soon the BSA became a formal chapter of the expanding AIA, and learnt like other architectural societies to combine conviviality with a keen nose for professional advancement. Of its clubbish proceedings at the turn of the century a member reminisced, 'The cultural topics debated were often of a de luxe type in keeping with the surroundings . . . but two subjects were perennial; how to get more money out of clients and revision of the By-laws.'[15]

*   *   *

The case of New York merits closer attention. Though the city could boast no Bulfinch, it was not short by 1800 on surveyor–builders able to design and erect houses and churches little behind the prevailing modes in Europe. Bulfinch's exact contemporary John McComb junior (1763–1853) is the best known example, in part because his drawings survive.[16] The McCombs father and son were principally masons, and in their capacity as designers called themselves surveyors rather than architects. But soon the smarter title began to lure the successful builders (or 'housesmiths,' the New York term) who presided over the rapid speculative building of the 1820s and 1830s that marked the first phase of the city's rampant expansion.

As in England, at this period the old building system of separate trades was generally

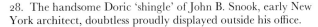

28. The handsome Doric 'shingle' of John B. Snook, early New York architect, doubtless proudly displayed outside his office.

giving way in New York to the more unified method whereby one head builder was firmly in charge. The builders were quick to capitalize on their gains. James Gallier, an English surveyor who emigrated to America following a bankruptcy, gives a jaundiced account of the 'sweating' he encountered in New York's construction industry when he arrived in 1832.

> The builders, that is, the carpenters and bricklayers, all called themselves architects, and were at that time the persons to whom owners of property applied when they required plans for building; the builder hired some poor draftsman, of whom there were some half a dozen in New York at that time, to make the plans, paying him a mere trifle for his services. The drawings so made were, it is true, but of little value, and some proprietors built without having any regular plan. When they wanted a house built, they looked about for one already finished, which they thought suitable for their purpose; and then bargained with a builder to erect for them such another, or one with such alterations upon the model as they might point out.[17]

For two years Gallier worked in association with Minard Lefever, a prolific designer and author of building manuals, at 'this horse-in-a-mill routine of grinding out drawings for the builders'. He adds: 'There was at that time, properly speaking, only one architect's office in New York, kept by Town and Davis.'[18]

History has by and large confirmed that the partnership of Ithiel Town (1784–1844) and Alexander Jackson Davis (1803–92), formally initiated in 1829, constituted New York's first true architectural practice. Their venture arose, it seems, from the kind of set-up that Gallier endured but deplored. Town had already made a reputation as an architect and engineer in New Haven when in 1827 he entered into some kind of business agreement with Martin Thompson, one of New York's leading builders. Associated too with Thompson was Josiah R. Brady, obscurely characterized by A. J. Davis as 'the only Architect in New York who had been a practical builder and ingenious draughtsman, writer of contracts and specification'.[19] Brady appears now and again to have employed the young Davis, who from 1826 ran a little draughting and perspective business of his own, perhaps a miniscule version of the type of *atelier* that the elder Pugin operated in London. At any rate it is plain that both Town and Davis were being employed to provide builders with drawings, probably at very modest remuneration.

Then early in 1829 the more experienced and confident Town made his move, thus recorded in Davis's diary: 'Since Town . . . is so pleased with my drawings in perspective . . . he kindly proposes an Association to practice Architecture professionally in New York, opening an office at 32 Merchants' Exchange for the transaction of business.'[20] This done, Town took himself off to London, Paris and Italy, assessing the vast advantage that would accrue to the young firm from first-hand acquaintance with the architectural fashions and methods of Europe. Soon reminiscences of Nash's London terraces, improved with clever touches from French and Italian house-planning, were rising along Lafayette Place on John Jacob Astor's estates. Builders were requesting more designs, perhaps even paying properly for them, while pupils were gathering to learn under Town and Davis before hastening too to 'hang out their shingle', to use the time-honoured American phrase. By the time Town died in 1844, the architectural profession in New York was thoroughly established.[21]

Town and Davis both strove to consolidate their professional gains by establishing themselves as gentlemen and artists. In a pamphlet of 1835 ('The results of some Thought on a favourite subject'), Town called for an Institution or Academy for the Fine Arts in New York. A meeting of December 1836 attended by Davis, William Strickland, John Haviland, Thomas Ustick Walter (all three from Philadelphia), Isaiah Rogers and Charles Reichard, and supported by Town, Lafever and Ammi Burnham Young, attempted to found such a society of architects. Plainly it was intended to stiffen the resolve of the New Yorkers by bringing in the most prominent practitioners from Philadelphia where Benjamin Latrobe and his pupils had done their utmost to provide a professional basis for architecture. But though Walter and others tried to keep up the momentum with a meeting in Philadelphia in 1837, the infant society could make no headway and for all practical purposes expired.[22] Distance, always a hardship for American professional societies, constituted one obstacle but was not the chief problem. The time was simply unripe for advancement of the professional ethic. Educated men of influence continued to look askance at the new pretensions of architects. A decade later, this is how the diarist George Templeton Strong still reacted to the buildings and behaviour of one of New York's premier architects, James Renwick junior:

Walked down with most windy of all the bags of conceit and coxcombry that ever dubbed themselves Architect, Jemmy Renwick, and most entertaining was the monologue with which he favored me—all about the 'points' of Grace Church and Calvary. If the infatuated monkey showed the slightest trace or germ of feeling for his art, one could pardon and pass over blunders and atrocities so gross as to be palpable even to my ignorance; but nature cut him out for a boss carpenter, and the vanity and pretension that are endurable and excusable in an artist are not to be endured in a mechanic.[23]

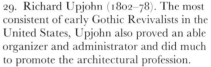

29. Richard Upjohn (1802–78). The most consistent of early Gothic Revivalists in the United States, Upjohn also proved an able organizer and administrator and did much to promote the architectural profession.

Before such criticism, the next generation of New York architects strove to impress upon the public its professional sobriety and artistic pedigree. A vital if ephemeral step in this process from the 1840s was the fashionable 'science' of 'ecclesiology'; for no one could fail to treat with due dignity any sufficiently grave designer of sacred edifices. The impact of the New York Ecclesiological Society, founded in 1848, was all the greater because unlike the institution of 1836 it fostered a positive architectural ideology, transmitted through the pages of its short-lived journal (1848–53). Before this, remarks Phoebe Stanton, there had been no American periodical on architecture; indeed until the late 1830s there had been precious little American architectural literature at all. In its eccentric way, therefore, the *New York Ecclesiologist* took up a torch that had only just been kindled by writers like A. J. Downing. In urging a wider interest in American architecture it was the ancestor of *The Crayon* and of the *American Architect and Building News*.[24]

Ecclesiology was an English importation, and many of its architectural exponents (Richard Upjohn, John Notman, Frank Wills) were English importations too. But American ecclesiologists differed from their English originals in being more candidly taken up with the kind of 'professional' problem that writers like Pugin were apt to scorn. No better example of this could be found than Richard Upjohn, 'Architect and Churchman' (1802–78), who came as close as anyone in the United States to the type of earnest English ecclesiological architect of the 1850s. Yet he arrived at his eminence by a characteristically American professional route. Already twenty-six when he arrived in the country, he was at first a cabinetmaker and carpenter at New Bedford, Mass. By the time he established himself in New York to build Trinity Church in 1839 he had matured into a thoroughgoing architect. As such, he became one of the first to crusade on such crushingly perennial topics as the iniquities of architectural competitions and the merits of a uniform fee-scale.[25]

Upjohn more than anyone else was the prime mover in constituting the American Institute of Architects; it was at his office that architects foregathered for the pilot meeting in 1857.[26] For all practical purposes the organization began as a New York society, and the city boasted the AIA's only chapter until 1869. But the influence of Thomas U. Walter from the old group of 1837 prompted a broader name and approach.

*   *   *

By the time of the AIA's foundation, the appeal of ecclesiology as a call to architecture had grown very weak in New York's increasingly secular and cosmopolitan society. So although Upjohn and his friends could contribute experience and respectability to the budding professional organization, they lacked the charisma necessary for further development. Happily for the AIA, another figure present at the inaugural meeting of 1857 possessed the perfect social and artistic pedigree for the task. This was Richard Morris Hunt (1827–95). A younger man than Upjohn and Walter, Hunt differed from them in two other vital respects. He had enjoyed the prestige, unique for an American at that time, of a training at the Ecole des Beaux Arts in Paris; and he was born rich, the first of a new genre of architect to be so.[27]

So respected did Hunt become in professional circles, and so pervasive was the influence of the informal atelier apeing French methods which he set up in 1858, that he and his disciples determined the direction of mainstream architectural thinking in America for the next seventy-five years. The story of the spread of Beaux-Arts ideals in America, especially through the establishment of architectural schools by Hunt's followers at MIT (1865), Columbia (1881) and elsewhere is familiar enough.[28] The more privileged, wealthy and promising pupils went to Paris itself in steadily growing numbers, to return aglow with the pure gospel. These men were to dominate the profession in New York as the nineteenth century drew to a close.

Remarkably, at a time when the unsentimental priorities of capitalism were starting to gnaw at the cities of the United States, the Beaux-Arts men openly advocated an architectural approach that was artistic in the extreme and often defied practicality and economy.* Examples of this cavalier approach, which seems rather to have enhanced than wrecked their careers, abound in anecdote and memoir. Hunt himself, on the evidence of his biographer, seems with strange frequency to have exceeded estimates, neglected supervision and disregarded instructions. More than once he was enmeshed in litigation; yet nothing marred the serenity of his career as the premier

---

* Because such attitudes emanated from the schools, records Grant Hildebrand, for most of the interwar years the great industrial architect Albert Kahn of Detroit would hire no college graduates with an architectural degree to join his huge staff of 300–400, believing that they might 'place self-expression over team co-operation'. (Grant Hildebrand, *Designing for Industry: The Architecture of Albert Kahn*, 1974, pp. 127, 132.)

30. Richard Morris Hunt as Cimabue, 1883. The perfect illustration of the Beaux-Arts architect's aspirations.

architect of the Gilded Age, the darling of Newport society.[29] The great H. H. Richardson was doubtless less slipshod than this, but a pupil of his who worked with his contractor Norcross on the Cheney Building at Hartford soon 'wondered at his ability in ignoring practical considerations when attaining artistic effects'.[30]

In that most fabulously successful of all Beaux-Arts firms, McKim Mead and White, the artistic principle was raised to a lofty and self-conscious ideal. 'Young men,' Charles McKim told students at Columbia who had been informed of the primacy of plan, 'the thing of first importance in architecture is—beauty.'[31] Joseph Wells, a key figure in the firm's early days, went further in his disdain for clients' priorities, pronouncing that 'the position of the creative artist with regard to the public in this century is that of a humorist trying to amuse the unamusable'.[32] Wells, in view of his sentiments, spent his time on details and was kept away from clients. But when an architect mustered enough assurance in putting this point of view to a rich enough customer it tended to work. Thus it was that McKim asserted his authority over the Pierpont Morgan Library before the most formidable of financiers.

> The first point to be settled was as to his authority to build according to his own conception. To Mr. Morgan he said in substance: 'I would like to build after the manner of the Greeks, whose works have lasted through the ages; but to do so well will be very expensive, and the results will not be apparent.' 'Explain,' said Mr. Morgan; and McKim explained: 'When I have been in Athens I have tried to insert the blade of my knife between the stones of the Erechtheum, and have been unable to do it. I would like to follow their example, but it would cost a small fortune and no one would see where the additional money went.' 'How much extra?' Mr. Morgan asked. 'Fifty thousand dollars,' said the modest architect. 'Go ahead,' commanded the man of capital.[33]

Stanford White got his way with methods decidedly less pompous than McKim's—in part through acting the playboy. A contemporary wrote: 'His relation to the merchant class and to the swell mob was of a personal, galvanic kind. He excited them, he buffaloed them, he met them on all sides at once . . .'.[34] And the contractor Paul Starrett enviously described his techniques:

> He treated a client as if the man was supremely lucky to have the services of the great Stanford White. He was full of whims and flashes, and expected his client to accept them as the signs of genius. He could build a building half way up, decide it didn't please him, tear it down, build it differently, make the owner pay the bills and like it.
>
> Unquestionably, White possessed a keen sense of beauty, but, like many another architect I have known, he could be very neglectful of the practical side of his buildings. He almost took the position that usefulness should be subordinate to appearance.[35]

No wonder Augustus St Gaudens caricatured the firm by showing the third partner, William Mead, struggling to anchor two kites! From this time on every large practice needed its Mead: the anchorman, the business or planning partner, whose role in the history of architecture has consistently been slighted. The flightier and more idealistic

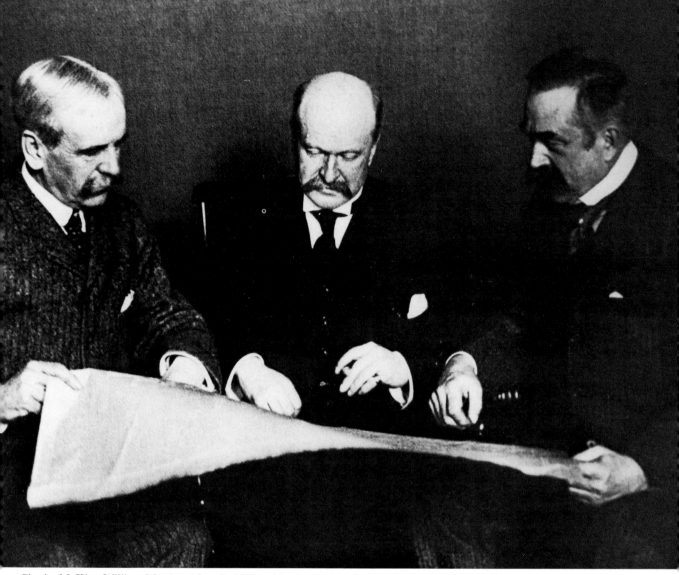

31. Charles McKim, William Mead and Stanford White, the great triumvirate and supreme arbiters of East Coast architectural taste between 1885 and 1910.

the design team, the more the anchorman had to pacify the formidable committees of profit-conscious businessmen who began increasingly to dictate the forms of urban architecture.

Why did McKim Mead and White succeed in persuading the American businessman to lavish money on architecture? Charles Moore, McKim's friend and biographer and no cynic as to the firm's ideals, candidly put its success down to 'the rapid increase in wealth and the consequent desire of the traveled wealthy for a share in old-world art and culture'.[36] The Beaux-Arts architect, in other words, was able at a moment of historic American self-consciousness to reassure his clients with a display of superior learning and polish. That was the reality behind such a foundation as the American Academy in Rome (at first the 'American School of Architecture'), started in 1895 on McKim's initiative so as to allow young Beaux-Arts stars to study there.

But clients of this kind, even in New York, were limited. The less privileged architects naturally failed to appreciate the artistic canons of Hunt and his school. They clamoured for greater professional gains of the type championed by Upjohn, not for visions of Paris or Rome. In New York, where Hunt and his disciples dominated its counsels, the AIA found itself treading water. Following a reorganization of 1866, chapters were inaugurated in Philadelphia and Chicago (both in 1869) and others followed elsewhere. But despite some progress in establishing a fee scale, architects away from the east coast were not in general drawn into an organization which, they believed, 'lacked pep and hustle'.[37] With increasing urgency they raised the issues of competition, of government architecture and of the licensing of architects, but the AIA was not getting results. By the 1880s things began to look bad: only thirty attended the 1885 convention in Nashville, while even on the institute's home ground of New York only a few more than fifty could be raised in 1887.[38] But by now another city, Chicago, had taken up the initiative. From Chicago, cradle of the modern office building and of the Prairie School, derives in great part yet another revolution in American architecture, that of the organization of the modern profession. As this achievement has earned scant recognition, it is worth examining in greater detail.

*   *   *

Fire, boom, slump, then boom, fast succeeding one another, wrought a revolution in Chicago's construction industry during the 1870s and 1880s. Management-oriented contractors arose, equal to the challenges of foundation-laying and steel-erection that were the preconditions of the world's first high-rise office buildings. Newly formidable labour unions began to make headway in the realm of construction. An ambitious periodical, *The Inland Architect and Builder*, dedicated to upholding the interests of Chicago in all things pertaining to construction, commenced in 1883. With these emerged a new, streamlined architectural profession, overtly in tune with the city's commercial ideal. Chicago architects of the period, a French observer said, 'brazenly accepted the conditions imposed by the speculator';[39] and the critic Montgomery Schuyler spoke of administrative ability as 'the one faculty that was absolutely indispensable to the success of a practitioner of architecture in Chicago.'[40]

Of the pioneering architectural partnerships of the day, those of Adler and Sullivan (1881–95) and of Burnham and Root (1873–91) dominated commercial building in Chicago and have preoccupied historians ever since. The Burnham and Root firm, which carried on with even greater success following John Root's death in 1891 as D. H. Burnham and Company and then after Daniel Burnham himself died in 1912 as Graham, Anderson, Probst and White, has been scrutinized with unusual intensity, the Promethean role of 'Uncle Dan' having been particularly well explained in two thorough biographies.[41] It was America's first fully organized commercial practice, the

32. Daniel Burnham (left) and John Wellborn Root (right) pose before their handsome corner fireplace in the library or reception room at their offices in the Rookery Building, Chicago. The studious, art-worshipping setting contrasted with a severely practical arrangement for the rest of the office.

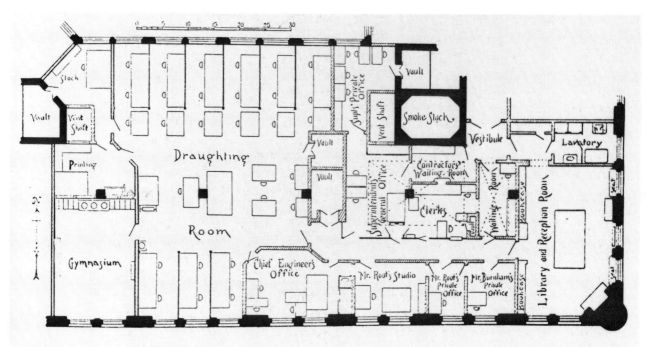

33. Plan of Burnham and Root office suite as fitted up on the top floor of the Rookery Building, Chicago, *c.* 1888–9. Note particularly the gymnasium, and the serried ranks of boards in the draughting room. Only Root has his own studio, but Burnham is closer to the library or reception room, whose grandeur is calculated to impress customers. Contractors have their own restricted waiting room next to the superintendents and clerks.

34. Plan of the Adler and Sullivan office in the Auditorium Building, Chicago, 1890. The office was situated on top of the building in a tower, the construction of which caused Adler some headaches, and it was open on all four sides. Adler and Mueller, the manager, have rooms close to the general office and the entrance; Sullivan and Wright, the chief designers, are juxtaposed at the other end of the office.

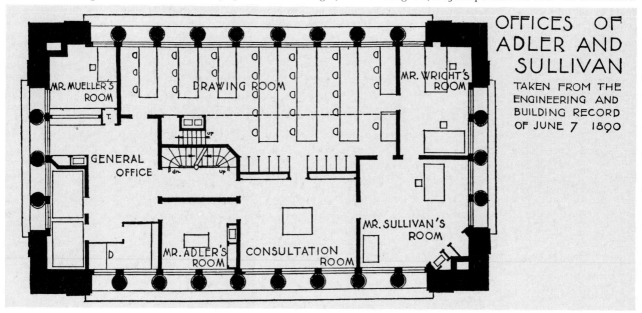

original from which the great architectural conglomerates of today directly descend. As early as 1889 a bright young architect visiting Burnham and Root's quarters could observe the portents: 'Here for the first time we saw a large thoroughly equipped office. It impressed us like a large manufacturing plant.'[42]

From the start Burnham, the capitalist idealist, dominated the firm's direction with his ambition. 'The only way to handle a big business is to *delegate, delegate, delegate,*' Louis Sullivan heard him urge upon Root, on discovering the latter lavishing precious moments upon detail.[43] In the early days Burnham was content to leave much of the designing to the talented Root, himself acting as 'the salesman'. When Root died, Burnham was bitter to find his strategy imperilled by mischance. 'I have worked, I have schemed and dreamed to make us the greatest architects in the world,' he soliloquized. 'I have made him see it and kept him at it—and now he dies—damn! damn! damn!'[44] But by dint of leadership and organization Burnham salvaged the practice, overcame the crisis when Charles Atwood, the talented partner whom he had chosen to succeed Root, died only four years after his predecessor, soon had offices in three cities and sped on to greater triumphs and international fame. The influence he came to exert transcended the fashions of architectural style or even of city planning that he helped set at the World's Fair of 1893. He altered the terms of architectural practice, enhanced the architect's professional status, and trained several of the men destined to be principals in the giant urban contracting firms of the new century.

Essential ingredients for Burnham's success were charm and suavity coupled with a compelling idealism and enthusiasm. Despite his ambition, self-conceit, and occasionally questionable methods, men of strong temperament and divergent views usually succumbed to Burnham the 'impresario'; Sullivan and Wright, for instance, were numbered among his admirers. 'His very being and looks were half the battle,' wrote Paul Starrett. 'He had only to assert the most commonplace thing and it sounded important and convincing.'[45] Prototypical even in his relaxations, Burnham anticipated the modern businessman's preoccupation with bodily fitness. To combat his large smoking, eating and drinking, he fenced, golfed and hunted, and proved 'almost evangelical in his zeal to have others keep themselves in shape'.[46] A small office gym was installed for the men, and at the age of fifty-nine Burnham himself took a course of 200 exercise sessions, mainly in callisthenics and jogging.

Dankmar Adler, principal of the other great Chicago practice of the period, has been overshadowed for posterity by his brilliant, mercurial partner Louis Sullivan. So alluring has proved the philosophy of architectural individualism, propounded by Sullivan himself in a series of 'inspirational' outpourings, and so intent have critics been to perceive buildings as the products of a single mind, that the Adler and Sullivan partnership has sometimes appeared as the latter's exclusive preserve. But even in the realm of design, responsibilities within the firm were always shared. Wright, it is acknowledged, created some of Adler and Sullivan's domestic work practically on his own; and after the partners split in 1895, Sullivan was unable to carry on without copious interventions from George Elmslie, Wright's successor as his right-hand man.[47]

Adler's role was in fact recognized by both Sullivan and Wright, if never in specific terms. Sullivan, rarely generous to other architects, said simply: 'Mr Adler was the "outside man". I did the aesthetics—Adler was a man of fine mind and excellent

35 (left). 'The Big Chief': a formidable-looking Dankmar Adler in 1898, from the first edition of Frank Lloyd Wright's autobiography.

36 (right). Louis Sullivan, Frank Lloyd Wright's 'Lieber Meister', photographed a few years before his death. This unromanticized portrait appeared in the first edition of Wright's autobiography but not in later editions, perhaps because it suggested neither genius nor vitality.

heart.'[48] Wright called his influence 'great and good, for he himself was a great builder. He was also a manager of men, a fine critic.'[49] If this sounds like Burnham and Root's division of labour, Adler did certainly undertake the brunt of getting and keeping commissions. But in addition he possessed outstanding skills in engineering which came to the fore in the Chicago Auditorium (1887–90). On the firm's general outlook, Sullivan's friend Claude Bragdon had this to say:

> In spite of his many graceful references to Sullivan as Master, it is probable that Wright would name Dankmar Adler, Sullivan's partner, as the more important influence of the two. Sullivan derived the fundamentals of his architectural philosophy from Adler, and it was the great good fortune of Wright and Sullivan, creative artists both, and therefore in the larger sense feminine, to have been impregnated, so to speak, at their most formative period with the virile and essentially male ideation of Adler, one of the greatest structural engineers of his time.[50]

Outside the partnership, Adler's stature within the profession in Chicago seems to have been almost as great as Burnham's. German by birth and drawn like Sullivan to

37. The delegates to the great St Louis convention of the Western Association of Architects, 1885. Burnham is unmistakable in the centre, in a lighter coat.

the German intellectual traditions of the mid-west,[51] he brought to the task of upholding the modern architect's interests all of Burnham's commercial idealism complemented by an unswerving capacity for committee work. Adler in fact was something of a disinterested workhorse. His practice was smaller than Burnham's, his ambition less intense. Consequently, when depression struck in the 1890s Adler and Sullivan were not so well able to weather the storm. They parted in some bitterness, Adler claiming that he could do better with a smaller practice. He even left architecture temporarily but soon returned, continuing to work until his death in 1900.[52]

Burnham and Adler, then, with help from their partners and subordinates, led the fight for the professional changes which the AIA could not or would not achieve. It is now time to see how.

Right from its inception in 1883, *The Inland Architect and Builder* began calling for an effective organization for the architects of the mid-west. The AIA's Chicago chapter, instituted in 1869, had degenerated into a club and stood condemned by the more active of local architects as 'a perfect failure'.[53] A convention of some 150 practitioners duly met in Chicago in November 1884 to inaugurate the Western Association of

Architects. The first proceedings revealed where the initiative lay—with the city's great commercial practices. Burnham chaired the inaugural meeting, characteristically exhorting his audience to emulate the western 'spirit of enterprise' and comparing their prospects to those of Athens, Carthage or Rome; Adler became treasurer, and Root took charge of a key committee. In February 1885 the same faction proceeded to combine at local level, starting the Illinois State Association of Architects. Other associations were arising at this time in adjacent states, but none achieved the importance of the ISAA. In this Adler and Burnham, again with help from their partners, proved the key figures at early meetings.[54]

The main practical goals on which the WAA and its constituent associations wanted action boiled down to three. They asked for effective rules on competitions; a share in government commissions; and architectural licensing or registration, in other words, a closed profession with entrance by examination. None of these aims, the Chicago group thought, was in the least inimical to good or artistic architecture; had they thought so, Sullivan, Root and others would have been early dissenters. To achieve what they wanted, Adler emphasized at the inaugural ISAA meeting, they were obliged to organize within the framework of capitalism. 'I believe in a business community like this, it is the body that appears to have money that is respected . . . If we wish to see the time when a person in order to practice as an architect, must pass an examination, we must appear before legislative bodies, and before the public as men of standing, and we are not so considered unless we have demonstrated our ability to earn money.'[55]

The fruits of the Chicago group's early labours were presented at the WAA's historic second convention, held at St Louis in November 1885 and dubbed by *The Inland Architect* 'The Magna Charta of a development and upbuilding of a new world architecture'.[56] The meat of the proceedings consisted of two mammoth committee reports. The first, chaired and drafted by Burnham, examined the problem of competitions in detail and spelt out a new code. The second, almost wholly Adler's work, comprised two bills to be submitted for legislation: one was for licensing architects at state level, the other for reforming the powerful federal post of 'Supervising Architect to the Treasury'.[57]

These proposals offered a much firmer basis for professional reform than anything hitherto concocted by the AIA. None was translated into law immediately. But the most far-reaching suggestion, Adler's bill for licensing architects, reached the statute book first, though initially in Illinois alone. Much not only of the drafting but of the research and lobbying for this bill seems to have been due to Adler. When touring Europe in 1885 to examine theatres in connection with the Chicago Auditorium, Adler enquired into the status of architects there, with the draft to be submitted at St Louis in mind. Doubtless he was concerned particularly with Prussia and other German-speaking states, where the tradition of the Technische Hochschule had made professional licensing common by the 1880s. At home, he was supported by Nathan Clifford Ricker, chief of the tiny University of Illinois architecture school, started at Urbana in 1873.[58] This was a help because the school's examination could be taken as a norm in weighing the necessary qualifications for licensing architects. After many years of trying, Adler and Ricker finally secured the passing of the Illinois State Licensing Law in 1897 which was introduced by a Chicago architect-turned-legislator, one Nothnagel.[59]

Considering that it was the first of its kind in America, the Illinois law seems to have provoked curiously few strong reactions. Probably this was because it was not sternly exclusive or hard to circumvent. Anyone could design a building for himself without being a licensed architect, so speculative projects were not covered. Architects practising at the time were able to register merely by paying a small annual fee, and to judge from early results the examination itself seems to have been hard to fail. Nevertheless the Illinois act was the first frankly masonic act of the American architectural profession. It was followed by licensing laws in Arkansas and California (both in 1901). Not until 1951 were all states thus covered.[60]

Though the WAA held vigorous conventions in 1886 and 1887, by the end of the decade it had been absorbed back into the AIA.[61] This came about not through any waning enthusiasm on the part of Chicago architects (though the city's labour problems, which were particularly intense in the construction industry and took an ugly turn with the notorious Haymarket 'riot' of 1886, do seem to have imparted an increasingly conservative tone to their pronouncements). Rather, Burnham and some of his disciples saw affairs increasingly from a national perspective, and so transferred their loyalties. On a hint from Root the AIA agreed to hold its 1887 convention in Chicago. Here Burnham revealed himself as the prime defector from the younger body and advocated amalgamation, with a strengthened AIA ensconced in new headquarters in Washington. In the same month Root was soothing the breasts of the locals at an ISAA meeting. 'The AIA recognized that they had been at fault in too great conservatism and the WAA in too great radicalism,' he told his colleagues.[62] Henceforward Adler became the main force to propel a sometimes reluctant WAA into the planned consolidation, which came about at a joint convention in Cincinnati in 1889. Ten years after, the newly forceful AIA transferred its headquarters from New York to Washington, as Burnham had suggested.

* * *

Once established in Washington, the AIA became the authentic voice of the organized American architectural profession, such as it then was. That is not to say that its writ went entirely unchallenged. For about five years just after the turn of the century a small rival organization, the Architectural League of America, flourished in the mid-west just as the WAA had done not long previously, but it soon lost importance.[63] Similarly, the AIA exercised little authority among west coast architects for a long time. Nevertheless by 1900 it stood as the nationally recognized representative of a nationally recognized profession. At this point the story outlined in this chapter could be closed. But it may be more illuminating to conclude with an episode that suggests with unusual clarity the nature of the AIA's early authority.

One of the three great issues that absorbed the architects of the WAA in the 1880s was the reform of government architecture. Compared to the grand problems of registration or competitions, it seems to have little relevance to the modern profession. Yet in its time it deeply affected the course of American architecture; for the results of this controversy helped block the emergence of a significant public sector within the profession.

Before the unification of 1889, both the AIA and the WAA had agitated on their members' behalf for a greater share of government commissions. They were fortified by the federal government's chronic incompetence in making provision for the post offices, customs houses and other official buildings increasingly needed in the burgeoning American cities.[64] More by default than by deliberate arrangement, these buildings had generally become the preserve of the 'Supervising Architect to the Treasury', a job that came into being at least half by accident.

Robert Mills had effectively worked as a government architect between 1833 and 1851, notably on the Treasury Building in Washington. So his post had come to be attached to the Treasury Department, the employees of the 'bureau of construction' having the lowly rank of departmental clerks. Ammi Burnham Young ran the office after Mills, erecting many decent buildings in the teeth of federal parsimony. After a report of 1862 from Thomas Ustick Walter asked 'why the government maintains a supervising architect to waste its treasure in the construction of expensive insecure buildings',[65] the post briefly disappeared, but it had to be resuscitated. The next important supervising architect, Alfred B. Mullett (1866–74), built prolifically and pompously all over the union but suffered from the frustrations of the post, the envy of colleagues in private practice, and the general corruption of the reconstruction era. Mullett, it was said, was 'as honest as President Grant was in his leadership of the country; but both had unscrupulous subordinates'.[66] Four times investigated and exonerated, Mullett later refused to have any truck 'with such a bunch of unprincipled men as the architects of Washington'.[67] His successor, W. A. Potter, was sympathetic to giving government jobs to private architects and urged the AIA to lobby for reform, but did not last long. After him, corruption and chicanery ran rampant under the aegis of James G. Hill.[68]

The AIA made a first attempt to alter affairs through federal legislation by promoting the Smithmeyer Bill of 1874, but this failed to pass.[69] The WAA's draft bill of 1885 rekindled enthusiasm, and eventually private practice appeared to have triumphed over recalcitrant bureaucracy when in February 1893 Congress passed the Tarsney Act. This act authorized the supervising architect to hold competitions for important buildings, but left discretionary powers in the hands of the Treasury Secretary, then John G. Carlisle.[70]

Six months later, Burnham was elected president of the AIA. Soon, as no competitions had been forthcoming, he and his colleagues started fretting and asking why. Supervising Architect Jeremiah O'Rourke, it soon emerged, had gone into a sulk and induced Secretary Carlisle to stall on implementing the Tarsney Act. The storm finally broke in 1894 when O'Rourke published his department's designs for a large federal building in Buffalo. At Burnham's word the AIA's new propaganda machine swung into action. Glenn Brown, then Washington correspondent of *The American Architect*, devoted a whole number of the magazine to a comparison of government and private structures, emphasizing the artistic superiorities of the latter.[71] Abuse was heaped upon the design for Buffalo, whose citizens were represented as rising up in outrage against impending monstrosity. Brown also made confident claims for the superior economy of private architecture.

Carlisle sat tight through all this. His obduracy stemmed hardly from commitment

38. Cartoon from *Life* caricaturing the non-implementation of the Tarsney Act, 1894. John G. Carlisle, the Treasury Secretary, rises from his seat of judgement, strikes down Art, and instead upholds his misshapen protégé, the Supervising Architect. Idiots or convicts appear to be doing the designing, while above are sundry ham-fisted and costly post offices produced by government architects, most lately that for Buffalo. The caption reads: 'Good Architecture Be——! Secretary Carlisle has decided that designs for government buildings shall be turned out by machinery as heretofore.'

to either public architecture in general or O'Rourke in particular, whom he eventually dismissed. Rather, the bullying of the AIA irked him, to the point where he declined further communication with Burnham. The AIA then changed its tactic and had a new measure, the McKaig Bill, introduced in Congress, but this too was blocked. Some private architects, Dankmar Adler for one, thought the AIA had badly mishandled the situation.

Instead of . . . treating the matter as a political measure and arguing from the standpoint of the politician, and proving to the politician Carlisle that it might be good politics to please the architects of the country at large and to utilize politically the new powers conferred upon him by the Tarsney law, they proceeded to bombard the shying Kentuckian with Olympian fulminations about the duty of the Government to the cause of art and all sorts of other things unintelligible and terrifying to the spoils politician.

The result was runaway, smash-up, an altogether unnecessary relegation of the Tarsney bill to the junk pile, three years of earnest effort wasted upon the McKaig bill . . .[72]

By a measure of luck the AIA's goal was for the time achieved in 1896 when Lyman J. Gage, a Chicago crony of Burnham's, replaced Carlisle. Gage implemented the Tarsney Act and advertised for a new Supervising Architect, agreeing that candidates should be vetted by Burnham and three other AIA stalwarts. As a result James Knox Taylor, formerly a partner of Cass Gilbert but by this date on the Supervising Architect's staff, was chosen. Though satisfactory at the time to the AIA lobby, Taylor's appointment was to prove embarrassing; for Taylor's views about government jobs changed radically once he was in federal employ.[73]

For the time being however all but the most avaricious of private architects were reasonably happy. Over the fifteen years from 1897 they profited handsomely from large government commissions under the Tarsney Act, among them jobs as notorious for delay and extravagance as any under the previous system. Cass Gilbert was paid $228,000 over the New York Custom House, McKim Mead and White $100,000 for the New York Post Office, and Arnold Brunner $146,000 for the Cleveland Post Office (a source of especial contention).[74] Some of these works were acquired in competition, others were awarded directly. In 1910 the position of private architects with regard to federal jobs was strengthened when Congress established a Commission of Fine Arts, with power to advise on the choice of artists, architects and designers for all major public buildings; Burnham naturally was one of the original commissioners.[75]

Shortly after this there was a surprising reaction. In 1908 the AIA had raised its fee scale from 5 per cent to 6 per cent, which many felt was poor value on big government contracts. Taylor therefore urged a congressional committee that his office should be given more work, and in 1912 'by an appropriation in the sundry civil bill' which the AIA had overlooked, the Tarsney Act was suddenly repealed.[76] The AIA was furious and a renewed row broke out, with figures bandied about on either side to no convincing effect. But the act did not return. After 1912 government commissions came to private architects through the Commission of Fine Arts or, alternatively, as one-off deals.

The campaign over government architecture ended in less than entire victory for the private firms and the AIA. But it did for ever reduce to the status of a second-rank organization a federal department which, despite its faults, had ample experience of large buildings constructed with results quite comparable with those of private practice. The campaign also neatly exposed the nature and prophesied the future direction of the AIA. Destroying the Supervising Architect's powers amounted, in the words of one politician to Dankmar Adler, to 'a move got up by a number of architects in the big cities to gobble up' federal commissions.[77] The policy showed that the AIA stood neither for the salaried architect, nor for the small independent practitioner, but merely for the 'architects in the big cities'. From Burnham's presidency onwards, the overt motivation of the AIA became not to advance the cause of art, as Hunt had advocated over the previous decades, but to gain ever bigger and more prestigious jobs for the great practices. The American architect, in fact, had finally organized himself into becoming a businessman.

*   *   *

The alliance fomented between the artists and businessmen of the American architectural profession in the 1880s and 1890s still holds good. Though the managerial and artistic approaches to architecture continue generally to appear mutually opposed, in many of the biggest and most profitable practices they have happily co-existed. The artists regularly place new things before their potential clients' eyes, whether by invention, importation from Europe, or public argument; the businessmen digest innovations in management and office technique, and pass these on into the mainstream of large private practice. Upon the firmness of this alliance depends the future of what continues to be a weak profession.

Yet (to revert to the start of this chapter) the bulk of building in the United States still takes place outside the limits of this unwritten agreement. So too, significantly, does much of what appears to foreign eyes especially rich, vital and indigenous in American architecture. The private house, for example, enjoys even now a life of its own unimaginable in Europe and often untouched by European taste. At one end of the market, the unruly individualism of Frank Lloyd Wright has given place to that of Bruce Goff and, less extremely, to that of thousands of practical, unconforming Americans who still design and build for themselves; at another end, catalogues of syndicated house plans stack the shelves of suburban bookstores and continue to be built from. Little of this has much in common with the world of official American architecture, which grew up around the defence of the profession. Another, more commercial example of vitality in American building is the much-analysed 'strip' or 'miracle mile'. In this case east coast art–architects, failing to tame the strip, have started to imitate it, thus fulfilling their historic role of broadening the range of architectural possibilities open to the 'respectable' part of the profession. Today the strip is certainly less savage than it was thirty years ago, but it remains essentially untamed: outside the agreed values of the American architectural profession, because outside the economic sphere of interest of both the big-business architect and the smaller art–architect. Yet these are the types of building ultimately most characteristic of American culture; they are the ones which seem to mean most to ordinary Americans and even, at present, to certain disenchanted east coast intellectuals.[78] The moral is plain: what is good for the American architect may not be good for the American public or, indeed, for American architecture.

CHAPTER FIVE

The Architect as Gentleman

Genius in architectural journalism, if there is such a thing, was nowhere perhaps more generously bestowed or more lightly frittered away than in Britain between the wars. Of course, most of such writing is ephemeral. But some of it will continue to be read as the minor work of authors known better for other things, yet deeply drawn to architecture. Among amateurs Evelyn Waugh, John Betjeman, Robert Byron and Osbert Lancaster all wrote about buildings with a gusto and wit unknown in English since the time of Horace Walpole. Among practising architects also, several combined knowledge of their craft with real literary ability. Two of these, H. S. Goodhart-Rendel and Sir Reginald Blomfield, will hold their place on account of their trenchant and readable books of scholarship. And two others, H. B. Creswell and Clough Williams-Ellis, deserve equally to endure, less for their learning than for the charm and delicacy with which they addressed the central problem of their careers—the predicament of the modern architect. A discussion of their writings forms the bulk of this chapter.

To the eccentric, lighthearted manner of these authors in treating so serious a subject, as indeed to this whole brief flowering of fine writing about architecture, the history of the British building press is germane. Its pioneers, J. C. Loudon of the short-lived *Architectural Magazine* (founded 1834) and George Godwin of *The Builder* (1842), were by temperament organizers and reformers. They traded primarily in neither architectural nor literary style but in fact, and their journals were formidably factual to boot. Aesthetic controversy, though afforded space in their columns, never sapped their belief that practical enlightenment and social progress should come first. And Godwin, over thirty-nine years of editorial control at *The Builder*, in fulfilling his own ideals made his magazine a necessity for architects, engineers, surveyors and builders alike.[1]

The *Building News* (founded 1855), Godwin's earliest and strongest rival, began from the 1860s to take a more strictly 'architectural' line by championing styles. But it did not much alter the balance of coverage established by *The Builder*. Later periodicals like *The Architect* (1869), the *British Architect* (1874) and the *Builders' Journal* (1895), while increasingly addressing the narrower audience of architects alone, remained imitations of Godwin's successful original. All in fact were useful, prosaic, ugly newspapers, anonymously concocted and ransacked for facts and hints by everyone in the building trades.

This system dissatisfied the late Victorian architectural élite. For members of the RIBA there were admittedly the Institute's own *Transactions* and *Journal*, but despite some valuable contributions these often smacked of parochialism. So in 1896 was founded the *Architectural Review*, still today acknowledged as the natural organ for fashionable British architects wishing to promote the artistic side of their profession. Despite an early change of ownership, the *Review* quickly settled down as a magazine run and written mainly by architects, that is to say by amateurs in the journalistic sense. It came out not weekly but monthly, it contained little or no trade news, and its articles were predominantly reflective or historical, often stretching to some length. In appearance the *Review* was much influenced by the late Victorian art magazines like *The Studio*. In format, type-face and most of all in quality and number of photographs, it was visibly superior to the weekly building press.[2]

Soon the more alert of the building papers began to follow this lead, particularly the *Builders' Journal*, which in due course acknowledged its true readership and turned into the *Architects' Journal*. Then, after 1914 the old-established leaders in the field underwent a marked decline in authority, appeal and size. *The Builder* continued, if with decreased prestige; the *British Architect* disappeared; while *The Architect* and the *Building News* merged in 1926 and changed to a two-column format with longer articles.

The new conditions encouraged architects to write more intelligibly, more directly and less technically about their subject. For many this was at first hard to do. Striving to avoid the provocative stylistic controversies of the mid-Victorians or the complexity of technical discourse, the contributors often lapsed into sentimentality, notably when developing their own ideas. So while the historical articles of the early *Review* are frequently enlightening, the texts of those on contemporary work less often have lasting worth.

Since the *Architectural Review* was less technical and more attractive than earlier building papers, it could draw upon educated middle-class writers and readers beyond the immediate world of the construction industry. This led to a tradition of articles by scholars and dilettanti of all shades of opinion. The tradition reached its apogee between the wars, when the *Review* was dominated by amateur writing. But architects of the period were far from inactive as writers. Many, following the self-effacing period of the Arts and Crafts Movement, wished again to communicate and propagandize more broadly. The cosiness of pre-war practice having vanished, architectural principle had to be hammered out anew. No less than their counterparts on the continent, British architects felt the need for a new and more socialized approach to their calling.

These two traditions, amateur and professional, gave birth to an architectural journalism new in literary richness and subtlety. But the best of its English-born writers could none of them slough off the past to go along unreservedly with the tide of root-and-branch modernism. To rival the brash, basically anti-intellectual tenets of *Towards a New Architecture*, British architects could produce no Pugin and British writers no Ruskin. At least theoretically many amateurs favoured radical beginnings. Yet they wrote most eloquently of the Regency or Victorian past, of the charm of the English suburb, or of travel in Spain and Afghanistan.

In a profounder sense architects too remained enslaved to the past. Arts and Crafts ideals in particular endured into the 1920s and 1930s. This tradition had taught that style mattered little compared to substantial and good workmanship. But it neither explained nor stemmed the inexorable modern demand for stylistic change. Collaboration had been another keynote in Arts and Crafts thinking. Yet instead of being understood as a modern alternative to individualistic professionalism, it was normally presented as a comfortable, old-world and preferably rural phenomenon, in which the classes played their accustomed roles and the architect–gentleman controlled and co-ordinated.

This idea of gentility is omnipresent in British architectural thought between the wars. Even the reformers believed in it. J. C. Squire the poet, feeling that architecture needed a broader public airing, instinctively set up the Architects' Club as a forum for gentlemanly discussions and dinners. The Mars Group, for all its radical posturings, was tarred with the same brush. To a degree the authors I have chosen to discuss, being practical architects familiar with the true conditions of building, were in different ways able to perceive the limitations of such an approach. But in their writings one single, nostalgic ideal stands out over all—the kindly, alluring, essentially harmless but increasingly anachronistic concept of the architect as gentleman.

*   *   *

In so far as Harry Bulkeley Creswell (1869–1960) is remembered today, it is as a 'humorist' and as author of *The Honeywood File* and *The Honeywood Settlement*, books that still enjoy a small vogue among those who care for architecture. There is a tinge of promise unfulfilled to Creswell's long career.[3] After university, he was articled in 1890 to Aston Webb, a rising star in the British architectural firmament. Creswell was devoted to Webb, whom he later described as

> truly an artist from his toes to the tips of his fragile lightly boned fingers, characteristically blackened with the soft H. B. lead with which he slapped his designings down on cartridge paper "because it bites so nicely," hissing through his teeth like an ostler curry-combing a horse.[4]

He stayed five years and clearly proved a capable pupil, destined for a bright future. He then worked as an architect superintending buildings for the Post Office in various places. At this time he produced his first pieces of architectural journalism; they appeared from 1897, chiefly in the *Architectural Review*, under the name of Bulkeley Creswell. They display a queer thoughtfulness, originality and heterodoxy, deploring for instance the esoteric side of art and betraying a penchant (then most unfashionable) for public-house architecture and underground lavatories.[5]

In 1900, having established a connection with a large boilermaking firm, Creswell set up in practice in Rugby, a Midlands town of small size. There quickly followed the one building which gives his name a small footnote in the history of modern English architecture. This was the Queensferry Factory near Chester (1901), later dubbed by Pevsner the 'most advanced British building of its date' on account of its flat roofs, plain surfaces and battered buttresses.[6]

39. H. B. Creswell in old age, sporting a spry look.

Probably Creswell thought much of it at the time, but in after years he was inclined to ridicule those who saw in it an intimation of 'modern tendencies', just as Voysey dismissed similar admiration of his houses. The attitude stemmed perhaps from embarrassment at the local progeny of his factory:

Although he [the architect] desired only that the building should look like what it was, the public desired more. Unable to accept it as looking like a town hall, or a bank, or a home for inebriates, or to trace in it the lineaments of Western architecture, the public not only explored the remotest wilds of Asia to seek a comparison with the Tibetan Rock Monastery, but adopted the salient feature of the boiler works as a local tradition; and workmen's villas, that sprang up in the vicinity, vied with one another in a display of superfluous and inconvenient battered buttresses.[7]

The Queensferry Factory was a splendid start but turned out to be a dead end. Rugby proved unpromising ground for expanding his practice, yet Creswell stayed there twelve years. There were a few small houses, odd commercial jobs and eventually a church, but never again anything like Queensferry. So he turned back to journalism, contributing some whimsical pieces for *Punch* from 1907.

In about 1911 Creswell returned to London and became consulting architect to the Crown Agents, a body with wide interests in the British colonies. This connection brought him a number of farflung jobs in the Falkland Islands, Sierra Leone, Mauritius and Ceylon.[8] But they seem to have come too late to recharge his architectural ambitions. During the war of 1914–18 the balance of his interests seems to

40. Willans and Robinson's boilerworks at Queensferry, Clwyd, designed by H. B. Creswell in 1901 and carried out by him in conjunction with H. P. G. Maule in 1903. Creswell's one claim to real architectural fame, the building enjoyed a modest *réclame* among 'functionalists' and was therefore duly derided by its author in his later years. 'The ideas now connoted by "functionalism and commodity",' he wrote in 1940, 'were then so familiar—stale even—that no verbal fantasies were necessary to enshrine them.'

have shifted towards writing. In 1917–18 he published two slight novels, *Thomas* and *Thomas Settles Down*. Architecture makes a halting appearance in the sequel when the hero Thomas Quinn decides to build his family a house. Inevitably he has 'harshtect trouble' which Creswell develops with relish, borrowing from his one architectural article in *Punch*. He sacks one architect who tries to make him build in 'Pseudo-Neo-Grec' but gets on splendidly with the second, as also with the builders and foreman. Appropriately Thomas ends up with a comfortable and traditional house. Here was the basis, as yet submerged, of Creswell's best later material.

From 1921 he began to write more or less regularly for the building press, notably the *Architects' Journal* and the *Architect and Building News* and chiefly under the pseudonym 'Karshish'.[9] Between 1922 and 1925 Creswell contributed a monthly 'causerie' for the *Architects' Journal*. Covering all manner of subjects, it never strayed far from his perennial concern, the dilemma of the modern architect caught between the demands of dignity and of good building, of acquired qualifications and of natural talent. 'Sir Christopher Wren F.R.I.B.A.', a piece written for the bicentenary of Wren's death in 1923, puts the point nicely:

If Wren were beginning his professional career today, British architects would sniff at the pretensions of a middle-aged President of the Royal Society in presuming ready-made eminence as an architect; and the Royal Institute, under any of its conflicting schemes of registration, would shut Mr. Wren out from the practice of architecture altogether . . . Mr. Wren might possibly possess all the essentials of a great architect, but he would be hopelessly deficient in those *in*essentials a knowledge of which is demanded of us all, and which it is the pride of all architects in large practice once to have possessed, and no less their pride to have since entirely lost and forgotten. It is extremely doubtful whether Wren at any period of his career would have been able to claim a good working knowledge of quantities, or of the ingredients and chemistry of paints, or pass tests in the law and practice of dilapidations, or even draw the Orders neatly to scale from Memory. What is an Aumbrye, Mr. Wren? The poor man does not, you see, know; still less is he able to state the nature and use of "Bricko," "Slabbo," "Poppo," "Cougho," "Sneezo," or any of those facilities with which modern building operations are endowed. . .[10]

So far Creswell had not found an authentic voice. Vigorous, perceptive and generally judicious, his journalism remained ephemeral because he could offer no cure to the architectural ills he diagnosed. The alternative was a special way in which to propound the problems, and here it was that he succeeded. In 1926–7 he contributed to the *Architects' Journal* a set of didactic essays on the 'tribulations of early practice'. To illustrate typical crises that might beset the young architect, Creswell lapsed here and there into fiction. The series having done well, he undertook another, this time wholly fictional. This was *The Honeywood File*, which appeared weekly from March 1929. It became instantly so popular that it was out as a book by Christmas, a month after the instalments ended.[11]

The Honeywood File is too charming to dissect in detail, but a brief summary can do no harm. It masquerades as the correspondence file of an architect, James Spinlove, and concerns the building of a minor country house, Honeywood Grange, for a crusty, pompous but ultimately fair-minded client, Sir Leslie Brash. The contractor is a sturdy, traditional country-town builder, John Grigblay, who along with Spinlove, Brash, his rivals Nibnose and Rasper, the district surveyor Potch and some others, features in Creswell's later novels. The letters are composed in a rich medley of styles, ranging from Brash's bumbling latinity and his wife's scattiness to the pith of Tinge, the quantity surveyor, and the oily obsequiousness of Wreek and Co., sanitary engineers. In between, Creswell interjects comments of praise and blame.

For all its general popularity *The Honeywood File* was intended as a technical fiction, parts of which have to be passed over by the ordinary reader. Architects on the other hand were meant seriously to profit from it and by all accounts did so, some saying that the book taught them truths about architectural practice entirely neglected in their schooling. Here they could see Spinlove making avoidable mistakes or scoring minor victories merely through the manner and phraseology of his letters. Here too the architect appears not as an isolated individual commanding affairs but as an instrument of the larger process of building, frequently beholden to those more experienced than himself, particularly Grigblay, the book's true hero.

Yet *The Honeywood File* was more than a little old-fashioned when Creswell wrote it. Then sixty, he not surprisingly often looked back to pre-war practice when country houses were still the meat and drink of the independent gentleman–architect's work. The technicalities and 'commercialese' not withstanding, the picture he paints is still the rosy late Victorian one of two gentlemen diverting themselves by building a house for pleasure. In the characterization of the dependable Grigblay and in the evocation of rural life in the 'home counties' there is much that is sentimental and soft-edged. All this makes the book more relaxing and pleasurable but detracts from its value as a commentary on the building world of the 1920s.

In 1930 Creswell composed a sequel, *The Honeywood Settlement*, in which among other events the patent paint ('Riddoppo') used by Brash against his architect's and builder's advice 'creeps' all over the floor, and Spinlove gets engaged to his client's daughter. In the same year he tried something a little more adventurous, the fictionalizing of an architectural dispute brought to arbitration. *Jago v. Swillerton and Toomer*, published as a book in 1931, concerns a parish hall given to the village of Grastopen by a *nouveau riche* squire, Colonel Jago; the hall has collapsed because of the peculiar properties of its American maple dance floor. Some of the details in *Jago* are even more technical than in *The Honeywood File*, so the work is seriously intended. But again Creswell adds sentimentality by transferring the story from town to country and drawing on class distinctions to differentiate Jago, his meek little architect Toomer, the shifty builder Swillerton and a knockabout cast of witnesses.[12]

Creswell composed several further architectural fictions, none so well remembered as the Honeywood books and *Jago*, and none so strictly didactic.[13] But his innermost feelings about architects and the practice of their profession are best revealed in a set of fictional articles which he never turned into a book. That is *Bernard Whistlow, F.R.I.B.A.: An Autobiography*, contributed to the *Architects' Journal* in 1931.[14] Perhaps it was never republished because it cut too deep. Creswell himself admitted:

> Bernard Whistlow's autobiography is an exact picture of life as I have experienced it within myself, and a true, if not entirely a literal one, in its episodes, and is coloured by no subjective purpose.[15]

In other words, Whistlow's experiences were more or less Creswell's and, he believed, those of many another architect of his generation.

The parallels of the story to Creswell's own career are close. Bernard Whistlow is the gangling son of a country rector, understood since boyhood illness to be 'the weed of the family' and so somehow marked out for architecture. In 1885 his father takes him to London and articles him to the great Graham Barstairs. Barstairs is undoubtedly Aston Webb, so much so that phrases from the description of him here recur in Creswell's later profile of Webb. One at least of the japes performed in Barstairs' office was to be claimed by Creswell, who recollected pouring water down Webb's private speaking tube 'to the eager listening ear of the chief draughtsman on the floor below'.[16]

Pupillage and office life are formative influences upon Whistlow-Creswell, and are described in sparkling, nostalgic detail. Eventually Whistlow builds up a little independence. A fine lady to whom he is introduced asks him to check her troublesome Belgravian drains; he remedies a potentially lethal situation but finds his client ungrateful. He passes the RIBA intermediate exams, turns up for 'certain desultory lectures' at the Architectural Association and even with some sense of futility attends the Royal Academy Schools 'under the evening newspaper and disparaging glance of Mr. Phené Spiers'. He leaves Barstairs, knocks about in various offices, and becomes clerk of works on an addition to a Post Office in a seaside town. This modest job introduces Whistlow to hitherto unsuspected realities about building, notably the social 'pecking-order' which permits him in his ignorance and innocence to command

41. Church hall at Bilton, Warwickshire, perspective by A. Douglas Robinson. This simple building, designed by Creswell during his Rugby days, became the inspiration for *Jago v. Swillerton and Toomer*. The buckling of the floor at this hall nearly precipitated Creswell into the disaster that befalls the fictional Mr Toomer, as the author explains in a postscript to the book.

men of rich experience and real virtue. Here, as in the Honeywood books, Bradshaw the builder and his foreman Richards good-humouredly withstand Whistlow's juvenile officiousness and manage to teach him a great deal. The lesson is not lost:

> It is my well-matured opinion that the builders of my country are, as a class, the most honest men of affairs in it; that I regard my intercourse with them and with their foremen and their workpeople as one of the happiest circumstances in my life. The impulse to do a thing well for its own sake, and not solely for the money to be gained from it, is especially noticeable in the old-established provincial firms in which the tradition of the Craft Guilds still lingers, and to be associated with those who engage in work on these honourable and manly terms gives zest to an architect's work.[17]

In 1899 Whistlow reluctantly takes a job as resident architect to the Eureka Plough Company, agricultural implement makers of Nollingborough in the Midlands. This corresponds to Creswell's own move to Rugby. Whistlow's position is not easy, for he has no experience of commercial architecture or of steelwork. The firm's engineers despise architects in general and the managers always employ the cheapest possible builders. Nor does the managing director at first acknowledge the status of his architect as the independent intermediary between building owner and contractor. Against the odds, Whistlow works himself gradually into a better position, but chafes against the restrictions of this salaried employment.

Private practice comes at last after Whistlow breaks into the local social circles through making a set of slick perspectives for a bazaar patronized by the Ven. Ambrose Brythwater, Nollingborough's aristocratic rector. In due course a country squire commissions a £17,000 'hunting box'. There follow some smaller domestic jobs and, more crucially, marriage, which 'more than any intrinsic capacities in myself, established me in practice, gave me an entrenched position in life, and found me fruitful opportunities to show what stuff might be in me.'[18]

The latter part of Bernard Whistlow's autobiography takes on a darker colour, reflecting perhaps some sense of struggle from Creswell's Rugby days. His wife encourages him in a more hardheaded attitude towards architectural practice (always travel 'first', not 'third'; always appear busy). So Whistlow dissolves a nominal partnership with an old office crony in London, not without acrimony, and remains in Nollingborough to play the 'social game'. This he pronounces

> indispensable for success for all except the most exceptionally gifted among architects . . . For a man to have any importance as an architect in the provinces, or to be conceded any skill or merit among those who are in a position to establish his reputation, he must attain a social position which allows him to mingle with the 'best people' and causes him to be envied and pursued by those who are lower down in the pecking order.[19]

The game means learning when to take off one's hat and when not, how best to play the gentleman ('it undoubtedly pays an architect to hunt'[20]) and of course whom to cultivate. Whistlow's largest job, the rebuilding of an aristocratic house, comes to him because his wife assiduously befriends the wife of the client's agent. But the architect has to reuse parts of the old house and in retrospect heartily detests the work. Then comes a string of disappointments, his wife dies, war intervenes, and the series concludes upon a melancholy note.

As gloom is not typical of Creswell's writings it would be unwise to exaggerate the quality. Nevertheless the career of Bernard Whistlow goes beyond the author's architectural predilections as manifested in his other books—domestic practice on an old-fashioned, gentleman-to-gentleman basis. It shows Creswell aware to the point of bitterness that architects must sweat to secure and increase their practices. Even the architect–gentleman, most fortunate of all, must abase himself ruthlessly before the social code. As for the salaried architect, he lacks dignity, power or opportunity, and is best advised to advance himself to independence as soon as possible. Such was Creswell's advice to the architectural profession of his day.

*   *   *

42. H. B. Creswell enjoys a joke. One of a set of generally unflattering caricatures—and captions—jotted down during the 1920s by H. de Cronin Hastings of the *Architectural Review*, mainly during meetings.

43. Clough Williams-Ellis dressed up as a 'toff': another mischievous cartoon by H. de Cronin Hastings.

Thrice an autobiographer, founder and creator of Portmeirion, knighted when a nonagenarian, Clough Williams-Ellis (1883–1978) may lay claim to the title of British architecture's most enduringly ebullient personality. Portmeirion apart, it is as a writer and tireless propagandist for his beloved art of architecture that Clough (the name by which he became universally known) will be longest remembered. Most of his buildings, always urbane, always intelligent, approximate too closely to pastiche and façadism to be the object of lasting curiosity. But (barring catastrophe) the wonderful Welsh fantasy village of Portmeirion will for ever incarnate that resurrected spirit of Georgian whimsy, now so distant, which between the wars held brief sway over much of British art and design.

Clough frequently insisted that he was born to be an architect. But he was equally naturally a writer and here his richest vein was himself. Hugely enjoying his work, he believed without immodesty that his own enthusiasm and experience were the best he could offer anyone who wanted to know what architecture was about or why beauty mattered. That was how *The Architect* (1929), his first, half-accidental essay in autobiography, occurred. Invited to explain his profession for a series on different types of life and work, Clough instinctively talked about himself. Here and in the more self-conscious *Architect Errant* (1971), which in great part derives from the earlier book, he revealed not only his architectural pedigree but perhaps more valuably his own reactions to it.[21]

Clough's father was an academic clergyman from an old Welsh family, buttressed by independent but not ample means and an array of family connections. When the son was about five, his father retired early to the Carnarvonshire family home where he had been brought up. The most powerful of Clough's several architectural memories of childhood concern the enlargement of this house in 1891–2. The eight-year-old on his own account spoke up on the subject with precocity,

> reproaching my parents for substituting pitch-pine for oak on the upper floors, for putting plate-glass in the stone mullioned windows, for crowning the roofs with glazed ridge tiles, for using hard, lobster-red bricks for the back chimneys and cast-iron drainpipes to support the back-door porch. Their plea of economy or "architect's orders" I grandly pooh-poohed. Altogether I must have been rather a tiresome little boy . . .[22]

To this and other early architectural proclivities his parents turned a blind eye. Eventually Clough was sent away to public school, thence in 1900 to Cambridge, and seemed destined for a scientific career. Then 'the old architectural itch' returned and he fled university. Forbidden by his family from taking articles as an architectural pupil, he spent a little time in electrical engineering but soon gave that up.

The next phase is curious but probably not unique. 'By looking up *Architecture* in the telephone-book, I came upon a subscriber called "The Architectural Association" in Tufton Street, Westminster; and that same evening I resolved to go straight round there to discover what manner of institution it might be.'[23] The principal, H. P. G. Maule, showed kindness to Clough and he was immediately admitted as a pupil. Yet before ever he had taken any instruction, 'a sort of second cousin' with 'considerable properties in various southern counties' gave him a position as 'a sort of A.D.C.' to a builder working on cottages for him in Sussex. Very quickly Clough had sown 'quite a little crop of architectural wild oats, mild quaker-oats that really harmed nobody yet taught me a certain discretion that I could scarcely have acquired so quickly in any other way.'[24] He went on with the Architectural Association, but only for two terms. Then again through 'family jobbery' came a small commission, enough for him to set up on his own. Through a mixture of luck, connections and talent the work came rolling in soon enough. In 1908 he was handed a large family property in Wales as his to improve and restore. In 1912 came the pre-war commission of which he was proudest, Llangoed Castle in Breconshire, a true country house in the old sense. Shortly afterwards he became engaged to Amabel, daughter of the maverick but influential politician, reformer and journalist J. St Loe Strachey. This was to be the most valuable connection of his career.

Doubtless this happy progression, based on so shaky a formal foundation, took more courage and hard work to achieve than Clough retrospectively was willing to admit or able to remember. But it was smooth enough for him to believe for the rest of his life that there was something almost beatific about being an architect. The thornier side of architectural reality he abruptly came to realize. War and the aftermath of war were one source of increased seriousness in him, as in other architects; another was the stimulus of an intellectual wife. Yet from his Edwardian beginnings he retained to the end a sublime confidence merely in being an architect.

Immediately after 1918 there was little opportunity for the pre-war type of private practice. Clough therefore plunged himself into causes, from which he was never again to be dissociated. First came the cheap cottages movement, championed by his father-in-law and his friend Lawrence Weaver. His earliest architectural book, *Cottage Building in Cob, Pisé, Chalk and Clay* (1919), was an offshoot of this. There followed the Design and Industries Association, the Councils for the Preservation of Rural England and of Rural Wales, and the National Trust. For all of these Clough fought and wrote eloquently. Though the style of the times and of his own personality discouraged solemnity, none of these causes was a mere dilettantish commitment. Nor did they fade away when his business began to grow again, especially with the starting of Portmeirion in 1926. In the late 1920s he announced himself, in the most delicate and gentlemanly way, a socialist.[25] In 1930, when foreign architects were being fêted in Russia, he made the pilgrimage with John Summerson (albeit in no very fervent spirit) and was even offered a job there—one wonders what he might have made of it. Returning in 1937 to observe the First All-Union Congress of Soviet Architects he was less impressed than Frank Lloyd Wright (with whom he travelled part of the way) and came home early.[26] Thereafter the socialism was submerged, but the civic duty stayed unimpaired. After 1945 Clough was briefly Chairman of Stevenage New Town and effectively campaigned for conservation of the countryside, especially in his beloved Wales.

So causes were important to Clough. Not being a natural administrator he viewed them as necessary but pleasurable adventures aimed at the judgment and sense of the educated classes. Confident in himself and sanguine about the good will and capacities of others, he radiates optimism in his writings. All this good cheer makes Clough hard to take seriously when he dons the mantle of a sort of gentlemanly Jeremiah prophesying environmental doom. *Britain and the Beast*; *England and the Octopus*; such picturesque titles hardly presage with real horror the tentacular choking-to-death of everything that Clough held dear. When for instance the Design and Industries Association at his behest undertook to expose the blighting of Britain's cities, the least good-natured idea he could come up with was a series of 'cautionary guides'. That to St Albans (1929) is a good example. It turns out to be an endearingly short and quaint pamphlet whose 'de-bunking', Clough assures the reader, is really quite harmless.[27]

The Pleasures of Architecture (1924), written with Amabel's help, was Clough's first general book on his profession and all in all his profoundest one. The title, the brisk style, and the robust but captious choice of illustrations belie a serious and in part novel purpose. The early chapters are sensitive but not specially original and rely strongly on the hackneyed concept of taste. Like others, he suggests that through the influence of Ruskin and Morris architecture in Britain began to escape the Victorian morass and has now entered an age of taste and enlightenment. Along with critics like Geoffrey Scott, he advocates the intenser exercise of architectural taste as the way to improve quality in buildings. But he then goes further, pleading for a much more broadly based discussion and understanding of architecture. Lutyens, Clough's architectural hero, had growled that too much was written and said about architecture: 'all this talk brings the ears so far forward that they make blinkers for the eyes'. Clough begs to disagree: 'people can be brought to a state of receptivity most easily by means of the written word, and that is the excuse for this book.'[28] To Clough public apathy about architecture is shocking:

> On how many newspaper staffs shall we find, besides the dramatic, literary and musical critics, an architectural critic? With how many casual dinner-party neighbours should we dare to substitute the latest London building for the latest London play as a feeler topic? How many schools have on their staffs an architectural master?[29]

These are questions that crop up constantly in Clough's writings. They reflect his amiable belief that any issue may ultimately be resolved, any reform instituted, if it gets sufficient hold upon educated opinion. *The Pleasures of Architecture* attempts to begin this task. In not the least grave of its pages Clough numbers the ways in which architecture may feature in English public-school curricula.

Above all he wishes 'educated opinion' to have some understanding of architects and their psychology as a means of gaining respect for this divine calling. A whole chapter of *The Pleasures of Architecture* is devoted to this question. The public has a notion of what a judge or a painter would be like. Why not an architect? Are architects so dull that they project no image? Clough takes a historic handful from the profession, starting with Wren and Le Nôtre and ending with character sketches of contemporaries (prudently concealed behind letters of the alphabet). The result, he admits, is a trifle embarrassing. The only shared characteristics he can discover among architects are inarticulacy, lack of charisma, respectability and pragmatism.

Most of this does not trouble Clough, who believes that he can explain why these qualities are needed by the successful architect without detracting from the 'magic' of his craft. Yet being the most articulate of architects, he is disturbed by the 'dumbness'. To dispel this he reverts to Lutyens' remark:

> Those whose work has the great reservoir of the subconscious energy upon which to draw will be the men to whom the general subject of their art seems so self-evident and obvious that discussion of its first principles appears either puzzling or contemptible.
>
> It was a very instinctive as well as a very great architect who made the complaint about 'all this talk making the ears stick out till they made blinkers for the eyes' which we quoted in a previous chapter. Dumbness might then seem secondary. That is, we might assume not so much that passionate but inarticulate men take to architecture as that a man would be so absorbed and so fulfilled throughout his entire nature because he was an architect as—like good dog Tray of happy fame—to 'have no time to say Bow-wow.' Probably in reality dumbness—if indeed it does go with architecture— has in its time been both cause and effect.[30]

Having taken his reader through this account of architects' psychology and urged architectural education for the young, Clough moves quickly on to houses. The progression is natural. To Clough, to Creswell and to most who had enjoyed pre-war practice, domestic architecture was the richest and most satisfying experience, the centre of an architect's spiritual existence. This conviction has a long and involved pedigree: a peculiarly English idea, it reached its climax early in the twentieth century when at last sufficient individual middle-class architects were building for sufficient individual middle-class clients for them often to collaborate on a more or less equal footing. So for Clough, propagandizing for broader public attention to his profession, the individual house of pre-war type provides the stage on which the architect can play his most vivid and sympathetic role. To fulfil the part banality is just as requisite as artistry, authority as important as subservience.

An architect, if he is to plan successfully, must receive almost as many intimate confidences as the family physician and the family lawyer together, and a good deal of his time must often be spent in very tactfully instructing his clients in the possibilities and limitations of building construction, the elements of architecture, and too often indeed in housekeeping, service, equipment, and the likes and habits of servants . . .

It was thought a great drollery that Mr. Andrew Carnegie should have at Skibo Castle a portrait with the inscription 'Our architect yet our friend,' but it is not clients only who sometimes feel the relationship a strain. But if inclined to complain of the ingratitude of house-building clients, architects should try to remember that the prospective housebuilder with limited money, so naturally, so inevitably sees his architect as Fate incarnate—the man who prevented him from eating his cake and having it too. But there are stiff-necked architects who some-times override their clients' wishes and build, not what the client said he wanted, but a design that the architect wanted to see carried out. Nor does this always work out badly. Sometimes a certain amount of domineering is right. Even if the client has been sure of his mind, he may have been wrong, for the architect has an abstract duty to architecture besides his duty to his client. It will always indeed remain a debatable question how much right an architect has to plead a client's wishes in extenuation of a bad building, or a beautiful building in extenuation of a ruined client. In some architects the aesthetic and in some the social conscience prevails.[31]

The theme of house-building recurs in *The Architect*, in the chapter concerned with the workaday side of professional life. First comes the usual medley of points: how to deal with 'tiresome wives', how to get a word alone with the foreman when the client is about, and so on. There follows an instructive example of what Clough conceives a typical opportunity in domestic design and how to deal with it. The site is semi-rural, of no more than an acre. Trees are to be kept and a small formal garden perhaps with a little garden-house or belvedere is obtainable. Since 'wattle-and-daub or earth walls are out of the question' the exterior is to be of brick but colour-washed 'just that faded apricot colour that so admirably sets off the mouse-coloured thatch of the hamlet—and our own roof can well be of thatch too.'[32] The neighbouring house, that of a retired bookmaker, presents a problem:

In the near corner of the adjoining plot to the east is a rather poisonous little

bungalow acting as a lodge to a villa further back from the road, happily hidden
by its attendant Wellingtonias. We particularly desire to be spared all view or
unnecessary consciousness of our neighbour and all his works, so we plan our neat
garage and engine-house close up against this bungalow, so that it is quite masked
from our forecourt.

(Not very neighbourly, perhaps, and we therefore rather nobly offer the owner
the alternative of reconstructing the exterior of his lodge—an offer, however, that
he rejects with indignation, as he chose it himself from plans submitted by the most
reputable local contractor and he still thinks it very stylish.)[33]

This revealing example is repeated in *The Adventure of Building* (1946), a slight work
subtitled 'something about architecture and planning for intelligent young citizens and
their backward elders'. (This book includes a 'self-measurement form' borrowed from
Amabel, through which schoolchildren may determine if they have the right qualities
to become architects.) And in a fictional epilogue, *On the Job*, the theme of the architect
as genial high priest of the great mystery and craft of house-building is elaborated and
updated so as to ensnare the young enquiring mind. The essentials are familiar. There
is the confident architect, the old-established builder with his capable foreman
(nicknamed 'The General') and the faintly scatty client, Mrs Hammond. This is how
the architect carries on on site:

Hullo! The top two panes of this larder window are shown with ventilation gauze
in them and you chaps have gone and glazed the lot. Silly. Have it put right, will
you—and no 'extra' to be charged for it, either.

Oh! and look here—someone's gone and fixed wooden plugs in this scullery
window to take a window board, when a *tiled* sill is specified. Make sure that they
are taken out before the tiles are laid, or it might mean dry-rot.

Plastering first rate, and just the surface I like, as you know. I suppose it's Harry
Davies? Wish there were more like him. Remember that church ceiling he
repaired for me near Chichester?—a lovely job.[34]

When Mrs Hammond turns up, the only point of altercation concerns the window
level in the nursery, which she fears may prove too high to allow her young twins to see
out properly. Our clever architect avoids lowering the window and spoiling the front
by promising a raised dais next to the window with a little play house beneath. Mrs
Hammond immediately enthuses:

Perhaps you could paint "W. Rabbit Esq." on the front door in your own nice
lettering? It will probably be the first words that the twins will ever read—and
you should jump at the chance of influencing the taste of two such intelligent
young persons in what you are yourself so keen about—the proportions of letters.[35]

---

44. Clough Williams-Ellis and Frank Lloyd Wright together at Plas Brondanw, the former's home, in 1956.
The two maverick architects first met *en route* to Russia in the 1930s and did not hit it off specially well; age
and independence of mind brought them closer together.

All therefore concludes well and the dialogue ends on the appropriate social note, with Mrs Hammond offering her architect some luncheon in return for a lift, as 'you must lunch somewhere'.

Of all the assumptions behind Clough's ideal architectural situation perhaps only one needs labouring. That is that he instinctively places his architect in a rural or semi-rural context. Clough was brought up in the country and his commitment to its protection and enhancement was one of the strongest currents in his long career. But he shared with the educated British bourgeoisie of his own and indeed of subsequent generations a deep-seated unease about cities. The thread of anti-urbanism can of course be traced well back into the Victorian past. It greatly enriched both British and American architecture, providing the impetus for reform both through the styles of the vernacular revival and through the broader achievements of the garden city movement, of which Clough was a loyal and active disciple. Yet, as with Frank Lloyd Wright's polemics in the United States, there was another side to the coin. In Clough's case his defence of the countryside often suggests that there is something irredeemable about urban and suburban places, urban and suburban architecture and by implication about being an urban and suburban architect. That of course was what most architects of his day really were. But by sticking to the country it was easier to go on peddling the myth of architectural individualism as if such situations were still typical.

Clough's inability to go much beyond this individualism was far from unique. But his is an interesting case because he struggled hard to understand the broader economic trends of the post-war world. His attitude towards planning controls is a good example. Potch, the district surveyor in *The Honeywood File*, is a mere cantankerous figure of fun. Clough on the other hand is, for an architect, unusually merciful towards such officials. Borough engineers, for instance, he chastises in the 'Devil's Dictionary' of *England and the Octopus* for their 'almost universal ignorance of the principles of architectural design';[36] but he blames this not upon them but upon councils who use them in the wrong capacity. Instead, he hopes for Oxbridge graduates qualified in achitecture filling key positions as city and county architects. And he adds: 'With an architect–artist in control in every town and county the face of England might be recharged with architectural significance. Do the Schools of Architecture and does the architectural profession take sufficient account of this?'[37]

As always, the thing is to be done by individual example. Even where government is invoked the strategy is similar. What, Clough asks in the same book, is to be done with the Black Country if coalmining and heavy industry collapse? Put through parliamentary powers, clear the old industrial sites and reduce each city to 'a compact and orderly township'.[38] Naturally only our special 'architect–artist', our gentlemanly architectural despot, can manage all this. The parallels with Wright's Broadacre City are uncomfortably close. In Britain, the culmination of this kind of thinking were the RA and RIBA plans for London of 1937 and 1938, originated by the senior members of the architectural establishment. In either plan, those parts of London that failed to meet the sponsors' aesthetic criteria or engage their social attention were to be ruthlessly sacrificed. A glance at such schemes is a reminder that it is as perilous to deliver over cities to individuals like Clough or Lutyens who have made their names

from country houses as to highway engineers or to the representatives of market
forces.

*   *   *

Our two examples fairly represent only one aspect of what architects in Britain thought
about their profession between the wars. Having practised in the securer days before
1914, both Clough and Creswell were in some measure seduced by that vision and
hoped that the profession could attain to it once more. No architect entering practice
after the war could continue long in that illusion. For any that did during the 1920s,
novelty obtruded after 1930 in the shape of the Architects' Registration Acts (1931 and
1938) and the coming of the Modern Movement.

Yet it is easy to overestimate the impact of these changes. Long fought for by the
businessmen of the profession, the acts excluded amateurs and 'cowboys' from the title
of architect, formalized the RIBA's control over whole areas of architectural
administration and strengthened the hand of large firms and partnerships.

"I DO NOT THINK IT POSSIBLE FOR DOMESTIC ARCHITECTURE TO
BE BEAUTIFUL, BUT I AM DOING MY BEST"

45. Professor-Architect Otto Friedrich Silenus superintends work on the new King's Thursday, country seat of the Beste-Chetwyndes, in *Decline and Fall*: an illustration by the author, Evelyn Waugh. 'The problem of architecture as I see it,' says Silenus, 'is the problem of all art—the elimination of the human element from the consideration of form.' When Waugh concocted this fantasy in 1928, Modern Movement ideas were still very new and few if any foreign architects had come to practise in England. Silenus was their harbinger.

Nevertheless they were slow to take effect. In the short term they by no means weakened the ideal of gentlemanly professionalism, for they enshrined within the construction industry those hierarchies of class which gentlemen–architects had previously been able to maintain only by suggestion. So long as there were enough personal customers to allow the old style of collaboration, the architect could continue to be a gentleman. And certainly expensive private houses of the right kind, while decreasing in absolute number, went on figuring prominently in British architecture's development up to 1939.

It has been well noted that modern principles of architecture, slow to arrive in Britain, first made a real mark in private houses. Maxwell Fry, Connell Ward and Lucas and the other pioneers often attempted larger projects. But in the end most of their houses were built while many of the bigger things were relegated to the plan chest. In a cultural climate generally hostile to European modernism, only a handful of bold, rich and relatively isolated individuals were prepared to risk the new way of building. To put it another way, only on this familiar ground of the private house allowing intimacy between client and designer, were modern architects fully able to exercise the coveted authority. And here it is the continuity with traditions dear to Creswell and Clough rather than any abrupt departure of style that is so striking. From this perspective, the new principles in no way threatened the old ways of thinking about the architect and his status.

This accords well with what is now known of the British pioneers of modernism. With exceptions, there was no rigid line between modernizers and traditionalists. Many architects were happy in the old tradition of eclecticism to flit from one style to another without sense of betrayal. Even the Mars Group, superficially the standard bearer of architectural radicalism, turns out not to have been so very radical. It did not pursue any profound change in the conditions of practice of the kind debated and tried in Germany or Russia, only the mere acceptance of new ideas about style.

Even within Tecton, the one revolutionary British group-practice of the 1930s, Berthold Lubetkin and Francis Skinner were alone in seeking any profounder reform within the profession. In the leftward-leaning Architects' and Technicians' Organisation (ATO), which broke away from Mars in 1935 at their instigation, the issues of patronage, official architecture and salaried architects were certainly debated, but the influence of the group remained slight. Outside Lubetkin's circle, British modernists rarely got beyond the bare professional platitudes that there would be new types of client, of building and of collaboration in the age about to dawn.[39]

So the thinking of Creswell and Clough, while not representative of the whole profession, is probably quite an accurate guide to the ideology of most architects who enjoyed artistic opportunities. Like much British architecture of that era, the attitude of the gentleman–architect charms, but it is also a little pathetic, for it has no future; it represents the fag-end of a tradition, as the more percipient architects of the newer generation were beginning to feel. The initiative had passed to other countries and to other styles of being an architect.

CHAPTER SIX

The Battle of the Bauhaus

Since his death in 1969, the reputation of Walter Gropius has been in decline. A period of eclipse often overtakes those whose ideas have become familiar to the point of cliché but have yet to be detached from us by the processes of history. Gropius is certainly suffering from such a phase. In the air of bitterness and resentment still informing criticism of the Modern Movement, the most persistent theorist and organizer of its heyday has reaped his due share of derision.

As an architect, ask some, was Gropius ever truly creative? The pioneering buildings on which his fame was founded, the Fagus Factory of 1911 and the Deutscher Werkbund Exhibition Building of 1914, may have owed much to his partner Adolf Meyer. After Meyer left him in 1925, Gropius participated to his advantage in several loose partnerships or associations, culminating in a much-publicized venture, The Architects Collaborative, founded in 1945.[1] But no later building (save perhaps the Bauhaus group of 1925–6) entirely fulfilled the promise of his early years or confirmed the overwhelming talent accorded him by early historians of modernism.

As a thinker and writer, anyone who studies what is available in English will speedily find Gropius frustrating.[2] His essays tend to be repetitive, equivocal and vainly idealistic, and they lack the whiff of rash excitement that pervades the works of Le Corbusier. Lastly, the deficiencies of Gropius as an educator are now easy to discern. Did not the principles evolved at the Bauhaus, once established in the schools of the west, achieve just that status of academic dogma that Gropius abhorred in previous education? And did not modernism, despite his pleas, fast lapse into a mere matter of style or superficial philosophy, with the disastrous environmental consequences so evident today?

When the pioneers of the Modern Movement emerge from the clouds of praise and opprobrium, Gropius will doubtless be once again widely, if temperately, admired. Yet posterity may be inclined to miss one aspect of his character which had incalculable effect upon his contemporaries' estimation of him: Gropius had lifelong charisma. His first wife Alma (whose turbulent entanglements with the composer Mahler, the painters Klimt and Kokoschka and the poet Werfel testify to an obsession with the dominating artist-figure) was but one of those stricken by the presence of the handsome architect.[3] His colleagues at the Bauhaus were unfailingly impressed, even when they disagreed with Gropius. Wrote the painter Lyonel Feininger, rarely his ally on artistic

46. Walter Gropius in 1920. The Director of the
Bauhaus was celebrated for his intense gaze.

matters: 'He works till three in the morning, hardly sleeps, and when he looks at you,
his eyes are like stars. I'm sorry for anyone who can't gather strength from him.'[4]

These special qualities, the winning blend of disciplined industry and fervour, alone
enabled Gropius's cherished creation, the Bauhaus, to survive as long as it did. With his
personality Gropius would disarm (sometimes literally) political enemies or fractious
students and smooth over ideological quarrels between the Bauhaus staff. But the
achievement was always a personal one. When, partly sensing his inability to control
affairs indefinitely, Gropius tired of the Bauhaus and deserted it in 1928, he left it prey
to the exposure of all the inconsistencies and uncertainties in his philosophy. Without
the depression and the rise of Nazism there would certainly still have been a crisis at the
Bauhaus. The comparative cogency of thought and aim displayed by Gropius's
successor as director, Hannes Meyer, a man of lesser charisma and adroitness at human
relations, guaranteed that.

After Gropius and many of his colleages had migrated to America, his genius for
personal authority found more compliant ground for its exercise. Without the historic
(if curiously unjustified) American sense of inferiority in matters cultural, it is
impossible to understand the overwhelmingly generous and respectful spirit with
which Gropius, Mies, Hilberseimer, Breuer, Albers and others were received and
speedily wafted to high positions in the architectural establishment. (Many, including
Gropius, had previously suffered a noticeably more churlish initiation into exile in
Britain.) The Harvard Graduate School of Design, for instance, where Gropius
became chairman in 1937, had been started some forty years before under the auspices
of a visiting Frenchman, E. J. A. Duquesne.[5] Now the new German method
supplanted faltering French traditions in the architectural curriculum. At the Illinois
Institute of Technology, Mies van der Rohe and Ludwig Hilberseimer came in to

introduce a more dogmatic, style-centred version of the same approach. The new education spread with such great rapidity that by 1954 the AIA regarded a Bauhaus-derived curriculum as orthodoxy for an American architectural school.[6]

Leaving aside their momentous influence on post-war architecture, the ready acceptance in the United States of Gropius and his colleagues led to distortions in the history of the Modern Movement and even of the Bauhaus itself. Their recognition, together with Gropius's essay *The New Architecture and the Bauhaus* (1935), consecrated for the English-speaking world a single, seemingly consistent theory and tradition—if not for the whole of modern architecture then at least for its German component. Of this tradition the American exiles, and Gropius above all, became the guardians. It was their Bauhaus, their retrospective outlook upon architectural progress between the wars, that has got into the history books.

But there are alternative views that lead one to question this stewardship. The Bauhaus, it is worth remembering, was primarily an arts-and-crafts school in which during Gropius's time the architectural strain ran thin. No true architectural course was taught there for the first eight years of its existence, 1919–27; once established, architectural teaching was for three years under the control not of Gropius but of Hannes Meyer, who became director in 1928. When Meyer fell foul of the political establishment and was ousted in 1930, he went to work in the Soviet Union. In this he was far from alone. Not only did colleagues from the Bauhaus accompany Meyer; so too did a corps of architects who had greater experience than did Gropius and his friends of actually applying to housing the principles of the new architecture. For every progressive architect who left Germany for the west in the 1930s, another could be cited who went east. Among major figures besides Meyer were Mart Stam, Ernst May, Hans Schmidt and Bruno Taut.

Unlike that of their counterparts in America, the experience of those who went to Russia was ultimately bitter and disappointing. They worked hard and long, but as Stalinism took hold they trickled back to scattered exiles in Mexico, Switzerland, Tanganyika, Turkey—wherever neither capitalism nor fascism openly prevailed. Many kept their socialist ideals only to eke out their post-war careers in relative oblivion, denied the attention of history or the blandishments of senior academic life. Yet these men's careers, if broken by political adversity, represent a strain of architectural ideology rooted in the German Modern Movement of the 1920s and, for a time, strong to the point of dominance in the Bauhaus itself. Fervent believers in the new methods and materials though most of these architects originally were, this was not their most important or enduring characteristic; for in Russia the shrewdest of them learnt, thirty years before their western colleagues, the drawbacks of too much faith in technology and, indeed, in a universal style. By consistently undertaking projects only of a strictly social nature, notably housing, and by discarding artistic individualism in favour of collaborative method, they pointed to a new conception of the architect which turned its back on romanticism as much, if not more, than the new formal vocabulary of style which they and their western colleagues equally professed.

Such an ideology was by no means foreign to Gropius's early pattern of thinking. Perhaps indeed Gropius will ultimately be best remembered for his lifelong devotion to the ideal of collaboration in architecture and design—a necessity, as he saw it, under

47. Members of The Architects Collaborative cling on to modern art outside their Harvard Graduate Center, 1949. Gropius's feet are closest to the ground.

modern conditions.[7] Yet this and other socially progressive ideas never gained complete primacy in his thought. His liberal, catholic temperament allowed other strands, sometimes incompatible, a place in his philosophy. Chief among these was a lingering fondness for the old concept of architecture as the mistress art, controlled and created by supereminent individuals and presiding over the lesser arts of painting, sculpture and the crafts.

So naturally, when there came the turmoil that forced the hapless German intellectuals of his generation to make their choices and resolve their philosophies, Gropius chose America. There an overtly capitalistic system obliged him to confine the social and co-operative elements of his thinking to limited, largely meaningless experiments like The Architects Collaborative, a firm which has never ventured far beyond the orthodoxy of modern big-time architectural practice in the west. And despite constant lamentation of the fact in his late essays,[8] Gropius's own thinking soon became confused with the cruder, less thoughtful views of men like Mies, who thought of modern architecture essentially as a style practised by and for individuals, all objective facts about the methods and conditions of modern practice notwithstanding.

*   *   *

Like so much connected with the Bauhaus, the story of architecture there is curious and somewhat quirky. Long ago it used to be assumed, on the strength of documents like Gropius's book *The New Architecture and the Bauhaus*, that the school was from the first formidably rationalistic. According to this way of thinking (which is associated particularly with Gropius's close ally and friend Lászlo Mohóly-Nagy), the reason for the long lack of an architecture department at the Bauhaus was that students had first to be familiarized with the 'language' of the new scientific objectivity (*Neue Sachlichkeit*). In the famous *Vorkurs* they would learn the nature of perception, and proceed thence to acquire further visual and manual skills in the later stages of instruction. Once these skills were widely enough disseminated, the task of teaching the new 'objective' architecture could be proceeded with.

All this hardly amounts to more than a rationalization of the chance economic and political circumstances in which the Bauhaus was born and staggered empirically from crisis to crisis. Its origins, it is well known, lay in the Weimar School of Arts and Crafts which Henri Van de Velde directed from 1902. Van de Velde, one of the first to try narrowing the gap between industry and the self-consciously 'artistic' crafts, believed that architects had a special mission: they were to encourage simple, standardized and easily manufactured forms throughout the domain of applied design. The Deutscher Werkbund was founded in 1908 by Van de Velde and his disciples, partly to carry out such a programme.[9] But its early members were less than fully conscious that true fulfilment of their programme would dethrone the artist and the architect from their positions of individualistic pre-eminence. Many indeed, especially the pupils of Peter Behrens of whom Gropius was the most notable, were drawn to machine production precisely because it could anonymously carry out the designer's will to the last detail. Their preoccupations, in fact, were less moral and social than aesthetic; they were concerned primarily with control and only secondarily with collaboration.[10]

Therefore when at the historic Deutscher Werkbund conference of 1914 Hermann Muthesius proposed that the main task of the architect should be to evolve standard building-types, Van de Velde, Gropius and with them all the painters in the Werkbund protested in shrill outrage.[11] Much later, Gropius claimed that their objections were 'more against the person of Muthesius than the content of his thesis. He was an unpleasant man who used tricky methods to get into the lead. His mind was also much too rigid and "unartistic".'[12] Yet plainly Gropius and his friends felt their personal interests threatened. Despite his commitment to rationalized methods and procedures of architecture, stated as early as 1910 in a memorandum on housing,[13] it is not with hindsight hard to see that Gropius was really preoccupied from the start with an architecture created in the old manner but offering a rational appearance.

When therefore Van de Velde, long exasperated by the anachronisms of court life and now finally frustrated by the onset of war, resigned his position at the Weimar School of Arts and Crafts and in 1915 recommended that Gropius, Endell or Obrist succeed him, he had no reason to think the school would alter greatly from its position as an advanced arts and crafts establishment, whichever of the three were chosen— even if, as was mooted, an architecture department were added. Nor probably did Gropius, coming from the front in Hussar uniform for an inconclusive interview with the Grand Duke of Sachsen-Weimar, envisage with any clarity the shape of things to come.[14]

But war disturbs men's minds. In 1919 when Gropius was finally appointed, the Weimar School and the corresponding Academy of Fine Arts had been closed for some time, so the discontinuity alone encouraged radical change. Ideological and artistic ferment were everywhere in the air; political chaos reigned. Ever a barometer of such currents, Gropius had every reason to be swayed. Once he had been 'buried alive under rubble and corpses for hours'.[15] Another time he had been shot down in a plane and the pilot next to him killed.[16] His personal life with Alma Gropius was in confusion. Like so many others Gropius grappled desperately with the psychosis of this post-war period, which Bruno Taut, another victim, was later to term an 'explosion of madness' that interrupted the development of a modern architecture.[17]

For the recrudescence of extreme, romantic individualism that stemmed from this collective trauma, 'expressionism' is the normal shorthand. In the applied arts its chief embodiment was the Arbeitsrat für Kunst, founded in 1918 with the radical Bruno Taut as its prime mover. After a few short months Gropius came to the fore, and he dominated its counsels in the period immediately preceding his appointment to the Bauhaus. In a lecture of 1919 he declared his current views on the profession: 'To be an architect means to be the leader in art. The architect alone can raise himself up again to this leadership in art, to the position of being its highest servant, the superhuman guardian and steward of its complete and indivisible existence.'[18] The *Arbeitsrat* group conjured up an artistic élite collaborating with spontaneous, mediaeval fervour on communal utopian projects of a type suggested by Bruno Taut's 'Cathedral of the Future', the great 'synthetic work of architecture' that was to symbolize the new society. In so far as it was possible, they strove to fulfil this utopian programme in the cultural institutions of post-war Germany, of which the Bauhaus was one.[19]

Though caught up by the new romanticism, Gropius by no means disavowed his pre-war commitments to rationalizing architecture. But he had to resort to some odd devices to patch up the inconsistencies. In a speech to representatives of the craft industries of Weimar, who not unreasonably feared what the much-vaunted new Bauhaus might portend for them, he argued that applied design must be plain and rational precisely in order to distinguish it from high art, which was by its essence sacred, inviolate and ethereal. This sophism, propounded several years before by the Viennese architect Adolf Loos, was better suited to the post-war period of crisis and was more or less canonized in the first Bauhaus programme. Thus while Gropius was placating suspicious citizens and politicians by assuring them that the aims of the new school's crafts courses were modest and practical, he was also urging his first students to undertake utopian design projects and declaring that conception, not execution, was paramount.[20]

As founded in 1919, therefore, the Bauhaus was practically a new institution based on the romantic, backward-looking ideals of the Arbeitsrat für Kunst, not a mere continuation of Van de Velde's school. Gropius was to write: 'The full consciousness of my responsibility in advancing ideas based on my own reflections only came home to me as a result of the war, in which these theoretical premises first took definite shape.'[21] But neither these original 'premises' nor the practical obligations under which Gropius laboured at Weimar were of help to the genuine advancement of architecture. For as well as the School of Arts and Crafts, the infant Bauhaus was required to digest Weimar's old Academy of Fine Arts. Not only was easel painting introduced into the curriculum (Gropius later denied that this had been so), but more or less pure artists having little interest in architecture's problems came to preponderate in the ranks of the early staff. The architecture department discussed in 1915–16 failed to materialize, nor was there serious instruction in the subject. In the autumn of 1919 the director of the local school of building trades did a little teaching on construction, and there were very occasional lectures on architectural history and statics; that was all. Students who wanted to know about architecture at first simply drifted along to Gropius's private office and asked their questions of Adolf Meyer. True, little building was being done at this stage in Germany because of economic and political conditions compounded by a desperate shortage of materials. Gropius himself had but one job, the odd Sommerfeld house in suburban Berlin, upon the interior of which some of the students were let loose. But architects were evidently soon going to be needed. What Gropius was doing was to nurture a monastic élite which could huddle together at the Bauhaus during this period of trial; when the new dawn came, they would burst upon the world with the new, utopian architecture. A variety of small jobs at Jena in 1921–2 provided a first inkling of this and helped to keep the Gropius private office going.[22]

These curious conditions began to change after Johannes Itten, the garlic-chewing educator who ran the preliminary *Vorkurs* on semi-mystical lines, departed in 1922 following disagreements with Gropius. Along with him disappeared other of the 'Inflation Saints', as the early Bauhaus gurus were once quaintly termed.[23] Following this first 'battle of the Bauhaus', Gropius and the whole school started moving slowly towards greater rationalism, strongly prompted by criticism from the state of Thuringia and the city of Weimar. This criticism, of very varying accuracy, intensified throughout the period 1922–4.[24] Some of it was simple. Weimar, 'a sleepy provincial town, full of tradition, museums and retired officials, a Stratford-on-Avon and Cheltenham rolled into one', as one student put it,[25] wanted in its obstinate way to see results from the Bauhaus and failed to do so. So an exhibition was planned for 1923. At the initiative of the students, not of Gropius, a plot was secured in connection with this show and a house built as the first unit of a projected housing scheme which would demonstrate the potentialities of the new architecture. This small building, the 'Haus am Horn', was designed by George Muche, put up by private firms under Adolf Meyer's direction, and furnished by Bauhaus students. Gropius did not himself have much to do with the house but helped plan the rest of the housing scheme, which was never built.[26]

This modest project encouraged the senior students to develop architecture at the Bauhaus further. In 1924 Muche and a group of Hungarian students of whom Marcel Breuer is best known started an architectural study group to look into the problems of housing; they made a number of designs, experimenting particularly with high-rise solutions. Still however Gropius would not relent and give architecture a formal place in the curriculum, but he did employ more 'Bauhaüslers' in his own office, which was beginning to get more jobs. By now he had frankly committed the school to increasingly social and practical aims, and his only excuse was its precarious political and financial position at Weimar.[27]

By this time Germany's economic recovery looked convincing and a national housing drive, financed by a tax on rent, was under way. In various German cities the new architecture was beginning to be applied to housing on a massive scale. In 1924

Berlin's city architect Martin Wagner founded the GEHAG building society, staffed largely by socialists, financed by trades unions, and dedicated to low-cost housing based on new building techniques. Bruno Taut, after an interesting but unproductive spell as Magdeburg's chief architect, came in to design several of the early GEHAG estates. The boldest programme of all, it is generally agreed, was sponsored by social-democratic Frankfurt, where Ernst May, an architect only recently converted to modernism, was put in charge of a new municipal construction department in 1925. Between 1926 and 1930 nine per cent of Frankfurt's population was rehoused by May and his energetic team, which included Anton Brenner, Karl Rudloff, Martin Elsässer and Grete Schütte-Lihotzky. The young Dutchman Mart Stam, operating autonomously, also developed a section of the city, while Adolf Meyer—now separated from Gropius—directed the Frankfurt planning office until his early death in 1929.[28]

Most of this was still to come when in 1925, under increasing hostility in Thuringia, Gropius negotiated the transfer of the Bauhaus to the more sympathetic city of Dessau and state of Anhalt. But it must have been an increasing embarrassment that the school had little to show for itself architecturally. There was still no architectural course and the number of good students and teachers interested in one remained low. Consequently the large task of designing the new Bauhaus buildings at Dessau and the seven-unit Bauhausmeister housing scheme that went with it fell entirely upon the private office of Gropius, Adolf Meyer having left him in 1925. Breuer and other of the architecturally oriented students helped with the school interiors, and Gropius later claimed that he 'brought the whole body of teachers and students into active co-operation' on the projects.[29] But it was by no means a grand, communal free-for-all. As part of the bargain he made with Mayor Fritz Hesse of Dessau, which paid for the buildings, Gropius also received a third large personal architectural commission. This was the first part of the famous Siedlung Törten, a smallish housing settlement in suburban Dessau which proceeded in stages from 1926 to 1930.[30]

In December 1926, to avant-garde acclaim, the Bauhaus was installed in its permanent buildings. Among architects, four specially significant figures attended the opening.[31] From Berlin came Martin Wagner, and from Frankfurt Ernst May. Mart Stam arrived from Stuttgart, where he was trying to transform the Deutscher Werkbund's model estate at Weissenhof, shortly to open, from the medley of modernistic buildings of different authorship that Mies had conceived into a serious, co-operative experiment in housing design. Finally, Hannes Meyer came from Basle to demonstrate the lively Swiss interest in the future direction of architecture. All these architects firmly held that the primary application of the new architecture must be social—a view to which Gropius, with his customary sensitivity to shifts in the ideological barometer, was now veering. Dessau had given him his first chance in years of designing housing. By now the little Bauhausmeister estate was complete, sixty of the Törten units had been finished and another hundred odd were under way. An employment office for the city was in the offing, and future housing commissions seemed likely.[32] In all these tasks the students could participate. With Hesse's backing, funding was also more secure.

At last, therefore, Gropius agreed from April 1927 to start an architecture course for the senior students. His first choice to run it seems to have been the brilliant, peripatetic

Mart Stam, then only twenty-seven years old. Stam declined on the grounds that he was not a teacher, so Gropius turned to Hannes Meyer.[33]

Though Gropius was later loudly to repent this decision, Meyer was a shrewd and natural choice, given the intensely social aims that he now envisaged for the architecture department. Meyer had just attracted international admiration for a striking design, made in partnership with Hans Wittwer, for the League of Nations competition of 1926. This doubtless brought his name prominently before Gropius, always excited by 'conception' rather than execution.

But for reasons which redound to the credit of neither man, Gropius never understood Hannes Meyer. Swiss, intense, somewhat rigid, Meyer was thoroughly suited by background to take on the Bauhaus job at a time when the problems of housing were dominating architectural thinking. As a young man he had (like Ernst May) studied housing in England, participated actively in the land-reform and co-operative movements in both Germany and Switzerland, and built a capable housing estate outside Basle.[34] Unlike Gropius, who was schooled in the aristocratic practice of Behrens and instinctively saw all problems of reform, whether social or aesthetic, from above, Meyer was a socialist before he was a modernist. But like others of his generation he was drawn in the 1920s under the stimulus of Le Corbusier and *L'Esprit Nouveau* to the extremism of the 'new objectivity'—summed up most simply as the belief that modern technology and method should absolutely determine visual form.[35] Though his devotion to this heresy was to prove slighter and less lasting than his commitment to socialism, it was at its height in 1927. 'Basically my teaching will be on absolutely functional-collective-constructive lines in keeping with *ABC* and "The New World",' promised Hannes Meyer to Gropius before starting work at the Bauhaus.[36] This referred to a confession of current faith he had just made in *ABC*, a Swiss architectural magazine run by the ubiquitous Mart Stam, Emil Roth, Hans Schmidt and Meyer's partner Wittwer. *ABC* was certainly socialist and pro-Russian in orientation. But Meyer's article was remarkable mainly for rabidly glorifying technology and deprecating art as insignificant or irrelevant to architecture. At the time Gropius must have known and at least half-acquiesced in these views, for Meyer was the opposite of secretive. Naturally a controversialist and endowed with an acerbic wit, he was to compose manifestos every bit as dogmatic and overdrawn as those of any previous Bauhaus ideologue.

Yet ultimately it remained Hannes Meyer's single, fanatical purpose to produce practical, thoroughly worked-out architecture from which the user was to reap all benefit and the designer little or none. This determination he applied straight away at the Bauhaus. For ten months he ran the new architectural course with great energy and what appears to have been little friction. Early in 1928 against a strong field Meyer won a limited competition for a school for the German Trades Union Federation at Bernau near Berlin. This sober complex of buildings became the stamping ground of the architectural department. So too a little later did a small new section of the Törten estate, for which Meyer was made architect by the city of Dessau. A group of students drew up the plans, which followed the lead of some of May's work at Frankfurt, but only five blocks of flats were built before Meyer's dismissal in 1930. Gropius continued meanwhile building his own areas of Törten, relying apparently more on his private

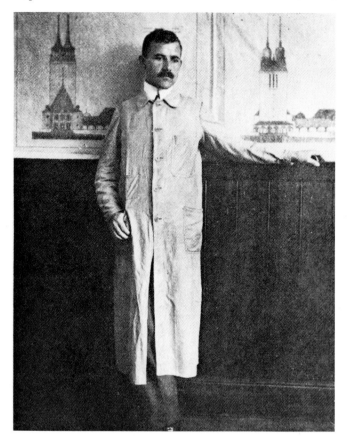

49 (facing page). Hannes
Meyer at the time he took over
directorship of the Bauhaus in
1928. Behind him, a plan for an
'ideas competition'. Note the
zip (invented 1925).

48. Hannes Meyer
(1889–1954). Portrait of a
young romantic, taken in 1913.

office than on the architecture department. It is perhaps of minor interest that while
there was unending technical trouble with Gropius's sector, leading to significant
friction with the city and eventually to the replacement of all the windows, Meyer's
brick-built apartments proved fault-free and are still in reasonable condition.[37]

In February 1928, following renewed tussles with local politicians, Gropius
announced his resignation of the Bauhaus directorship in order to devote himself to
private practice, particularly housing. Mies van der Rohe having cannily declined the
post, Gropius recommended Hannes Meyer as his successor. Among the students there
was uproar; but when one howled 'Hannes Meyer as the Director of the Bauhaus is a
catastrophe' Gropius retorted that he was being hotheaded. Meyer quickly
responded to criticism with a frank address in which he contrasted the romantic epoch
of the Bauhaus in Weimar with the practical tasks confronting them in Dessau.
Gradually the turmoil subsided. Meyer was installed as director in April and moved
into Gropius's house, to what seems to have been reasonably general approval.[38] But
the outcry does suggest that Meyer's views were well understood within the Bauhaus
and that Gropius cannot, as he later claimed, have been much deceived as to his
intentions. Here however is Gropius's account of the matter.

It is true that I esteemed Meyer at first, but my change of opinion later on was not
on 'principles', but personal.

I erred in my judgment of his character and am to blame that he became my successor—for I did not recognise the mask over his face. When I appointed him, I judged the financial position of the Bauhaus to be relatively assured and its connections with industry to be well established. Meyer's reputation as an architect with strong public interests had attracted me, and during the first period of his work with the Bauhaus, I never doubted his qualifications. I liked his work for the Trade-Union School at Bernau which he had done with the modest and gifted Wittwer. Nevertheless I never made true personal contact with him for he was taciturn and—as turned out later—purposely concealed his personal views and intentions, as you will see from the following.

From the experiences of Weimar I knew that the inclusion of political activities in the Institute itself would inevitably bring about its end. From Weimar onwards I took the official point of view that party politics was the individual's private affair but that the Institute was not to be identified with any party. Without this policy the Bauhaus would have been dashed to pieces even in Weimar and its conception and work would never have been brought into effect. Before I suggested Meyer as the new director, I spoke with him about this important point and received his assurance that he shared my view that the Institute had to be kept out of political life. He was as emphatic as I in this matter. Then he was appointed and the mask fell. With his outlook of political materialism, which he had concealed from us, he undermined the idea of the Bauhaus and brought the Institute between Scilla and Charybdis and finally brought himself to ruin.[39]

Meyer began firmly as director, quickly expanding the architecture department. Hitherto instruction had been far from complete, for 'it was usually found advisable to let the most promising of the architectural pupils round off their studies by attending complementary classes at various technical institutes.'[40] Meyer now brought in Ludwig Hilberseimer to direct design, Anton Brenner (from May's Frankfurt team) to run the building studio, and Mart Stam as a regular guest lecturer and critic. Other additions to the architectural staff were Meyer's ex-partner Wittwer, chief draughtsman and expert on technical services; Alcar Rudelt, director of structural engineering; and the Norwegian Edvard Heiberg, specialist in housing estates. In other areas Meyer's every change leant in the direction of more science and less irresponsible theorizing. Lectures on sociology and economics were planned; there was even a talk by a sex educationist. Moholy-Nagy left with Gropius, and Breuer departed soon after. In their stead came Walter Peterhans to direct photography, and Count Dürkheim to lecture on psychology. The financial base of the Bauhaus was also improved by increased revenues from the sale of products and more rational co-operation with industry.[41]

None of this saved Meyer from the effects of the renewed political instability that overtook Germany from 1929. The Bauhaus had always been attacked from the right, and in this respect Meyer was much more vulnerable than Gropius. His views at this period can be gleaned, once allowance is made for the habitually satiric and exaggerated language of Bauhaus propaganda (always a gift to the school's political opponents), from manifestos he wrote for the students on building and its relationship to society. They reveal an avowed materialist, a socialist and a virulent foe of all types of artistic formalism.[42] As the threat of Nazism grew he began to allow—indeed it would have been cowardly to forbid—increased political activism among the students. A small Marxist group developed and grew, allegedly under Meyer's protection. In March 1930 he was visited by a major local politician of the SPD, technically still a leftist party, and told indirectly to dissolve the 'communist cell at the Bauhaus'. This Meyer seems to have done without significant trouble within the school. But in July rumours of the cell's existence resurfaced in the papers. A personal subscription of Meyer's to a collection for International Workers' Aid seems now to have been enough to cause an increasingly panicky Mayor Hesse to act. Along with the museum director Ludwig Grote, Hesse visited Meyer, who acknowledged the donation. According to Grote, Meyer also said: 'You know perfectly well, Dr Grote, that I am a scientific Marxist.'[43] In a letter of Swiftian venom later addressed to Hesse, Meyer recounts what now ensued.

On my return from the opening of the Bauhaus travelling exhibition in Zürich, I came to see you on July 29, 1930. There was great excitement in Dessau. The ninety workers' flats in the Dessau-Törten estate, the first project to be jointly designed by our building department, were ready for occupation. Thousands flocked to see them. Unqualified recognition in every newspaper. A two-and-a-half room flat with a kitchen, bathroom and amenities for 37.50 reichsmarks' rent a month! At last an achievement in keeping with the role of the new Bauhaus.

The job had been done under my guidance but was actually carried out by a group of young students. I stepped into your room with a feeling of relief. You referred to the investigation of Bauhaus affairs which the Anhalt government was demanding as a result of the false report from the town authorities—and called for my immediate resignation. The reason: it was alleged I was bringing politics into the Bauhaus. A Marxist (you said) could never be the Director of the Bauhaus. Immediate cause of dismissal: a voluntary contribution as a private person to the International Workers' Aid Fund for helping the distressed families of miners on strike in the Mansfeld coalfield. It was no use my reiterating that I had never belonged to any political party. It was no use explaining that a 'Bauhaus Dessau' group of the German Communist Party was an impossibility from the party organization point of view, no use my assuring you that my political activities were of a cultural and never a party character. You cut me short and interpreted my nervous smile as agreement.

And so I was liquidated from behind. Just when the Bauhaus was closed for the vacation and all my intimates in the Bauhaus were far away from home. The Bauhaus camarilla rejoiced. The local press of Dessau was overcome by a moral delirium. The Bauhaus condor Gropius swooped down from the Eiffel tower and pecked at my directorial body and, reassured, W. Kandinsky stretched out on the Adriatic beach. It is finished.[44]

The rest of the Bauhaus story is well enough known. With Meyer gone Hesse looked for guidance to Gropius, who without regard to the constitution of the Bauhaus pressured Mies into accepting the post he had refused two years before. For the two credibly functioning years that remained of its existence, the school stuck to architecture as its main purpose but slid back into formalism. As Gropius later admitted under cross-examination, 'Mies' own interests hardly touch the social sphere, and you are right in seeing here a discrepancy with my own thought.'[45] Philip Johnson has gone further, alleging that Mies only finally left Germany in 1937 'because Hitler liked pitched roofs'.[46] But though far from an ideal choice, he had been implacably opposed to Meyer and for the time that was what counted. 'Life is oxygen plus sugar plus starch plus protein,' Meyer had asserted in one of the more childishly materialistic passages of his manifestos. 'Try stirring all that together,' growled Mies, 'it stinks.'[47]

An outcry ensued among the students after Meyer's dismissal, anger being directed particularly at Gropius, who had interfered though no longer formally affiliated to the school, and at Kandinsky, who some believed had acted as an informer. Mies called in the police to restore order, but never really succeeded in depoliticizing the students. 'Mies is a wonderful architect,' wrote one student, 'but as a man, and particularly as the Director, he is very reactionary.'[48] In spite of many desertions from the architecture department Hilberseimer stayed on and kept it together. It produced a few city planning schemes but accomplished little else. Gradually the political climate deteriorated and Nazi students came to the fore. In October 1932 Mies met the same fate as Meyer; Dessau terminated his contract. For a time he tried to resuscitate the school in Berlin, but the task was hopeless. The Bauhaus quickly disintegrated.

*　　*　　*

One day in October 1930 a Pullman car bristling with architects glided into Moscow. They were led by Ernst May, who in view of the Depression had left his post in the Frankfurt Stadtbauamt, signed a contract to work for the Soviet Government and brought with him the pick of his team. Seventeen in all, they included Mart Stam, already at thirty-one an architect of extraordinarily varied experience, and Hans Schmidt, later to be the group's memorialist.

These were the advanced guard of a migration over the next two years by many German-speaking architects of 'modern' persuasion. Some were drawn to the Soviet Union out of political enthusiasm, others by loathing of the artistic reaction in their homeland; all were in need of the work no longer to be found in the west. May's party was followed shortly by Hannes Meyer, smarting still from his recent sacking. Round him soon gathered a group of some half a dozen faithful ex-students and colleagues from the Bauhaus. Others arrived a little later, like Fred Forbat, who had been to the fore in the earliest days of architectural experiment at the Bauhaus, Kurt Meyer, the city planning expert from Cologne, and Bruno Taut, now no longer the pathological dreamer of manifestos but the experienced designer of many a large German housing estate.*[50]

The 'May Group' is much the most celebrated of these small bands of exiles. It came at official Soviet invitation, it remained united for some time, and its doings were minutely reported back in Germany. The opportunities tendered to the team under the Five Year Plan of 1928–32 were exceptional. May, Stam and their colleagues were asked to produce town plans and to design housing for a whole series of new industrial cities of which Magnitogorsk, an ambitious steel-producing centre in the Urals, was the first and foremost. There ensued projects for Makeyevka, Nizhny Tagil, Avtostroy, Kuznetsk, Stalinsk, Karaganda, Balgas and Orsk. Representatives of the May Group also submitted a scheme in the competition of 1932 for the replanning of Greater Moscow.[51]

By contrast Hannes Meyer and other members of the 'Bauhaus Brigade' underwent experiences more closely akin to those of most other foreign technicians drawn to Russia at that time. Several of them worked at first in Giprovtus, the bureau responsible for buildings connected with higher education, but most were soon dispersed among Soviet architectural brigades. Those employed upon town-planning schemes had fewer opportunities to create new cities but worked chiefly upon

* The sources do not agree precisely on the composition of the main 'brigades' that went to Russia. Christian Borngräber, the most recent and detailed author, gives the following names. 'May Group': Hans Burckhardt, Max Frühauf, Wilhelm Hauss, Werner Hebebrand, Walter Kraatz, Karl Lehmann, Hans Leistikow, Albert Löcher, Erich Mauthner, Ernst May, Hans Schmidt, Wilhelm Schütte, Grete Schütte-Lihotzky, Walter Schutz, Walter Schwagenscheidt, Mart Stam, Ulrich Wolf. 'Meyer Group' (or 'Bauhaus Brigade'): René Mensch, Klaus Meumann, Hannes Meyer, Konrad Püschel, Béla Scheffler, Phillippe Tolziner, Antonin Urban, Tibor Weiner. Others add to May's party the names of Gustav Hassenpflug and Eugen Kaufmann, and to Meyer's group those of Edvard Heiberg (Norwegian) and Josef Hausenblaus (Czech). Among those who went separately or in small groups were Fred Forbat, —Gerwin, Kurt Liebknecht, Jaromin Kreicar, André Lurçat, Felix Samuely, Hinnerk Scheper, Josef Spalek, Bruno Taut and Rudolf Wolters.

50. Mart Stam, portrait photograph of the architect as a young man. In his latter years Stam retired as a recluse to Switzerland.

piecemeal projects for improving and extending old ones. Among a whole series of cities to whose development Meyer contributed only two appear to have amounted to significant new schemes: one for the competition of 1932 for Moscow and the other for Birobidjan, the anticipated capital of the Far Eastern Autonomous Republics.[52]

The tangible results of these brave men's labours were few. Though development plans, site plans and even housing designs abound, beyond a few forlorn blocks of flats, a school here and a clinic there, pathetically little that they conceived was actually realized. It was their fate to offer an interpretation of the new architecture in a country that was huge, hard for an outsider to comprehend, notorious for its human and natural ingratitudes, and as yet unsteadily governed. Vainly and irretrievably they lavished their ardour on abortive, farflung projects on behalf of an experimental system of government that could hardly yet provide its people with the bare necessities. Lecturing in Berlin in 1931, May spoke of building in the USSR as a life-and-death struggle.[53] Conditions were primitive, the administration incompetent, the materials and labour inadequate. From the start many Russians disliked the foreign experts, resented their privileges and inflated salaries and, with much justification, criticized their schemes.

To cap all this, in 1933 (the year that Hitler came to power) began a new Five Year Plan, and with it a darkening of the Russian political outlook, both external and internal. Foreigners, particularly Germans, were appreciated no longer. Few new contracts were signed, and some old ones were rescinded. May and Stam slipped back west in 1934. Hannes Meyer stayed on till 1936 and Hans Schmidt till 1937, but neither accomplished much after Kirov's assassination in December 1934 ushered in the era of the purges. From that catastrophe the remaining foreign architects were not immune. Werner Hebebrand was arrested in 1937 and deported next year, while Antonin Urban fell victim to Stalinism, dying in 1938 at the age of thirty after two years in prison.[54]

Well before this accumulation of adversities overwhelmed their careers, the challenge of building and working in Russia had deeply touched all these men. Their reaction varied with their architectural outlook and political alignment. Rudolf Wolters, for instance, spent a year in the Novosibirsk district under an individual contract in 1932–3. On his return he published a vivid but bigoted memoir of his experiences, *Spezialist in Sibirien* (1933). Wolters was no admirer of the Soviet Union and indeed became one of the chief architectural mouthpieces of the Third Reich.[55] For him the whole episode was a sorry tale of privation, incompetence and ignorance— all of which he ascribed ultimately to Jew-Bolshevism. He returned smugly satisfied of German superiority.

Among the May Group there was a strong current of political sympathy with the aims of the Soviet Union. But it was never dominant enough to outweigh the commitment to technological modernism that its members imported with them. Most of the criticism that the group quickly attracted concerned this 'formalist' baggage brought from Frankfurt. Their plans for Magnitogorsk and Kuznetsk and the first blocks at Stalinsk were attacked for their aridity. As early as 1931 an article complained of the 'barrack-style residential stereotypes à la Ernst May, whose designs have been sharply criticized and rejected by the youth workers' press and the architectural societies alike'.[56]

Though some of this hostility to the imported new architecture can be put down to a heated debate being carried on at this time on the nature of Soviet town planning,[57] a great deal more of it stemmed from the recent history and organization of Soviet architecture. With added social drama, the progress of Russian architecture between the wars in many ways parallels that of Germany. In both lands a period of utopian experiment, stylistic and institutional, gave way to another in which the starkness of social need prompted administrative reforms and the revision of many preconceptions; then followed a third, destructive phase of reaction in which all suffered.

Soon after the Revolution, Russian architecture had been submitted to a course of radicalization profounder than anything that Germany could then offer. The critical early institution was Vkhutemas, the Higher Artistic and Technical Workshops, founded in 1918 with the blessing of Lunacharsky, Lenin's western-oriented 'Commissar of Enlightenment'. Vkhutemas was an amalgamation of the respected Moscow School of Painting and Architecture with the Stroganov School, an arts-and-crafts college linked ideologically to the Deutscher Werkbund. The three-year architectural curriculum, started in 1920, reflected the constructivist experiments of its two chief instigators, Nikolai Ladovsky and Konstantin Melnikov. In its early years it was in fact as markedly romantic, individualistic and self-centred as may always be expected when architects have much that is new to think about but little to build.[58]

The new architectural societies offered a similar complexion; they expressed the concerns of the Moscow élite and quickly became prone to factionalism. Asnova, founded in 1923 by Ladovsky and others, was unrepentantly 'formalist' and aesthetic in orientation. Its slogan, 'Tailors measure man but only architecture can take the measure of architecture,' was hardly calculated to appeal to the mature Marxist-Leninist. Asnova's chief rival OSA began in 1925 as the vehicle particularly of Moisey Ginsburg. It subscribed to the glorification of western technological modernism and of mass production, as expounded in Le Corbusier's manifestos. Undoubtedly OSA's line, as propagated through its periodical *Sovremennaya Arkhitektura* (1926–31) was more social and collaborative than Asnova's. Its proponents saw their role in developing a socialist economy as that of an avant garde encouraging new western techniques like prefabrication. But much of their activity was utopian and superficial. Few of OSA's best-known adherents had much experience of building extensively in a country as technologically backward as Russia, and most of the daring schemes they produced remained perforce on paper.[59]

By 1928, when the first Five Year Plan ushered in an era of positive, planned construction to replace the caution of the N.E.P. years, these organizations were threatened by their quarrelsomeness, irrelevance and 'inability to assimilate the large numbers of more conservative provincials recruited into the field through the open-admissions policies of the earlier twenties'.[60] Increasingly the state needed architecture, and a new policy replaced the loose liberalism of Lunacharsky, who resigned in 1929. Architects began to be diverted into the burgeoning state bureaux from private practice, which was finally abolished in 1932; and Vkhutemas was reformed into the broader Vasi, the University of Architecture. The government also began looking into the feuding of the architectural societies and to throw its weight gradually behind a new faction, VOPRA, the Association of Proletarian Architects, founded in 1929. VOPRA was at first not concerned so much with style or technology as to evolve a more strictly Marxist interpretation of the role of the architect; for this reason Hannes Meyer became a member. But its ideology was soon perverted. The chief force in VOPRA emerged as Karo Alabjan, under whose leadership it became the focus of resentful outsiders who resented Muscovite dominance within Asnova, OSA, and the old-established Moscow Society of Architects. Eventually Stalin's aide Lazar Kaganovich was instructed to sort matters out and knock heads together. In accordance with the recommendations of Kaganovich to the 14th Party Congress, the factions were replaced in 1932 by the Federation of Soviet Architects (SSA) with Alabjan as editor of its official organ. Two years later this group provided the nucleus of the Soviet Academy of Architecture (BAA), founded in 1934.[61]

One of the sources of resentment among the VOPRA group seems to have been the employment of foreign avant-garde architects, of whom the Meyer and May groups were merely the latest, most committed representatives. Since about 1925 the links of OSA and Asnova with western modernists, and particularly with the architects of Weimar Germany, had been intense. In 1925–6 Erich Mendelsohn built a dyestuffs factory at Leningrad and visited Moscow; Bruno and Max Taut both kept in touch with developments in Moscow; and Le Corbusier was called in for the Centrosoyuz office project there, designed in 1928–9 and built with alterations in 1934. Between 1929 and

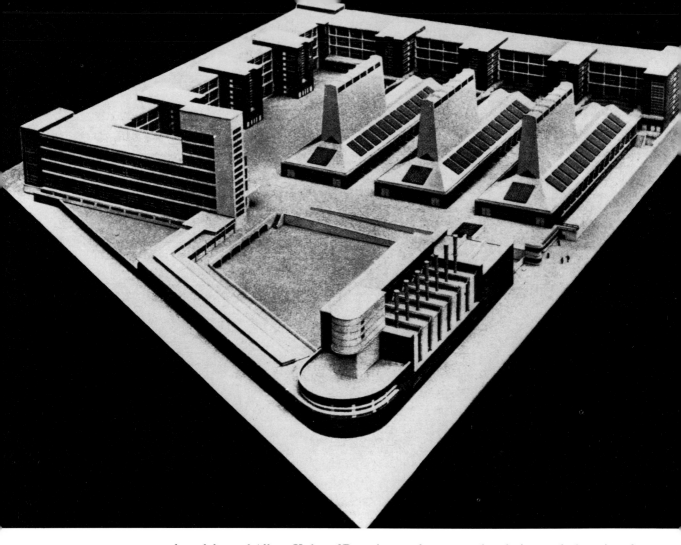

1932 the celebrated Albert Kahn of Detroit was also engaged to design a whole series of factories and to educate Russian technicians in the process. Then in the early 1930s two great Soviet competitions preoccupied the underemployed architects of the west. First came the Ukrainian State Theatre competition (1930), for which Gropius, Breuer and many other European architects submitted entries. There followed the notorious Palace of Soviets competition (1931–4). For the first stage of this débâcle Le Corbusier, Mendelsohn and Perret all sent in stylistically adventurous projects, only to see a coarse neoclassical scheme by Boris Yofan declared the winner and an American Beaux-Arts entry (by George Hamilton) the runner-up.[62]

In 1932 Gropius visited Russia and was bitterly disillusioned; he came back 'greying and shaken by what he had seen and experienced'. On his return, at the most delicate possible point in the evolution of Soviet architectural institutions, the influential Congrès Internationaux d'Architecture Moderne (CIAM), set up four years previously to represent the whole western Modern Movement, took a drastic step. Indignant at the result of the Palace of Soviets competition they at the last minute cancelled their forthcoming third conference in Moscow, opting instead for the comforts of a luxury Mediterranean steamer the following year. Twenty-six foreign architects working in Moscow, most of them doubtless members of the Meyer and May

51 (facing page). Model of the dyestuffs factory designed for the Leningrad Textile Trust by Erich Mendelsohn and built in 1925–6. This very large complex was one of the first modern buildings actually constructed in the Soviet Union, and probably the first Russian building of consequence to be built by a foreign architect since Behrens's German Embassy of 1911.

52. Hans Schmidt (b. 1893), a photograph of the Swiss architect in East Berlin, 1963. Schmidt was the best 'survivor' among the various German-speaking architects who made the pilgrimage to Russia.

groups, protested in vain.[63] The significance of this act was that it officially dissociated the Modern Movement in the west from architectural developments in Russia, crudely interpreting and condemning them in terms of style when as yet no ukase on matters of architectural style had been issued. Despite the recrudescence of neoclassicism there was plenty of stylistic variety in official architecture; modernism was tolerated until 1936, when rigidity became the rule in virtually all fields of Soviet life. In 1932 Bruno Taut was still hopeful enough to move his practice to Russia; and as late as 1934 so prominent a western modernist as André Lurçat could be enticed into a three-year stay under the second Five Year Plan and build quite successfully.[64] Even in January 1937 Frank Lloyd Wright, star guest at the first All-Union Congress of Soviet Architects, found much greater variety of view than he had expected. (In Wright's case, however, large doses of flattery and some skilful 'squiring around' by Alabjan plainly impaired his perceptions.)[65]

The overthrow of the Muscovites by Alabjan and his allies, followed by the rash action of the CIAM, certainly compounded the problems of the foreign architects. But at the same time imported modernism was being much more drastically undermined by something less whimsical than ideological fashion—the 'objective conditions' caused by the chronic shortage of technical expertise, machinery and materials. Almost

53. Housing at Stalinsk built by foreign architects. A view published in one of several articles in Russian architectural periodicals criticizing the work of the foreigners.

from the start these difficulties had forced a reversion to wooden construction and single houses at Magnitogorsk, and similar circumstances occurred everywhere.[66] Such experiences soon caused the politically more serious of the architects like Hannes Meyer and Hans Schmidt to rethink the relationship between socialism and style. This quickly led them to qualify their commitment to modernism. The dogmatism of western technologies and styles, they soon saw, was hopelessly wrong for Soviet conditions. Commenting on the technical deficiencies of their work, Meyer reminisced:

> The Soviets treated these foreigners as precious precision instruments, wrapping them up in cotton, lodging them in the few modern houses, giving them the privilege of almost luxurious food, and paying them very high salaries. These foreign experts brought with them from Europe and the United States the last word in super-mechanized and standardized building, and the collision between their ideas and the actual situation of the Soviet building industry at that time, was often cataclysmic. Many essentials were lacking: steel for concrete reinforcements, plywood, cement, glass, hardware; nails and screws seemed worth their weight in gold. The most customary mode of construction was of wood. The few 'occidental' projects that were carried out proved to be ill-adapted to the climate. In the sub-tropical zones, the Russian insects tended to infiltrate very quickly through the great quantity of joints in even such excellently constructed wood buildings as those of the American Jewish IGOR-group (which I saw in Birobidshan in 1933).[67]

The styles which the westerners purveyed were hardly more popular. The poor condition of several of the prominent Moscow works of the constructivist era reflected adversely on modernism. In remoter localities the Russian working man was frank in his yearning for decoration, his pleasure in craftsmanship. At Magnitogorsk, Hans Schmidt recalls, the workmen mocked the plainness of flats built by Stam and his colleagues in comparison with the richness of royal palaces.[68] Increasingly it became the preoccupation not just of VOPRA's neoclassicists but even of men like Meyer and Schmidt to adjust the interiors of the new housing to proletarian prejudices. 'Chippendale furniture,' Meyer later wrote, 'here an expression of conservatism, is there a step forward in the development of the highest quality of cabinet work.'[69]

No western architect of intelligence who worked in Russia returned with as crude or confident an understanding of style as he took with him. None abandoned the Modern

Movement altogether. Even Meyer, who expressed his conversion in a form almost as extreme as that with which he had pledged his faith to technology a decade before, applied a discernibly 'modern' vocabulary in his few later works. But undoubtedly, had these architects had the chance to teach the lessons they had learned about the limitations of the new architecture, it would profoundly have affected the post-war course of the Modern Movement. The tragedy is that that chance was never vouchsafed. When they left Russia, few were willing or able to go back to Nazi Germany, and in those countries where they did find refuge there was little building of significance for a decade, until well after the war was over. By that time the confidence of the less politically minded of these architects seemed to have been sapped; few of them attempted work of any great ambition or audacity again. Some of course were dead; Bruno Taut, for instance, eked out a solitary exile first in Japan and then in Turkey, where he died in 1938. Ernst May lived for some years as a farmer in Tanganyika. Eventually he resumed architecture and did some work in East Africa before returning in 1952 to Germany, where he practised for a time. Mart Stam returned to his native Holland in 1934 and worked quietly there until the war and indeed subsequently; but the spark had gone, and eventually he retired into somewhat mysterious solitude in Switzerland. Hans Schmidt alone retained his authority as a recognized voice for a socially responsible form of modern architecture. After nearly twenty barren years in Switzerland, he took an influential post in East Berlin where he lives still in honoured retirement.[70]

The story must end with Hannes Meyer, the most potent symbol of an alternative modernism that might have been. He spent three years back in Switzerland before

54. Wooden housing at Birobidjan, projected capital of the ultimately abortive Far Eastern Autonomous Republic. Housing of this type, produced by Hannes Meyer and his team, represented a step back from the technologically oriented buildings designed by the German architects when they first arrived in Russia.

55. Bruno Taut in exile in Japan, 1934. Taut later moved to Turkey, where he died in 1938.

moving to Mexico, where he worked for a decade. Then, becoming ill, he returned to Switzerland again and died there in 1954, aged sixty-four.[71] In his later career he adhered to the opinions he had come to as a result of his experiences in Russia. He strenuously opposed 'formalism' and continued to believe in the Soviet Union, whose architectural achievements he extolled in an article of 1942 dedicated to Shosta-kovich.[72] Along with this went a certain softening. He became less of a strict materialist, less inclined to claim architecture as a pure science, less opposed to the concept of art as having some place within the modern architect's philosophy. He drew and engraved prolifically in his last years. But to the ethic of self-glorification he remained adamantly hostile. Co-operation must be the architect's guiding light: 'Building is an activity profoundly connected with social-economic needs and the superimposed spiritual structure. And the architect is always of necessity a collaborator. He does his work together with economists and industrialists, with workers, artisans and housewives.'[73]

During the last decade of Hannes Meyer's career his chances were few and his opinions little heeded. Meanwhile the Modern Movement, or at least the version of it that was acceptable to the post-war capitalist world, was being at last accepted everywhere. For the time being Walter Gropius was once again the brightest star in the

56. Ernst May in 'exile' in Africa. May (holding camera) is portrayed together with colleagues and the English governor at the opening of an African cultural centre at Moshi, *c.* 1950. For three years May was a farmer in Tanganyika; then he was interned in South Africa; then he ran an architectural practice in East Africa for a few years before returning to Germany in 1952.

architectural firmament. Of Meyer, Gropius wrote in retrospect: 'Hannes Meyer was a treacherous character, which I did not recognize early enough. I believe that Hannes Meyer's inner downfall was his denying art as such. It narrows the field if the rational point of view is made the only factor.'[74]

The causes given for Meyer's comparative failure are shrewd. The accusation is shoddy and prompted by the challenge that the consistent example and philosophy of Meyer and his colleagues continue to pose to the orthodox western architect. Gropius himself was too vulnerable and uncertain to admit this, but such a consistently aesthetic architect as Philip Johnson has seen it: 'Hannes Meyer was a Communist, and was a damned good architect, and the more I see of Hannes Meyer the greater man I think he was. But I don't like what he *said* . . .'[75] Naturally: for in the breadth of radicalism of such an architect, reaching far beyond questions of style to the scope and nature of the profession, lives on a reproach and a threat from which the modern practitioner can never entirely avert himself, however skilful and sprightly his stylistic twists and turns.

CHAPTER SEVEN

The Architect as Entrepreneur

It has been a theme of earlier chapters in this book that the powers, attributes and aims assumed by architects have often been at odds with reality. The questions to which this chapter addresses itself are: Is this still true today? Has the more self-aware and self-examining profession of the late twentieth century made a more honest appraisal of the possibilities and limitations of architects? What are the most permanent shifts in direction which have occurred since 1945, how far have architects accepted them, or indeed how far are they bound to accept them? The answers offered have been arrived at from no more than a very partial study of the profession in Britain and the United States alone. So this chapter is a comparatively slight sketch which will unquestionably, with the benefit of hindsight, need amendment.

*   *   *

Few people might agree as to who has been the most illustrious of British post-war architects, but the most notorious one is easy to name: John Poulson. Following his bankruptcy and imprisonment in 1973–4, Poulson came to symbolize certain objectionable features in British business and politics during the 1960s. As the controller of companies which dealt corruptly with powerful politicians and officers in many local authorities and public institutions, his name stands for a web of malpractice ramifying in many directions.

In such a web, the small creature at its centre is soon lost sight of before the broader network which his disgrace reveals. So it has been with Poulson. The demise of the great men who succumbed to his blandishments and of the tight, municipal oligarchies which he exploited, is remembered; his own works and the exact nature of his operations were soon forgotten. Even in architectural circles, where investigations might have been expected and morals drawn, the career of John Poulson was quite swiftly dismissed. Poulson today for the British profession is not much more than a catchword, or a bogeyman.

Yet the example of Poulson has undoubted relevance to the future of British architecture. For despite his downfall, the type of architecture which he practised and of which he was something of an innovator, is becoming commoner, not rarer. It is easy to explain why: Poulson at his zenith was described as 'the head of the largest architectural firm in Europe'.[1] What in fact he had done, with spectacular if short-lived success, was to transform himself from a mere architect into an entrepreneur. How had this occurred?

Until about 1957–8, J. G. L Poulson was a middling firm of architects based on the Yorkshire town of Pontefract.[2] Poulson himself had done well to get so far, having never had any very special abilities of his own. He had been an articled pupil in a small Pontefract firm from 1927, but according to various contemporaries, 'couldn't draw plans for toffee', 'couldn't design a brick shithouse', 'couldn't even draw a straight line'.[3] Yet he had ambition enough to set up on his own at the age of only 22 in 1932, gradually got a few jobs and so expanded, never doing much (if any) designing himself.

The aftermath of the Second World War opened new horizons for Poulson. He secured some larger jobs through a Ministry of Works official who helped him get building licences in the difficult post-war period; and some first contacts in the north-east of England enabled him to open an office at Middlesborough in 1951. In 1954 he built himself a spruce modern house outside Pontefract. With the abolition of building licences in that year, boom time began for architects and the Poulson practice started to take off. Modern office buildings were going up all over Yorkshire and the north-east, and big public housing projects and hospitals were in the offing. Poulsons were among the few sizeable firms of architects in the north, and after a few years were able to profit from the new 'negotiated contract' system used by many public bodies, whereby in order to expedite projects, established experts in a given field were employed without full exploration of alternatives. By 1958 the firm's fee income had reached about £100,000.[4]

Up to this point, Poulson owed his success mainly to the fact that he was a plain, hardheaded businessman. He was ruthless with his staff, among whom there was constant turnover, but amiable, pliant and flattering with useful contacts and clients. His method was 'to promise almost anything to the client together with a totally unreasonable delivery date for his drawings', remark Martin Tomkinson and Michael Gillard in their excellent book on the Poulson scandal.[5] Nothing was to change in these habits, but in 1958 an innovation occurred when Poulson, on the advice of his first important political ally, Sir Herbert Butcher, established Ropergate Services. This was a service company ostensibly supplying the architectural firm with its office and transport requirements at a fee which would greatly reduce its profits. As company profits were taxed at a lower rate than architectural partnerships, this was of great benefit to Poulson. However the arrangement contravened the rules of the Architects' Registration Council of the United Kingdom (ARCUK), the body which administered the 1938 Registration Act to which Poulson had to adhere if he wished to continue calling himself an architect. Following negotiations between Poulson and ARCUK, he resigned as a director of Ropergate Services in 1960 but remained its chief shareholder; on this basis, the company eventually commenced trading in 1963.[6]

The assets built up in Ropergate Services allowed Poulson to finance borrowing for a number of companies which he promoted from 1964 onwards, mainly in order to chase the prestigious overseas projects which politicians henceforward were constantly urging upon British architects, engineers and builders. The most significant of these were Construction Promotion (formed with Leslie Pollard in 1963–4), Open Systems Building (1964) and International Technical and Construction Services (1966). Mainly through these companies, Poulson advanced sundry sums and gifts to directors and 'consultants' of one kind or another, backed by a fee income which by 1963 had passed the £500,000 mark—a fabulous sum by standards of the time. In the same period, Poulson in 1965 divided his firm into J. G. L. Poulson (architects) and J. G. L. Poulson Associates (civil and structural engineers). Thus by the late 1960s, he was able to offer clients a complete design and technical management service. Despite the earlier difficulties over Ropergate Services, Poulson seems to have had no real problem with ARCUK or the RIBA over these arrangements. Where he wished to avoid infringing professional rules, he simply allotted a controlling interest to his wife or to trusted allies, while keeping effective command himself.[7]

By 1969 the whole of the Poulson empire was in trouble, on account of his grandiose habit of advancing sums to consultants and contacts in expectation of jobs which never materialized or which lost money. Almost all the foreign ventures turned out ill-judged; only one, the huge £250,000,000 mining complex and harbour at Mocamedes, Angola, proved truly profitable. Poulson finally became bankrupt in 1972, and at the hearings enough evidence emerged for criminal proceedings to follow on.[8]

The misdemeanours for which Poulson was tried and sentenced in 1974 amounted, in simple words, to corruption in connection with public works contracts in Britain. Poulson 'schemed, bullied, bribed and cajoled his way to obtaining the all-important contracts', say Tomkinson and Gillard, who catalogue the many instances in their book.[9] Picked out for special attention at Poulson's trial was George Pottinger, a civil servant central to the development of the state-subsidized Aviemore Holiday Village, the project which Poulson regarded as the pinnacle of his career. The two became close friends. Poulson sent Pottinger on free holidays, advanced him money and designed him a house free of charge. Pottinger, who saw Poulson as 'a Napoleonic figure at the height of his career', helped him over difficulties at Aviemore and even wrote speeches attacking the Wilson Labour Government for Poulson and his wife to deliver. Among other recipients of the legendary Poulson generosity were national politicians, councillors, an executive to the National Coal Board, a surveyor who had worked for British Railways, and a district health officer. All were connected with work which he had or hoped to get. Poulson's philosophy about such gifts was simple: 'I am in a position to assist you by being efficient and effective and not just another typical example of the English architect,' he once wrote to John Cordle, M.P.[10]

In 1972 (after the bankruptcy but before the trial) Poulson was formally expelled from the RIBA for 'professional misconduct'. These charges against him, distinct from the criminal ones, dated back to 1970, when the 'blowing' of the Poulson story first attracted the RIBA's investigating committee. In the event, the committee avoided the then-unresolved and delicate question of payments to public figures (which certainly contravened RIBA rules) and concentrated upon Poulson's relationship with his subsidiary companies. So he was expelled on the technical grounds that he 'had a substantial financial interest in building construction companies, and was exerting direction and control over them while he was acting as a consultant architect, in that he supplied working capital to the companies and remunerated their directors, and was otherwise directly concerned in the conduct of their business.'[11] Thereafter the case was officially dropped; no further enquiry followed.

This decision was not without its critics. Some felt that the RIBA had acted against Poulson feebly and too late, that it waited for facts to come instead of ferreting them out. Malcolm MacEwen (previously the RIBA's information officer and author of a book very critical of the profession, *Crisis in Architecture*) argued for holding a full enquiry. How was it that no architect on Poulson's staff or connected with him had 'sneaked', he asked? Compared to such methods and conduct, the RIBA's investigating committee spent most of its time on trivial professional infringements. Because the RIBA had neither the will nor the power to look into serious offences, continued MacEwen, it was abetting misconduct and encouraging its repetition: 'If another Poulson is operating today, his chances of evading discovery and punishment are much better than Poulson's ever were, particularly if he remains sane.'[12]

But others, particularly architects with experience of modern commercial practice, felt differently. By the standards of international business, Poulson had done nothing exceptionally wicked, however inept or misguided or greedy he might have been. Had not the accident of financial failure prised open the can of worms, none of these misdemeanours would have come to light. In how many other matters of business, of government and of building might not similar derelictions have been hidden, simply by cleverer organization and accounting? The malignancy which Poulson brought to the surface was known to spread deep within the construction industry, if not among architects. In this context, the RIBA's charges against Poulson looked like blows from children who see a competitor trip and then assault him along with bigger boys.

There were deeper reasons for the RIBA's equivocation over Poulson. The rules under which he was expelled, and likewise the ARCUK rules which had caused difficulties when Ropergate Services was established, had been formulated in the 1930s when the concept of the independent professional architect untouched by business interests was in the main unchallenged. But during the decade of the 1960s when Poulson was at his zenith, the RIBA and many of the organs of the profession had, at least in public statements, abandoned some of the trappings of such a professionalism in order to foster any kind of growth in architecture, benign or otherwise. Poulson himself had been applauded in the building press for his go-ahead policies and his commitment to profit and efficiency. It was now profoundly illogical for the RIBA to turn on him for a technical and outdated reason, when to all intents he had been encouraged to pursue his kinds of priorities. For the believers in this new aggressive architectural posture, the culprit was not so much Poulson as those like MacEwen who sought to drag architects back to old-style professionalism. What was needed, claimed one RIBA member, was not an enquiry but 'a policy of positive public relations'. MacEwen's time as information officer should have been spent not in attacking these new directions but in 'hounding the press, radio and TV with good news about the profession. He should have pursued every critical article and letter in the papers with a riposte. Every time a building was mentioned without the architect's name being quoted, he should have been in touch with the editor straight away.'[13]

What was the origin of such attitudes?

*   *   *

A good starting point for the growth of the managerial and entrepreneurial ideal in British architecture is 1962, when the RIBA published *The Architect and his Office*, a survey of the whole profession. Before then, very little detailed information about architectural practice was available. So the survey set out to show what British architects, especially those in private practice, actually did.

The Architect and his Office looked at a sample of offices of RIBA members, who at that time represented about three-quarters of all architects registered under the act of 1938. In 1957, 52 per cent of these members had been in private practice, 28 per cent in local government employment and 6 per cent in industrial and commercial firms, including builders; the remaining 14 per cent either taught, were abroad, had retired, or were in other jobs.[14]

The survey came to two simple and important conclusions. Firstly, it suggested that most private architectural firms were far too small. Nearly 70 per cent of Britain's 3,000 private offices employed less than six 'professional' staff, and only 13 per cent more than ten. Why so many small offices had continued in business for so long was obscure to the investigators: 'Either they offer their principals a satisfying way of life which compensates for the relatively small returns, or alternatively . . . the principals have a supplementary source of income.'[15]

Secondly, the survey found the management of private architectural offices in Britain to be incompetent and unrealistic. Few practices (and very few small ones) showed financial understanding or could co-ordinate jobs well. Most were geared chiefly towards drawing and those related skills which are conceived as essentially architectural. Yet these occupied only just over half of all architects' time; for principals in large offices this could fall to a mere tenth of their time. Meetings, correspondence, discussions and administration took up the rest, yet these were rarely planned for.[16]

The Architect and his Office placed the blame for these failings squarely upon architectural education, and testified to 'universal complaint of the lack of knowledge, particularly the failure to coordinate design and construction'.

> How many architects at the bottom of the ladder visualise that advancement to the top is likely to mean spending nearly half their time on meetings and correspondence? Does the present system of architectural education take account of this pattern of development into which the majority of architects now have to fit? Or is it still influenced unduly by the idea of the one-man practice, turning out young architects who hold the belief that they are ready and equipped to take the full responsibility of practice as soon as they have the minimum office experience laid down by the R.I.B.A.? Many experienced practising architects, and others in related professions to whom we talked, considered this misguided belief to be responsible for much of the dissatisfaction which the young and recently qualified architect creates, and which he himself feels in his early days in an office.[17]

The recommendations of this report profoundly influenced British architecture in the 1960s. It urged the RIBA to diversify architectural education, draw the profession closer to others in construction (notably engineers), change its scale of charges so as to decrease fees for large jobs and increase them for small ones, liberalize the rules governing the soliciting of work, and help where possible to draw back service skills like lighting and heating to architects' offices. Above all, architectural management was to be improved.[18]

The RIBA obediently tried to implement as many of these suggestions as it could. But by so doing without questioning the report's premises, it sowed the seeds of future dissension. *The Architect and his Office* had been preoccupied with the issue of how private practice might become more profitable and efficient, because the RIBA had traditionally addressed the interests of principals, not of its membership as a whole. Yet of this membership about a half was outside private practice altogether, and at least another quarter consisted of salaried architects in private offices. Since in the larger and more profitable offices 'unqualified' technicians were starting to supersede salaried architects, a more prosperous private practice was not necessarily in the latter's interests. At the same time, the structure of architectural employment in Britain was also moving slowly away from private practice.

The RIBA therefore embarked on a process of managerial reform without ensuring that its policies accurately reflected the changed structure and interests of its membership. *The Architect and his Office* confirmed that the special problems of salaried architects had been ignored, but its recommendations took scant heed of the fact. This mistake was bound to cause trouble.

*   *   *

The British property and redevelopment boom of the 1960s did what the RIBA on its own could never have done in boosting the new attitudes about profit and organization in architectural practices. The firms that were able to wax fat in this era were in actual fact not so many in number; Oliver Marriott, for instance, estimated in 1967 that a half to three-quarters of the new London office blocks built over the previous decade had been built by only ten firms of architects.[19] Nevertheless these firms exerted an influence upon professional attitudes out of all proportion to their numbers. The example of Poulson, who battened mainly on public commissions, has been given already; to balance it, something should be said about the procedures of Richard Seifert, the cleverest and in many ways most respected commercial architect of the period.

Like Poulson, Seifert set up in independent practice with very little experience in the early 1930s, and worked only in a small-time way before the Second World War. The causes of his success lay in his immensely hard work, his practicality, his discretion, and in one other simple secret. 'One thing I learned particularly during my wartime experience was to fully understand and comprehend any statutory documents,' he once told a reporter.[20] To another he said: 'I find it difficult to understand how an architect can possibly advise his client to their best advantage if he does not know the law . . . I know the law because I make sure I understand it. It is absolutely essential.'[21]

When building controls in Britain were lifted in 1954, this knowledge paid dividends. Office developments which sprang up in city centres had to comply with the considerable technicalities of the Town and Country Planning Act of 1947 and its

57. Colonel Richard Seifert.
The most successful post-war
British architect at the
height of his powers, *c.* 1965.

various amendments, in which many architects remained complacently untutored. Seifert became celebrated for his ability to manipulate the clauses on 'plot ratio'—the rules which governed to what height a building might go in relation to the surface area of its plot. At Drapers Gardens, a development in the City of London, he was able to build higher and secure another 10 per cent of office space for his client by virtue of a sub-clause in the 1947 Act which had been intended for quite other purposes. At the better-known Centre Point, Seifert's capacity with intricacies of law made him appear a benefactor of the London County Council rather than its opponent, and thus gained approval for his scheme.[22] In a third case, the small Avon House in Southwark, Seifert countered the restrictions of the late 1960s on more offices by putting up a building which met all the regulations for warehousing and commerce, but which could be changed into offices once the restrictions were lifted.[23]

These skills (which most other architects were too high-minded or too idle to acquire) can be presented, according to taste, as technical victories or anti-social tricks. They were certainly the ingredients of architectural success; in 1967 Richard Seifert and Partners had six offices with nine partners and 240 staff.[24] Seifert himself constantly maintained that his actions were guided wholly by professional responsibility. Sir Hugh Casson has glossed this as 'an unswerving loyalty to his client. Most architects feel that their loyalty lies also to society in general. I am sure that Col. Seifert regards this as presumptuous.'[25]

In retrospect at least, Seifert showed symptoms of broader responsibilities as well. By the mid 1970s he was, like others, deploring high-rise blocks for living and shoddy commercial buildings produced in the rush for development profit. In particular he condemned the measure which for ten years after 1954 had allowed developers to claim compensation not only for abortive costs on rejected schemes but also for development value and profit. Because of this, many urban commercial developments were built which should never have been allowed.[26]

*   *   *

Seifert himself continued to run his practice very simply throughout the years of his pre-eminence, without any special managerial methods.[27] But many of the bigger offices, urged on by the RIBA, began to take on the new language and procedures of business. Some sense of the distance which architects travelled in this period may be gained from comparing two books on professional methodology separated by only eight years. Maurice E. Taylor's *Private Architectural Practice* (1956) perpetuates the comfortable homilies of the inter-war profession: if you want to get jobs, join a club, play golf and make sure your office looks smart. Brunton, Baden Hellard and Boobyer's *Management Applied to Architectural Practice* (1964) has a drastically different tone:

> The new style efficient architect practises his full delegation, co-ordinates his staff into a tightly knit highly flexible organisation, and maintains all his recording and controlling techniques. He seems all set to go towards an orderly, busy and profitable future. One day his predicting techniques cast a shadow, the programme foretells of a sizeable gap in his work load which his flexibility cannot fill. The Fee Forecast shows a corresponding plummeting of expected income, and the liquidity checks shows that the cash position is such that there is no margin to weather any falling of receipts if over a prolonged period . . .[28]

Between about 1958 and 1964 the RIBA worked zealously to promote this 'new style efficient architect'. But thereafter its nerve began to fail and its policies to vacillate, as opposition to the great rebuilding programmes grew, contradictions emerged in the philosophy of managerial architecture, and the economic boom subsided. Almost immediately, another and less confident strand started to appear in the professional argument, one on which architects were broadly in agreement: whatever changes in organization took place, the architect should maintain or even extend his 'leadership' in the construction industry. Better co-operation with others was never to lead to loss of control.

Again and again architects returned to this issue of control. In 1960, in a debate on the profession's position, W. A. Allen emphasized that relations with other building professionals should be improved, then immediately added: 'some single group must see to the smooth collaboration of the whole array of interests, professional and industrial, and the main duty is clearly ours'. In the ensuing discussion, only an engineer could be found to remark that the 'strategic quality of thinking' needful in such a co-ordinator might not necessarily be an architect's.[29] Later, in 1968, when the RIBA had lost its earlier sense of purpose, two of the doyens of the profession, the Lords Esher and Llewellyn-Davies, produced a policy document (soon known to the initiate as 'The Lords' Prayer'). This addressed with some candour the issues of fragmentation of skills in the building industry, of architectural control, and of 'comprehensive building management':

> There are three reasons why architects should set themselves to provide this comprehensive service. The first is that they are there, trained however imperfectly to think more comprehensively than other relevant disciplines, with a cast of mind that veers habitually (unlike the engineer's) from the particular to the general. The second, less disinterested, is that if they do not achieve this capability they will find themselves sooner than they expected on the fringes of decision-making rather than at the centre, acting as stylists for other people's products. The third is that experience in countries where architects occupy this fringe position, shows that such societies get inferior buildings in every sense of the word.[30]

This obsession with control was an old theme in the profession's history. But the fears of this period were not unrealistic. Though private architects in Britain have long supervised more building work than in most comparable countries, that share was sharply declining in the late 1960s, from 40 per cent of all new construction between 1964 and 1969, to only 26 per cent between 1970 and 1974.[31] (That this was only a phase induced by the amount of public housing built in these years by municipal practices was hardly realized.) Meanwhile the bigger, more managerial private firms were contracting out more and more service skills to outside concerns, and relying increasingly on technicians with non-architectural training to do all kinds of jobs, from draughting to computer-programming.

Nor was this remedied by greater general prosperity among architects. Throughout the 1960s British architects smarted from the findings of the 1956 Pilkington Commission, which worked out that they earned less than actuaries, barristers, solicitors, graduates in industry, dentists, doctors, accountants, university teachers and—worst of all—surveyors and engineers. The RIBA brought in changes in its fee scale to help meet this situation. But then, horror of horrors, in 1968 the Government's Prices and Incomes Board investigated architecture on the grounds that the type of mandatory fee scale operated by the RIBA was against the public interest.[32]

This question was eventually referred to the Monopolies Commission, dragged on through the 1970s, and has still to be finally settled at the time of writing. But in the course of this dispute, the RIBA retreated significantly from its aggressive managerial posture of the 1960s to cower in the familiar shadow of protectionism. The free market might be worshipped, but the defence of the profession came first. Without a mandatory scale of charges, it argued, architects would be at the mercy of powerful clients who would 'shop around' until they found someone willing to take a lower fee; this would drive yet more architects into the public sector, depress average earnings and lead to shoddier buildings. The Monopolies Commission was unimpressed by this line of argument, and issued a report which led in the long run to the dismantling of mandatory charges in favour of a 'recommended' fee scale. So in the end, architects lost ground on one of the few issues to unite the profession.[33]

*   *   *

Because of this conflict between the ideal of managerial efficiency and a weak profession, attempts to legitimize entrepreneurial activity in British architecture were generally thwarted during the 1970's. From the entrepreneurs' standpoint, such half-hearted and sluggish moves towards reform as there were were frustrating. The out-datedness of the old professional attitudes was most apparent in export markets, whither British architects were being asked to turn their attentions. Here a modicum of moral flexibility was needful if jobs were to be got and kept, especially in the Middle East. The RIBA would only advise architects to adhere to the 'responsible professional customs' of the countries concerned.[34] Yet many had few such customs, and could not be penetrated unless architects joined consortia which included contracting; these the RIBA officially did not countenance.

At home, architects eager to take up the challenge of development, to advertise, to incorporate, to become directors and contractors, faced an opposition consisting of old-style professionals, salaried architects and small-scale principals, few of whom stood to gain from alterations in the rules of ARCUK or the RIBA. Among these, salaried architects were the most important group. When the business boom of the early 1960s petered out, it gave way to a period of public works, especially in the field of housing, in which salaried architects in municipal departments assumed a greater importance than ever. In 1971, for instance, 80 per cent of the RIBA membership was salaried; and at a referendum held in that year this membership conclusively rejected the RIBA's managerial policies.[35] In the same period, a Salaried Architects' Group sprang up to uphold the interests of the neglected majority and to counteract existing factions on the 'right' of the argument, like the Architects in Industry Group, the London Association of Private Architects, and the Association of Consultant Architects.

The grievances of salaried architects and other skilled subordinates in British offices were of long standing and had several times previously led to attempts at combination and organization.[36] But with the expansion of large practices and the diminution of small ones in the 1960s, the experience of the ordinary salaried architect took a turn for the worse. In 1962 *The Architect and his Office* had feared that young architects were entering practice after a training that had ill prepared them for the realities of the profession and were beginning to feel alienated. Ten years later, evidence that this was so was abundant. In London, for instance, an architectural 'lump' had grown up, consisting of freelance assistants hired by agency who passed from office to office. Here, a participant describes his reasons for working in this fashion:

From every sensible point of view, I would be better off as a permanent. But the truth is, something shocking has happened to architects.

The day of the gifted amateur may have passed, but the day of the ungifted

58. Lewis Womersley, City Architect of Sheffield, lording it before his grandest creation, the Park Hill Estate, in 1962. Womersley was among the most powerful of local-authority chief architects thrown up by the British public housing boom of the 1950s and 1960s.

professional—in the quasi technical sense anyway—is certainly on us. To a frightening extent, the clients are certainly the masters, and I have yet to meet the architect who will gainsay a client. Ironically, these clients are spurious. They have no intention of personally using the buildings they commission, for they are usually ignorant entrepreneurs with strongly developed anti social instincts, or cautious committees whose true function is to pauperise buildings to a level acceptable to their political masters. Buildings produced in these conditions, either by craven lickspittles in the private sector or pliant nonentities in public offices, do not really warrant involvement . . .

When I enter a fresh office and find the usual hysteria about getting 'it' ready for planning permission, or byelaws, or a committee or board meeting, I can only say—after a swift glance—my God! Who, or what, done it? And I am constantly astonished that trained, apparently balanced and competent men take it so seriously. I find myself immediately on the outside . . .[37]

This piece noticeably makes no distinction between public and private offices. For by 1972 many assistants found local authority practice just as alienating. Here too the twin fetishes of the 1960s for size and for 'corporate management' had grave results for architects. In the newly stratified mega-departments, designers were kept even further from committees and clients and 'treated like clerks'. In sorrow, Louis Hellmann described in 1973 how the admired Architect's Department of the London County Council, where Robert Matthew had devised and Leslie Martin perfected a flexible group-system of practice, soon fell into 'Stalinist' managerial perversions when the authority became the Greater London Council. Managers who revered private practice imposed technical decisions from above without consultation, tried to block all communications between designer and user, and feigned participation when revolt threatened from below.[38]

For a moment in the 1970s, it seemed as if the salaried architects would prevent the further encroachment of business attitudes in British architecture, and stabilize the profession around a more or less socialized ideal. In the event they proved too irresolute and apolitical. At the time of writing, it appears that the battle to legitimize the entrepreneurial approach has been won, not indeed because the boom conditions of the early 1960s have returned, but because of a change in political climate combined with the much severer, prolonged slump of the late 1970s. So savage have been recent cuts in public works, particularly in housing, that the large municipal architects' departments have been drastically reduced in size; the Greater London Council's, for instance, has dwindled almost to insignificance. The private sector too has been squeezed, to the point where only the most profit-conscious, business-orientated practices have been unscathed. Salaried employees, insecure in their jobs because of the number of out-of-work technicians and architects ready to take their places, do not have so much power as they did before. In such circumstances the RIBA, more out of desperation than zeal, goaded by government to abandon monopoly and less fettered than before by the reservations of its salaried membership, has cast fears to the wind and permitted members to do more or less what they like, if that will obtain more work. Poulson, in fact, has been finally forgotten.[39]

*   *   *

The problems of the modern British profession were lucidly diagnosed in Malcolm MacEwen's *Crisis in Architecture* (1974), the most savage denunciation of official policy in the RIBA's history. Having worked for the RIBA through the 'decade of management', MacEwen believed that the Institute had abetted British architects to abandon their social responsibilities and cut themselves off from public opinion. They must now regain moral respectability, he urged, by dissociating themselves from property speculation and returning to the service of the community.[40]

Unfortunately, MacEwen's particular suggestions for institutional reform were not convincing. But a more coherent programme did emerge shortly afterwards from the New Architecture Movement, founded in 1975. NAM still labours today under the disadvantage of being a little more than a network, with an *ad hoc* organization, a sporadic output and an uncertain future. Yet since its foundation it has consistently been the only pressure group within architectural politics in Britain to grasp issues beyond the scope of self-interest, and to combine its suggestions for reform with some deeper understanding of the relation between architects, the construction industry and the general public.

NAM has concerned itself with a variety of immediate tasks. It campaigned with some success to spread unionization among salaried architects and technicians. It also put lengthy evidence to the Monopolies Commission to counteract the RIBA's defence of its fee scale. This submission argued that the prevailing fee system was part of a nexus of arrangements serving to segregate architects from their real clients, the users of buildings.

> The fee system acts as a barrier to those architects whose capacity or conscience favours small scale initiatives in preference to the corporate or bureaucratic clients whose sectional interests at present totally bias the market . . . The fact that . . . direct community architecture is practically non-existent, indicates that 'public interest' in the market for architectural services is only fractionally served. In the troika of medical, legal and architectural professions, the architectural profession is conspicuous in its failure to develop alternative systems of remuneration to prevent this sort of distortion.[41]

The other and broader issue that has interested NAM is the reform of the Architects' Registration Council of the United Kingdom (ARCUK). This body holds the key to the institutional future of British architecture. Under the terms of the Architects' Registration Act of 1931, ARCUK was set up to regulate the membership, conduct and education of the British profession. This act was a compromise, five bills having been unsuccessfully put to Parliament between 1926 and 1930. The rock on which these previous bills had foundered was that the RIBA was itself to be the profession's controlling body—a proviso even then unacceptable to Parliament as monopolistic. The RIBA therefore yielded and accepted a nominally independent registration council in the shape of ARCUK. But from the first, the RIBA appointed most of ARCUK's members and so controlled the profession. Of 68 members today, 41 are nominated by the RIBA; the rest consist of representatives of government, unions, other professional bodies within construction, and 'unattached architects' (i.e. registered architects who are not RIBA members).[42] Historically, ARCUK policies broadly have been those of the RIBA, though in law the bodies are wholly distinct. Were the proportion of registered architects who are RIBA members to decline drastically, the Institute would lose control of ARCUK. But the practical benefits that still accrue from membership of the RIBA make that as yet unlikely.

For the past few years, NAM has worked to increase its influence by securing most of the seats allotted to 'unattached architects' on ARCUK. The group's success has made it the second most important voice on ARCUK and has invigorated deliberations there, but the body still falls short of anything like independence. NAM therefore has a plan for its constitutional reform. Of the new 60-member council, just under half would represent the profession and over half would be chosen from the rest of the construction industry and the wider community. The architectural representation would be split between principals, self-employed architects, salaried management, salaried architects, technicians, teachers and students, according to current proportions within the profession.[43]

As things stand, the RIBA is unlikely to allow power to be wrested from its hands. Yet if Parliament finds time (in the past it has not attached urgency to the problems of the architectural profession) it may see things differently. A state-appointed body has already decided that the RIBA fee scale is unjustly monopolistic. From here the step is short to reconsidering the issue of registration.

Possibly, reform may also be generated from within. The RIBA, like other professional institutes, is no-one's favourite body: too quick for some, too slow for others, alternately pussy-footing and heavy-handed, neither a true trades union, nor a learned society, nor a disinterested champion of public good. Yet through its history there has run a strain of liberalism or enlightenment that has, for instance, impelled it to publish such a devastating self-indictment as MacEwen's *Crisis in Architecture*. If the discrepancy between its own policies of the past twenty years and the real interests of most of the membership can be made to sink in, it may not be long before the RIBA itself is pressing for reform of ARCUK.

But, some may say, does any of this matter? Can the internal bickering of the profession in any way affect the quality or production of architecture? The answer is yes. The type of managerial profession widely advocated in the 1960s has not improved British architecture; so much can be grasped without countenancing the inflated claims of some architects for the significance of their contribution during that period. Profit-bent principals, unaccountable managers and alienated assistants, in whichever sector, have not made good buildings. Nor, despite the lip-service that the entrepreneurs have paid to better liaison with other skills in the industry, is it likely that advertising, incorporation, directorships and consortia will help much. But a reformed controlling council of the profession, with a majority drawn from the whole field of construction, could help towards modernizing what by common consent is one of the country's most backward industries.

The alternative is a yet more entrepreneurial profession. Where that might take British architects is best surmised by looking, as so often, westwards across the Atlantic.

*   *   *

Among the phenomena of recent American architecture one of the most startling has been the success of John Portman of Atlanta. Bold, large, simple in outline, complex in organization, above all profitable, his buildings have been frequently described; but a brief account of his progress may not be out of place.[44]

Portman studied architecture in the 1940s at Georgia Institute of Technology

(Georgia Tech). His early office experience in New York and Atlanta was chiefly commercial. Having practised on his own from 1953, he in 1956 joined forces with his ex-professor Griffith Edwards, a partnership which lasted until 1969. From these years date his first unusual achievement, particularly his conception of the Peachtree Center, a core of urban redevelopment in downtown Atlanta which was to be not only designed but also controlled personally. His earliest building here was the Atlanta Merchandise Mart (1961). There followed the Atlanta Hyatt Regency Hotel (1966–8), which brought Portman's name into architectural prominence as the pioneer example of the 'atrium-type' hotel built round a dramatic internal open space. To Peachtree Center he afterwards added three slim office blocks, an addition to the Hyatt Regency in which what was to be a recurrent motif, the cylindrical tower, first appeared, and then the seventy-storey Peachtree Plaza Hotel (1975–6), in which that theme was developed.[45]

After the Hyatt Regency, Portman also began to branch out in other cities, designing hotels (based always on the atrium type and sometimes on the cylinder) at Chicago Airport, Los Angeles, San Francisco and Detroit. At San Francisco and Detroit these hotels became the focus of larger schemes of reclamation on the model of the Peachtree Center, which by the 1970s was an assured commercial success. As yet none of these three schemes is complete. But by the end of the decade Portman had passed from being a mere architect to recognition as one of America's most revered planners. A recent project for a 'Great Park' for Atlanta betokens yet further expansion into such fields.[46]

Other American architectural firms have certainly succeeded in recent years in greatly shaping city centres (e.g. Harrison and Abramowitz at Albany). Portman's achievement is different in kind because he has exercised more control and achieved his goal in at least three separate cities, leaving aside unbuilt redevelopments and individual buildings. How has this been done?

The answer is that Portman has consistently acted as his own developer. To this he evangelically attributes his success (a book promoting him is even entitled *The Architect as Developer*). Following his first commercial venture, a medical office building which lost him $7,500 because he could not control the real estate angles, Portman realized that he could only build what he wanted by commanding the techniques of development. On this basis, by the usual process of complex deals, the Peachtree Center was 'assembled', so that from the Atlanta Merchandise Mart onwards Portman effectively 'developed' most of his own building sites. Naturally, others were in varying degrees involved. Trammell Crow of Dallas provided much finance and expertise for the early part of Peachtree Center, the Rockefellers are important partners at San Francisco and at Detroit the controlling interest has been Henry Ford's.[47]

The focus of the Portman office differs from that of the traditional architect. The 200-odd staff are divided between three companies: John Portman and Associates, the architectural practice; Peachtree Purchasing, which handles contract buying for hotels and other commercial buildings; and Portman Properties, which assembles, develops and administers sites. Portman himself oscillates between design and development. The firm designs enough traditional buildings to give the architectural office some independence, and Portman personally 'sets the basic design concept' for

59. John Portman holding forth over the top of a model showing a small morsel of his Peachtree Center, Atlanta.

each building. But the intricacies and tactics of development naturally absorb the greatest proportion of his time.

Portman continues to see himself primarily as an architect and conceives the profession as having a high destiny. His theory, as advanced in *The Architect as Developer*, is that architects must grasp the chance to become 'master coordinators for the physical development of entire cities'.[48] This they can only achieve by understanding patterns of growth, knowing markets and property values, and above all by appreciating the 'financial climate that makes it right to do something or not to do something'.[49] Good architecture, he avers, increases values and makes developments successful, for only the designer by 'weaving elements of sensory appeal' into his projects can humanize the calculations of the speculator. Thus architecture and real estate work to mutual advantage and to the whole community's benefit.

How far Portman's own developments bear this out is hard to say. Profit, the most easily ascertainable criterion used to judge them, touches on one side of the question alone. In his favour, his buildings have proved in the simplest sense successful and popular. Against him, his schemes confront the problems of urban renewal, his chosen field of combat, only indirectly. He remains as a developer bound fast by profitability; his great projects, so far as they have yet gone, serve only the affluent middle classes and the corporations that rent his office and hotel space. Prosperity, by the orthodox theory of capitalism, is to percolate downwards through the social hierarchy as a result of the jobs created by these developments. The concept of the architect–co-ordinator, as appeared in the British context, is also fraught with a contradiction. It urges architects to reach out and co-operate with others while keeping their own pre-eminence. Why Portman thinks architects as a class so well fitted to this demanding role he does not say.

*   *   *

John Portman's career merely provides the most visible example of a species of architect–entrepreneur that has been springing up all over the United States since the 1950s. Not all of these take the same form. Some are developers in the Portman mould, some have turned their practices into limited liability companies, and others have moved over to 'design and build'. But all, less equivocally than in Britain, have embraced the managerial and marketing approach so dear to American business philosophy. An article of 1971 in *Fortune Magazine* was probably the first to draw the American public's attention to this conversion. Besides Portman it singled out among others Charles Luckman Associates of Los Angeles, acquired in 1968 by a large corporation which wished to diversify into real estate; CRS Design Associates of Houston, perhaps the first architectural team to incorporate; and RTKL Inc. of Baltimore, which had recently merged with a California software computer company. Common to the firms mentioned in the article was a commitment to marketing architecture aggressively.[50]

The causes of this revolution are essentially just the same as in Britain: a fear that the traditional architect's role was dying. But in the United States the problem has proved more acute and the solutions proposed more drastic.

The American architectural profession's hold upon the construction industry has always been more tenuous than that of its counterparts in Europe. Only a fifth to a quarter of all American building in dollar value is supervised by architects, and only one per cent of all private single-family houses is designed by them.[51] A survey of the profession conducted by the American Institute of Architects in 1950 found, as in Britain, that there were too many architects in too many inefficient small firms chasing too few jobs.[52] From this period engineers, who are less exactly distinguished from architects in the U.S. than in Britain, began increasingly to encroach upon the architectural preserve in the form of architectural-engineering (A-E) agglomerations. A study published in 1968 showed, for instance, that in rankings of 'design firms' by level of earnings the highest that a purely architectural firm could come was twenty-second.[53]

One special constituent of these recent changes in the American profession has been a reaction against the cultural influence of the prima-donna art–architect. Such influence has been especially strong in the United States, where individualism is so vital a part of the prevailing ideology. To an extent this situation persists. Perhaps more than in Europe, architectural pundits still hang on the latest pronouncement or value the smallest sketch of the recognized darlings of the hour.

Such 'prima-donnas' have by no means all been impractical idealists. The use of the tool of 'art' to entice or intimidate a client has certainly been familiar in American architecture, from Sullivan and Wright downwards to Philip Johnson. A recent example of a clever architect whose career falsified the realities of practice to his own advantage is Louis Kahn, an artist of great aesthetic persuasiveness, yet one whom Philip Johnson himself could call 'a total phony, a worse phony than I am.'[54] What Johnson meant comes out in a curious book written about Kahn by his long-time engineer, August E. Komendant. In this book, admiration of the man's artistry struggles with bitterness that he could neither acknowledge help received (and Komendant claims to have given much) nor work properly with others.

> It was typical of Kahn not to give credit to any one of his associates, regardless of how great or extensive their contribution to a project was. But in this respect Kahn was not an exception, it is common to almost all architects . . . All artists and geniuses have a very strong personal ego. For this reason probably Kahn never allowed anyone in his office, or even in the university, to become his successor. He would have felt himself challenged and overshadowed by such a person. Only very secure persons, with ability and progressive views, teach and develop their successors to one day carry on their ideas and work. Kahn was not such a person . . .
>
> Kahn never discussed economy in his class; it was a dirty word for him. He advised students that an architect's first task after receiving a commission and the program accompanying it is to change the program, not to try to satisfy it, but to put it into the realm of architecture . . . Such advice, if carried out without contemplation, was a disservice to students and made them arrogant.[55]

So complete has been the hold of the 'prima donnas' upon the 'higher' level of theory in American architecture that the existence of other views still goes almost undiscussed in academic circles. Often indeed those who have criticized developments in American architecture and planning over the past twenty years have singled out this 'aesthetic' ideology as their particular foe. For instance Robert Goodman's *After the Planners* (1971), which in looser form offers a similar critique of the profession in the United States as MacEwen's *Crisis in Architecture* does for Britain, argues that the 'aesthetic' approach to architecture actually helps to alienate and repress.

> The more architecture can be described in the morally neutral currency of 'aesthetics', devoid of political content for the people affected, the more élite and the more removed from the political review of ordinary people become the experts who use this currency. Meanwhile, as those who practise architecture criticize architecture, those who teach architecture and those who learn about and 'appreciate' architecture continue to see it in 'aesthetic' rather than political terms, the more useful this 'aesthetic' becomes to those who rule. For the rulers are no longer repressing people with their highways and urban-renewal projects; they are supposedly bringing them progress and culture.[56]

*   *   *

Clearly, 'art' can only work as a means to elevate the architect, get him work, and leave him in control within strict limits. Though these limits embrace the most prestigious and visible of projects—notably certain types of public building and the private houses of the rich—they are not enough to employ a whole profession. They are certainly insufficient to fulfil the avowed aim of the Society of American Registered Architects, to 'return the architect to the position of leadership in the new building industry'.[57] The more pragmatic among American architects, realizing this, have come to believe that the gap can be filled only by self-promotion of a cruder kind.

The theme of promotion in the professional literature of American architecture is not new. But in the past it emanated chiefly from small practices. The eight books written between 1941 and 1957 by the Boston house architect Royal Barry Wills are amiable and clever examples of the genre. Nearly all are aimed at getting Wills's and other architects' names before the public; and *This Business of Architecture* (1941), for example, offers twenty-three civilized hints on how to get new commissions.[58]

From the 1960s however the tone of such books changes, their numbers increase and the status of many of their authors is much higher. An attractive example of the genre preferred by Wills, mixing autobiography with business hints, is *Architecture A Profession and A Business* (1967) by Morris Lapidus of New York. On the basis of long experience going back to the Beaux-Arts days, Lapidus argues that the era of the 'individual masterbuilder' is over and that from now on group practice will predominate. Whether through birth, marriage, political connexion or training in corporate management, the young architect (he exhorts) should strive to become a principal in one of the few firms that do most of the work. 'Architecture must be sold just like any other commodity,' he says: 'excite, titillate and interest your possible client, but don't oversell.'[59]

Wendell E. Rossmann of Phoenix fleshes out much of this advice in *The Effective Architect* (1972). To obtain commissions Rossmann suggests mailing campaigns combined with 'the swing around the country' to visit city managers, bank managers or school-district superintendents. He advises architects too on the procedure for 'the first personal contact', 'the follow-up' and, when a client finally chooses between architects, on the interview. He justifies all this 'professional publicity' as a modern necessity if architects are to be accepted by the public.[60] In common with other writers of this type, he believes that architects historically have held high status (he cites Ictinus, Erwin von Steinbach and the great Renaissance men), but that this status has been undermined recently by the depredations of engineers and builders.

> In the past, the public had to deal with the architect regardless, because he was also engineer and builder. Our society, being quite cognizant of the surrender of some of his authority to others, will now almost instinctively seek out the contractor for advice first . . . The architect's last bastion is art. The very sober subjects of engineering and construction are now in the hands of someone else. The architect is left with the difficult defense of the artistic value. Aesthetics, previously accepted as part of the whole package, must now be taught to society singly. The teaching will require much time and effort.[61]

In so far as the nature of this 'teaching' is explained, it turns out chiefly to be self-promotion and advertising of the kind that builders and engineers already use; for, Rossmann reminds us, 'the very lubricant of business in these United States is publicity'.[62]

The most vigorous of this series of books is *Architecture by Team* (1971) by William Wayne Caudill, self-styled 'hardnose practitioner' and founder member of the Texan practice Caudill Rowlett Scott (now CRS Design Associates). In the same vein of autobiographical self-promotion as Lapidus, Caudill tells the story of his firm. Caudill Rowlett Scott was from its inception (1946) 'organized for growth'. The first step was specialization, the building type chosen being schools on the strength of early commissions. By 1957 the firm was big enough to 'incorporate'. For this step, then virtually unique for architectural practices in the United States, Caudill claims several advantages: tax gains, protection from liability, better relations with corporate clients, and smoother professional development. At about this time the firm had offices in three cities and undertook no job worth under $500,000 (Caudill quips that he was obliged to design his own house because he couldn't afford his own firm). In 1970, when the starting price had advanced to $3 million and the staff amounted to 240, the firm launched Computing Research Systems Corporation (CRS 2) as a 'hard-line, fast-riding outfit developing new ways to adapt the computer to architectural practice'.[63]

Caudill's book vehemently promotes the 'team' in opposition to the individualism which he drank in as a young man at architectural school and still finds all-too-prevalent there:

Frank Lloyd Wright, Le Corbusier, Mies van der Rohe were my idols. Walter Gropius, Richard Neutra, and Alvar Aalto were also my gods, down the mountain a piece from Olympus. There was a third, a lower, level of younger architects who, had they lived in another era, might well have taken the place of the greater deities. But the third level of architects have not a chance in this day. Nor will they . . . From now on the great architects will be on great interdisciplinary teams.

Although the idea of the prima donna is dear to the hearts of many professional architects today, it is still more dear to those who write about architecture in the mass media—not to mention the professional press. The hero is still on his pedestal in the eyes of the architectural historian and the newspaper fine arts-architecture critic. The temple builders are still considered the rightful newsmakers, the headliners; and writers continue to cater to these little architectural gods . . . Not along ago I read a newspaper account of the opening of a public building in which the architect was given quite a spread. If quoted correctly, within two short paragraphs the architect said, 'I did this,' or 'I did that,' six times, and 'my building' twice. Yet did he really do the building? Didn't he get just a little help? Did he program the needs of the client by himself? Did he draw every line? Make every engineering calculation? Specify the cement, aggregate, and texture of concrete? Estimate the cost? Nurse the building through construction? . . .[64]

The sincerity of Caudill's crusade on behalf of teamwork in architecture carries over into his description of different systems of group practice evolved within the firm. Yet the book does not venture to say how far team practice of this type merely bolsters the success and profitability of the firm, or how far it truly serves a client's interests.

Finally, an account of the recent American literature of architectural promotion would be incomplete without mentioning the contribution of management consultants. Two books of this kind are Weld Coxe's *Marketing Architectural and*

Engineering Services (1971) and Gerre L. Jones' *How to Market Professional Design Services* (1973). As their authors are on home ground, they discuss marketing techniques with greater confidence and objectivity than their architect counterparts. Both studies are at their most interesting when they pass beyond the 'sales psychology' of presentation and communication to describe what Jones calls 'promotional tools and strategy'. They suggest, for instance, employing commission agents to chase up potential clients by means of 'bird-dogging' and 'doorbell-ringing', and even using professional 'Washington reps' to help acquire federal work.[65] Jones in particular provides insights into political lobbying. One technique is 'piggybacking', whereby a favourable review or article is republished several times. He cites an article read verbatim from *Building Construction* into the *Congressional Record* by Senator Hugh Scott of Pennsylvania; the piece concerned a new Washington building by architects from his state, Vincent G. Kling and Partners of Philadelphia (one of the earliest firms to adopt an aggressive marketing strategy). Jones also suggests how political contributions may be made without publicity and how favours may be secured from politicians.[66] The need for this kind of advice should not be doubted. According to F. Carter Williams, who in 1974 led an AIA committee to investigate political contributions by architects, some state agencies at that date exacted a precise percentage of fees to the party in power in return for the award of commissions.[67]

*   *   *

How did the American Institute of Architects respond to the clamorous forces calling the profession into the market place? At first it did so slowly and weakly. Traditionally the AIA has been the mouthpiece of the larger architectural practices, and therefore has stood well disposed towards business techniques and orientation. But it is not so powerful as the RIBA in Britain. To many architects a symbol of the remote and resented federalism, the AIA only in the 1960s exceeded in membership 40 per cent of all architects registered under the various state acts.[68] Its powers of reformation and representation have been correspondingly limited, and it has more usually drifted along with the prevailing ideological current than given a lead. An illustration of this is the chopping and changing which have attended the AIA's main instrument for regulating members' conduct, the Standards of Professional Practice.[69] Since such a code was first adopted in 1909, five years have hardly passed without some change loosening or tightening the rules concerning advertising and publicity. In 1945 these rules were made more stringent than ever before, yet many ambiguities and grey areas remained. This confusion reflected real uncertainty among American architects in the 1940s and 1950s about their public image and responsibilities. A tract of 1957, for instance, endorses in one place Wallace Harrison's notion that 'architecture today is produced by men sitting around a table, and the man who makes the most intelligent suggestion is in point of fact the architect, whether or not that is his title.' Then on another page it salutes the American architect for 'standing in many a tight Thermopylae, and defending civilization against the incursions of the barbarians.'[70]

By the 1960s the barbarians, heeding Harrison's counsel, were pouring through and the AIA was obliged to do something about it. It moved faster on development than on advertising and publicity, relaxing the code in 1964 so as to allow members new powers to act as 'co-ordinators' of the type represented by Portman and others.[71] This change was reaffirmed in 1971, and in the following year the AIA published *Development Building: A Team Approach* to encourage architects to go entrepreneurial. Simultaneously it endeavoured to protect the profession from contamination. The changes of 1964 and 1971 reinforced prohibitions against contracting and against working with package builders and other 'unregistered persons who offer architectural services'.[72] In other words, closer links with others in construction were yet again to be countenanced only if architects were in charge.

On the issues of marketing and publicity, the AIA has given way more recently. Today its code explicitly endorses the marketing techniques suggested by the management consultants who specialize in 'A–E' work, like direct mailing and the employment of commission agents. By 1977 these consultants themselves were helping the AIA sponsor 'architectural training laboratories' and 'marketing workships', and assisting in the evolution of the first MBA course for the 'design professional'.[73] In 1978 the AIA finally capitulated to the logic of the situation and voted to permit 'dignified advertising'. The same year saw the commencement of a three-year trial period during which AIA members may be principals in construction and contracting.[74] So far in fact had the status of the architect eroded that the AIA wished at almost any cost to secure 'a piece of the action'.

Recently the AIA's hand has been forced not merely by existing usage in the profession but also by the threat of legislative interference. For just as architects were finding themselves crowded out by others in the construction industry, the option of greater protection rather than more aggressive marketing was being spirited away from them by the strengthening of anti-trust legislation. The AIA has long been in the shadow of its more powerful sister bodies the American Bar Association (ABA) and the American Medical Association (AMA); its first code of 1909 was even modelled on that issued in 1908 by the ABA. In the 1970s these more powerful lobbies came under the eye of consumer groups as barriers to free competition. Supreme Court cases of 1975 and 1977 decreed, respectively, that the ABA was not exempt from anti-trust laws and that prohibitions against advertising in the legal profession violated the First Amendment.[75] These decisions obliged the AIA to go along sooner or later with advertising and the dismantling of further controls on its members. Following the 1977 decision, for instance, the New York State Board of Regents (the state's licensing body for all professionals) voted to allow architects to advertise, at a time when the AIA ban on advertising still stood.[76] In 1979 another AIA rule, that members should not supplant others once hired, was held by a District of Columbia court to violate competitive bidding and therefore became a dead letter.[77] At present even the publication of suggested minimum fees by the AIA is for the same reasons impossible.

*   *   *

Despite superficial variations in style, the processes of architectural commercialization described in this chapter are markedly similar in Britain and the United States. Very probably the same tendency would be found in the architecture of any advanced industrialized nation of the capitalist world. So inexorable a trend deserves more than the 'moral' response it so easily elicits from its critics. Such reactions depend often upon a rigid respect for the ethics of old-style professionalism or for the sacrosanctity of art. Unlike doctors or lawyers, architects have not 'cornered' their professional market. They are, and always have been obliged to sell their wares. In their day the conceptions of architecture as 'art' or 'profession' were just as instrumental in promoting these wares as any latter-day management consultant's manual. All that has happened is that these conceptions are no longer enough to hold or increase architects' share of the market.

Yet despite the enthusiasm and success of the entrepreneurs, architects of all kinds continue to be disquieted by the tendency I have outlined. In an essay on the modern American profession, Bernard Michael Boyle quotes some dark ruminations of Nathaniel Owings, co-founder of America's most successful post-war practice, Skidmore, Owings and Merrill: 'What had we become? Certainly not designers in the classic sense. We were entrepreneurs, promoters, expediters, financiers, diplomats; we were men of too many trades and masters of none.'[78]

There are vestiges of conservatism in this. Architects hanker for the halcyon days when practices were small, comfortable affairs run by people with money enough of their own not to need to do much better than break even. They perhaps fear too that the great business gamble may not succeed—that when pitched into the open market besides builders, engineers and surveyors few of them may have the methods, skills and discipline to hold their own. Protection, from the professional point of view, may still be the wiser option than out-and-out commercialization, though in the U.S. at least there can hardly be a turning-back now.

But disquiet has a simpler and juster basis too: fear for the quality of the product. As the forces of late capitalism make themselves increasingly felt, profit for the professions becomes a motive more compelling than status and class, and the interest of architects falls into line with that of others in the construction industry. 'Total design', says Boyle speaking of Skidmore, Owings and Merrill, 'was conceived as a device of control as much as of service, a constituent of the service package which was the office's product.'[79] Art, when used wisely and maturely, helps to make buildings attractive. Professionalism interpreted to mean responsibility and disinterestedness, helps to ensure that they are well built. But the laws of the market require only that they be profitable to someone, be he entrepreneur, architect or builder. In this transaction neither the user nor the passer-by has a place, except by accident. The wider community thus loses its involvement with the process of building.

Architecture is still a liberal profession and attracts people whose thoughts transcend self-interest. But if commercialization continues apace that can hardly be maintained for long. If the next few generations of architects cannot define some new relationship between the public and the process of building, they will lose that special sense of identity which the profession has treasured for so long.

CHAPTER EIGHT

The Influence of Imagination in Architecture

'Know thyself,' admonished the Greek sage. Do architects know themselves? If not, they cannot expect to predict or plan their own futures. Yet throughout the profession, people purvey and sustain a misleading impression of what it is to be an architect, buttressed in large measure by illusions of what it has been to be an architect. Earlier chapters of this book have tried to clarify the historical perspective; this one addresses the same questions from a theoretical standpoint, recapitulates some of the main themes, then draws a few morals and conclusions.

*   *   *

The chapter's title comes from a lecture given by John Ruskin before the infant Architectural Association in 1857. In it, the subtlest English-speaking critic ever to weigh the claims of architecture summed up his mature views upon the architectural profession. For his audience of young men, already ardent to lead British architecture along the romantic path of Gothic, Ruskin's message was as clear and thrilling as a clarion's; they must *imagine*. Industry alone, he proclaimed, would never avail to make an architect great; practicality and utility could not raise him above the level of a mere builder; mathematical skill would be perceptible to few among future generations. Human imagination and sympathy alone would make his work endure. And he pressed obstinately on towards a familiar conclusion that has made Ruskin's name a byword among architects for eccentricity and irrelevance. Building, he affirmed, could not be great architecture without sculpture and decoration, and no architect was truly worthy of his title unless he was also a sculptor and decorator. The central and most sacred part of architecture, in fact, was the least essential.

This paradox encapsulates the issue that has lain unresolved in the preceding chapters. Time and again, architects seeking self-definition and self-justification invoke the bewitching powers of art. Yet time and again the deepest analysis of how they have become what they are, or the frankest account of how they spend their time, seems to have little to do with art. Ruskin's way with the dilemma was drastic. To probe the depths of value in architecture, he argued, we must disregard not only the trappings of architectural practice but even the plain, plodding procedures necessary for sound building. Given the state of the world and the needs of the people, sound building should never be neglected; indeed it may be as much as an unlucky age can produce. But it should not be confused, thought Ruskin, with architecture, which relies upon imagination to stir our hearts and minds. Nor was it enough to arrange masses pleasingly or to proportion façades harmoniously. An architect to be imaginative had to adduce the works of natural creation and so kindle the spark of affinity in a fellow creature. This was why, in Ruskin's eyes, representative decoration was the principal part of architecture.

Though extremest in Ruskin, this species of architectural 'reductionism' is common enough. The same foundation underpins every systematic interpretation of architecture for which the criteria are exclusively aesthetic. 'A bicycle shed is a building; Lincoln Cathedral is a piece of architecture.' So runs the celebrated opening sentence of Nikolaus Pevsner's *Outline of European Architecture*, in which Ruskin's representative decoration cedes place to 'spatial expression', a criterion hardly less esoteric. A more recent and cautious contribution to the theory of design, Roger Scruton's *The Aesthetics of Architecture*, travels a similar path. This book seems at first to reject 'reductionism' and to endorse the proposition that 'architecture is identical to building—a special case of the activity of design'. But later the reader discovers that certain classes of building more than others satisfy in their variety of appeals the sophisticated observer, avid for 'aesthetic experience'. These buildings, then, become the 'higher' architecture, to the creation of which the architect is specially bidden to bend his pencil.

No matter, then, how much these writers bicker about the nature of the aesthetic criteria involved, they all agree that architecture is only special when it is the product or the object of 'imagination'. Here, the bias of recent English-speaking upholders of this theory is specially illuminating. Scruton and his disciple David Watkin, for instance, have endeavoured to rehabilitate 'imaginative experience' in architecture, after what they perceive as a period of neglect during the heyday of the Modern Movement, when materialism reigned and the only touchstone for good architecture was the solution of practical design problems. But even the most superficial reading of twentieth-century architectural theory shows that the aesthetic point of view has been far from neglected. Certainly older criteria, whether of the classical or of the Ruskinian variety, met everywhere with rejection. But no architect of standing in the Modern Movement could plausibly be accused of not having done his utmost to replace them. An easier charge to prove against such men is that of formalism—that in their striving for aesthetic expression they betrayed those other ideals of functionalism and practicality that they so vociferously upheld.

This example gives rise to some simple questions. How is it that the purely imaginative standard for architecture has dominated for so long, when the facts of everyday architectural practice cry out against it? Can standards which exclude or fail to account for so much that we normally think of as architecture really have broad validity? Can it be wise or right to tell the workaday modern designer that he or she may hardly have the chance to grasp at architectural significance more than once or twice in a lifetime?

The explanation lies, of course, in the mystique attached in our time to art. It would be hard to penetrate and pointless to denigrate the power and allure of artistic expression—that irreducible, strange, comforting and liberating aspect of individual human motivation. Yet so often and so automatically has architecture since Vitruvius been categorized along with the purer arts, that it is worth the effort of wrenching it away for a moment. That done, we can see what oddities occur when theories and terms invented for other pursuits (painting, perhaps, or music) are extended to architecture. An earlier chapter, for instance, touches on the bizarre consequences that ensued when the young Goethe transferred the theory of genius from literature to architecture (see pp. 19–23).

'Imagination' is just such another term. When Ruskin speaks of imagination, he does not use the word loosely but in a precise and technical sense borrowed from English eighteenth-century aesthetic theory. From Shaftesbury and Addison he derived the idea that imagination was the highest human faculty, uniting aesthetic and moral sensibility. From Reynolds he took the late-classical notion, that an artist should first make a thorough study of tradition and then bring his creative imagination to bear upon it and so speak to the world. Here were thoughts richly rewarding for the individualistic arts of literature and painting. But unlike a poem or a picture, no building (unless like the works of Boullée it remains on paper) stops at being the mere imaginative expression of an individual addressing the imaginations of others. However highly this power is valued it will never make a sufficient theory of architecture. It will always remain a system transferred by analogy from other pursuits, not one that is fashioned to fit the whole case and circumstances of architecture.

Architectural biography in particular has favoured the imaginative approach, because here the individualism natural to the purer arts finds its easiest outlet. Nevertheless even in this realm, when imagination is accorded priority, what actually happens in the architectural process is frequently falsified. What truly occurred when Frank Lloyd Wright built a house is soon forgotten when it becomes the mere object of aesthetic experience. Likewise, a fantasy such as *The Fountainhead* which glorifies architectural egoism misconstrues constructional reality and insults the practising intelligence of designers.

Here someone may interject that the only fitting way to react to a fine building like Falling Water is imaginatively. That, after all, is how Wright would have wished it. Rejecting it, we are left with pedantry and sterility of the soul. Only if we receive it into our imaginations, does the architecture live.

For many buildings of course the aesthetic approach must come foremost. But this primacy, this reverence for the individual imagination, does not oblige us to stop there. Perhaps a simple, human analogy serves best. Often we are drawn to a person by outward qualities of beauty or sensuousness whose mystery is never explained and always remembered. Yet we think it foolish (or perhaps merely innocent) not to search for deeper qualities, let alone to restrict our friendships to such persons. It is a sign of richness in architecture, not of poverty, that much remains when the types of response appropriate for painting or music are exhausted or found wanting. In the purer arts, deep study can perhaps enhance such responses, but it cannot change the fact that they primarily address the individual imagination. Architecture on the other hand often responds feebly to the readiest imagination. But in compensation there are other things intrinsic to the subject which lie entirely outside the province of imagination. Of any building one may ask: what was its purpose? whose hands built it? from what was it made? how did it weather the test of time? Of course these questions are asked about paintings and symphonies too. But they hardly have the direct relevance that they do in architecture and other of the applied arts.

Analogy with the pure arts, therefore, has perverted the proper meaning of imagination in architecture. Thus far I have spoken only of the theory of architecture as art. But another theory, equally deficient, has recurred throughout this book: that of architecture as a business. The shortcomings of this idea hardly need pointing out. For although it corresponds more closely with the world in which most architects operate, it has never acquired much dignity and hardly amounts to more than a practical prop. It is perhaps especially helpful in the short term, for the ambitious but thoughtful architect intent upon goals near at hand.

These two theories, apparently so much at loggerheads, have in fact sometimes co-existed quite happily in the same architect. The power of art, it has several times been said in earlier chapters, is often enough most helpful for architectural business. But there is another and currently more important relationship between the two ideas. For to affirm that everything in architecture that is worth anything belongs ultimately to the 'creative' imagination is a gift to the coarser proponents of commercialism. It elevates the power of pleasing above all others, so leaving the field of everyday architectural design, conduct and practice vacant to anyone wanting to possess it. In responding to the call of artistic conscience, the imaginative architect can ignore the claims of client, staff, workmen, even perhaps of sound building.

In traditional architectural thinking this gap is supposed to be filled by 'professionalism', which mediates between art and commerce. But having neither the spiritual appeal of art nor the worldly lure of profit, professionalism has always been weak. Once institutionalized, professionalism quickly passes over into mere protectionism. At its best it prevents architects from becoming preoccupied with any one of the constituents of good architecture and reminds them of the necessity of others. But at its worst, professionalism unites the exclusiveness of art–architecture with the greed of the commercial approach. When for instance the modern architect is urged on account of his artistry and his breadth of knowledge to become a 'co-ordinator' and leader in construction, the exhortation amounts to little more than an attempt to use the high ideal of art to secure more and better jobs.

If architects wish to preserve the better elements in professionalism and to prevent their calling from degenerating, except in a few instances, to a mere trade, they must find a way to break the barriers limiting the concept of imagination to art and design. In other words, they must raise to the level of ideal those aspects of architecture whose worth is plainly perceptible to everyone. A start might be made if we could resuscitate that objective of 'sound building' which, Ruskin ultimately concluded, was as much as could be achieved in his day. This limited and lowly ideal perhaps seems insufficient to draw in the dedicated adolescent to the cause of architecture. Nevertheless for some time after Ruskin wrote, say between 1890 and 1930, it did inspire a significant group of architects in Britain, the United States and Germany. Modernism in architecture grew chiefly out of this idea but, partly through the power of art, perverted it by glorifying novelty and technology and by interpreting what was supposed to be method as style.

If we are once again to take seriously the ideal of 'sound building' it will be as well to understand its meaning, its strengths and its weaknesses. It never excluded art in the ordinary sense of that word, since all architects who subscribed to it understood that it was right to bring genuine, easily accessible aesthetic pleasure to the senses. But its more thoughtful exponents also believed that within the domain of art lay also all that was best in architectural professionalism: simplicity and economy, respect for client and user, knowledge of techniques and materials, and so forth. This enlarged sense of art as *techne* corresponds well not only with the realities of architectural practice but also with a noble tradition of writing on the philosophy of art, stretching from Plato to Collingwood.

One further doctrine was central to the ideal of 'sound building': collaboration. If modern architecture were ever to be reformed, Ruskin had insisted, the architect must somehow get on terms with his fellow workers. But here, in proceeding beyond individual example the ideal met with economic reality and generally failed. Collaboration was constantly promulgated but in practice enjoyed only limited success, as some episodes in this book suggest.

Today's conditions mean, of course, that the objectives of 'sound building' could not be reformulated without much revision. One grave sin of the old philosophy of building, at least in England, was its conservatism. Being against innovations in style as arbitrary and meaningless, its proponents easily lapsed into opposition to new technology, new building types and new procedures. Many of them designed little except houses, which did not strenuously test their ideas. Lacking experience of larger and more novel structures, they left the way open to the brash new style-mongers who succeeded them. Today we badly need architects who can not merely display architectural technology but understand it fully and if necessary harness it. A reinterpretation of 'sound building', therefore, would have to recognize the continuing technological development of the building industry. If this is an exacting demand, there are other tasks which should prove easier than they once were. Equal collaboration and partnership, for instance, flew in the face of the social, professional and commercial structure of building at the turn of the century. But nowadays class boundaries are more fluid and the building industry is more fragmented. In the face of such realities, the entrenched isolationism of the professions is starting to crumble.

Of course a renewed ideology alone cannot avail the modern architect. Of all activities, building is the most vulnerable to economic pressures, the least susceptible to isolated reform. Without an improved social system there can be no permanently better architecture or permanently better architects: which is why frustrated architects so often have recourse to fantasy and to art. The greater difficulty that confronts architects in western countries is that they have increasingly to work within the narrowest constraints of profit and loss. It is idle to suppose that the occasional escapade outside these bounds, however highly praised, can be of general significance. Nor does it solve the problem, except perhaps for an architect's conscience, if he devotes himself only to 'social' or 'community' architecture. In terms of 'sound building', a well-detailed housing estate certainly weighs more in the balance than a shoddy office block. But in the absence of any institutionalized context for social architecture similar in some way to the facilities offered by law centres or public health clinics, the decision as to which of these is built and, ultimately, as to who designs them, does not lie with the architect. He is the prey of economic forces which he cannot significantly influence, even if he aspires to be a Poulson or a Portman.

The only task that architects can fruitfully undertake in these circumstances is to reconstruct their professional ideology in the light of their true position. This task cannot be done in detail for them by historians or critics; it is up to architects themselves, and more particularly to the thousands of salaried staff who everywhere constitute the majority in the profession yet fail to make themselves heard. All that can be done from the outside is to point to what is practicable and, barring social revolution, inevitable: a smaller architectural profession, in which imagination and artistic ability are more evenly balanced with technical and managerial experience, in which collaboration with other specialists takes on a more realistic, less high-handed meaning, and in which 'sound building' is valued above 'high art'. This balance has excellent historical precedent. It was from just such a state of affairs that the architectural individualism so much admired today evolved in the eighteenth century; and it was to just such a state of affairs that Philip Webb and his disciples in the Arts and Crafts Movement, reacting to Ruskin's despair of achieving anything worth having in architecture, yearned to revert.

Finally, can architecture survive as a special and unique profession if the 'imaginative' element is curbed? That is possible only if some such goal as 'sound building', in itself an uncharismatic target, can be raised to the level of ideology still enjoyed in the schools by the endless debate about styles. Otherwise, duller people will dominate and the profession will become indistinguishable from others serving the construction industry. If a generation's imagination can be fixed upon something above the game of styles, novelty of appearance, and paper projects, and remain equally resolute in the face of the allurements of commerce, we may at last get a profession worthy of the claim of leadership in that industry.

NOTES

ABBREVIATIONS

ABN	*Architect and Building News*
AIA	American Institute of Architects
AJ	*Architects' Journal*
AR	*Architectural Review*
ARCUK	Architects' Registration Council of the United Kingdom
Asnova	Assotsiatsiya Novykh Arkhitektorov (Association of New Architects)
CIAM	Congrès Internationaux d'Architecture Moderne
ISAA	Illinois State Association of Architects
JSAH	*Journal of the Society of Architectural Historians*
NAM	New Architecture Movement
OSA	Obshchestvo Sovremennykh Arkhitektorov (Association of Contemporary Architects)
RIBA	Royal Institute of British Architects
Vkhutemas	Vysshiye Gosudarstvennyye Khudozhestvenno-Tekhnicheskiye Masterskiye (Higher Artistic and Technical Studios)
VOPRA	Vserossiiskoye Obshchestvo Proletarskikh Arkhitektorov (All-Russian Association of Proletarian Architects)

NOTES TO CHAPTER ONE

1. American novels with architectural heroes of interest include Robert Grant's *Unleavened Bread*, 1900, and Edna Ferber's *So Big*, 1924. Among English examples are *A Laodicean*, 1881, by Thomas Hardy; *The Man of Property*, 1906, by John Galsworthy; and *The Roll Call*, 1918, by Arnold Bennett.

2. The film was directed by King Vidor, with the following cast; Gary Cooper as Howard Roark, Raymond Massey as Gail Wynand, Robert Douglas as Ellsworth Toohey, Henry Hull as Henry Cameron, Patricia Neal as Dominique Francon, and Kent Smith as Peter Keating. The character of Guy Francon was omitted from the film.

3. Ayn Rand, *The Fountainhead*, 1943, Part 4, Ch. 18.

4. Joseph Patterson was an important architectural patron of Raymond Hood, who designed for him not only the *Daily News* Building (1928–30) but also an East Side apartment house (1928) and a country house at Ossining, N.Y. (1930). For Patterson's eccentricities, see Walter H. Kilham junior, *Raymond Hood, Architect*, 1973, p. 105.

5. 'Psyching Out Ayn Rand', *Ms. Magazine*, Sept. 1978, p. 26.

6. Ayn Rand, preface to later editions of *Atlas Shrugged*.

7. The biographical information in this and subsequent paragraphs derives from Nathaniel and Barbara Braden, *Who is Ayn Rand?*, 1962, pp. 149–239.

8. For E. J. Kahn, see Arthur Tappan North's brief and uninformative monograph, *Ely Jacques Kahn*, 1931; Walter H. Kilham junior, *Raymond Hood, Architect*, 1973, pp. 80, 88; Cervin Robinson and Rosemarie Haag

Bletter, *Skyscraper Style*, 1975, esp. pp. 16–17.

9. Ayn Rand, *The Fountainhead*, 1943, Part 1, Ch. 1.

10. *Ibid.*, Part 1, Ch. 3.

11. *Ibid.*, Part 1, Ch. 6.

12. *Ibid.*, Part 1, Ch. 14.

13. *Ibid.*, Part 1, Ch. 13.

14. These comparisons are meant merely to be suggestive. I am grateful for advice from Walter H. Kilham and from Richard Chafee, who thinks the relationship between Francon and Stengel refers to that between James Gamble Rogers and Otto Faelton. Mr Chafee also reminds me that Cass Gilbert did not attend the Ecole des Beaux Arts.

15. The figures of Ralston Holcombe and Jon Erik Snyte both have characteristics in common with Bertram Goodhue. On Goodhue's division of his staff according to style, see Wallace K. Harrison's reminiscences in *The New Yorker*, 20 and 27 Nov. and 4 Dec. 1954.

16. Rand, *op. cit.*, Part 2, Ch. 11.

17. Beaux-Arts Ball Programme, 23 Jan. 1931 (in archives of National Institute for Architectural Education, New York).

18. Rand, *op. cit.*, Part 4, Ch. 4.

19. See especially Frank Lloyd Wright's account of the affair in *An Autobiography*, 1932 edition, pp. 335–41.

20. Frederick Gutheim, *Frank Lloyd Wright on Architecture: Selected Writings 1894–1940*, 1941.

21. Nathaniel and Barbara Braden, *Who is Ayn Rand?*, 1962, pp. 225–6.

22. Rand, *op. cit.*, Part 3, Ch. 6.

23. *Ibid.*, Part 1, Ch. 13.

24. Frank Lloyd Wright, *Modern Architecture*, 1931, pp. 47–8.

25. Frank Lloyd Wright, *An Autobiography*, 1932 edition, pp. 31, 57.

26. *Ibid.*, pp. 101–2; Rand, *op. cit.*, Part 3, Ch. 1.

27. Gutheim, *op. cit.*, p. 11.

28. *Ibid.*, pp. 59–76, esp. pp. 64–8.

29. H. Allen Brooks, *The Prairie School*, 1972, *passim*, esp. pp. 42–4.

30. Gutheim, *op. cit.*, p. 50.

31. Frank Lloyd Wright, *Two Lectures on Architecture*, 1930, pp. 40–1.

32. Frank Lloyd Wright, *An Autobiography*, 1932 edition, p. 342.

33. *Ralph Walker, Architect*, 1957, pp. 58–9.

34. Rand, *op. cit.*, Part 1, Ch. 2.

35. *Ibid.*, Part 1, Ch. 13.

36. *Ibid.*, Part 2, Ch. 6.

37. *Ibid.*, Part 4, Ch. 8.

38. *Loc. cit.*

NOTES TO CHAPTER TWO

1. J. W. von Goethe, *Von Deutscher Baukunst*, 1772. For complete translations and commentaries see Elizabeth Holt, *A Documentary History of Art*, vol. 2, 1958, pp. 360–9; and G. Grigson and N. Pevsner in *Architectural Review* 98, 1945, pp. 156–9. An invaluable commentary is contained in Paul Frankl, *The Gothic*, 1960, pp. 417–26.

2. J. W. von Goethe, *Dichtung und Wahrheit*, Book 9, translated e.g. by John Oxenford, *Goethe's Early Life*, 1904 edition, pp. 320–2.

3. For modern scholarship on Erwin and Strasbourg see F. X. Kraus, *Kunst und Alterthum in Elsass-Lothringen*, vol. 1, 1876, p. 376; Hans Haug, *La Cathédrale de Strasbourg*, 1957, pp. 59–61; Hans Reinhardt, *La Cathédrale de Strasbourg*, 1972, pp. 21–2, 78, 210.

4. See esp. Logan Pearsall Smith, *Four Words*, Society for Pure English, Tract XVII, 1924, pp. 22–48.

5. Frankl, *op. cit.*, pp. 417–26.

6. L. P. Smith, *op. cit.*, p. 27.

7. Haug, *loc. cit.*, and Reinhardt, *loc. cit.*

8. *Dictionary of National Biography*, sub Allan Cunningham.

9. John Summerson, *The Life and Works of John Nash Architect*, 1980, p. 183.

10. Allan Cunningham, *The Lives of the Most Eminent British Painters, Sculptors and Architects*, vol. 4, 1831, p. 1.

11. *Ibid.*, p. 11.

12. *Ibid.*, pp. 64–8.

13. On Alan of Walsingham, see e.g. James Dallaway, *Observations on English Architecture*, 1806, pp. 25–6; A. Kingsley Porter, *Mediaeval Architecture*, 1909, vol. 2, pp. 181–92; R. E. Swartwout, *The Monastic Craftsman*, 1932, pp. 158–61.

14. Robert Lowth, *The Life of William of Wykeham*, 1759, pp. 19, 218.

15. Horace Walpole, *Anecdotes of Painting in England*, ed. James Dallaway, vol. 1, 1828, p. 206.

16. James Dallaway, *Observations on English Architecture*, 1806, p. 45.

17. Walpole, *op. cit.*, p. 211n.

18. C. R. Cockerell, *On the Architectural Works of William of Wykeham*, 1846, pp. 4n., 8, 11.

19. L. F. Salzman, *Building in England down to 1540*, 1952, pp. 9–10, thinks it 'reasonably probable' that Elias of Dereham designed Salisbury Cathedral.

20. For the life of Montalembert see Mrs Oliphant, *Memoir of Count de Montalembert*, 2 vols., 1872.

21. For Rio, see his *De la poésie chrétienne*, 1836, tr. 1854; *De l'art chrétien*, 4 vols., 1861–7; M. C. Bowe, *François Rio, sa place dans le renouveau catholique en Europe*, 1938.

22. Oliphant, *op. cit.*, vol. 1, pp. 241–5, 343–5; see also the anthology of Montalembert's writings on art and architecture in J. P. Migne, *Troisième et Dernière Encyclopédie Théologique*, vol. 17, 1856, esp. cols. 1007–52, 1142–68, 1179–88, 1189–1208.

23. Oliphant, *op. cit.*, vol. 1, pp. 270–9.

24. Montalembert, *Chronicle of Life of St Elizabeth of Hungary*, tr. Ambrose Lisle Phillipps, 1839, pp. xlii–xliii.

25. Migne, *op. cit.*, col. 1214, reprinted from *Annales Archéologiques* for 1847. The essay was reissued in almost identical form in Montalembert, *History of the Monks of the West*, vol. 6, 1877, Book 18, Part 5.

26. Oliphant, *op. cit.*, vol. 2, pp. 319ff.

27. G. G. Coulton, *Art and the Reformation*, 1928, p. 28.

28. *Ibid.*, Chs. 2–4; R. E. Swartwout, *The Monastic Craftsman*, 1932, *passim*.

29. Coulton, *op. cit.*, pp. 64, 515–16.

30. Swartwout, *op. cit.*, p. 87.

31. Paul Frankl, *The Gothic*, 1960, pp. 564–77.

32. *Ibid.*, pp. 522–5, 572–3.

33. The French publication of 1858 by J. B. A. Lassus was greatly augmented by Robert Willis in his notes to the *Facsimile of the Sketch-Book of Wilars de Honecort*, 1859.

34. *RIBA Transactions* 10, 1859–60, pp. 38–51.

35. G. H. Moberly, *Life of William of Wykeham*, 1887; Sir William Hayter, *William of Wykeham Patron of the Arts*, 1970, p. 13.

36. E. S. Prior, *The Cathedral Builders in England*, 1905, p. 86.

37. J. F. Bentley to Charles Hadfield junior, 30 Dec. 1899 (letter at RIBA kindly communicated to me by P. Howell).

38. Ralph Adams Cram, *The Gothic Quest*, 1907, p. 124.

39. F. J. Furnivall, *Early History of the Working Men's College*, 1891 (written 1860), p. 9. Furnivall's reprint of *The Nature of Gothic* also included two small excerpts from the third volume of *The Stones of Venice*.

40. John Ruskin, *The Seven Lamps of Architecture*, 8.8–10.

41. *Ibid.*, 5.24.

42. John Ruskin, *The Stones of Venice*, 2.6.21.

43. E. T. Cook and Alexander Wedderburn, *The Works of John Ruskin*, 1903–12, vol. 5, pp. xxxvii ff.

44. *Ibid.*, vol. 24, pp. 406–7.

45. John Ruskin, *Lectures on Architecture*, preface and 2.60–1; compare *The Two Paths*, 4.123; *Ariadne Florentina*, 2.56–60; *Mornings in Florence*, 1.2.

46. See especially Ruskin, *The Seven Lamps of Architecture*, preface to edition of 1855, and advice to J. D. Sedding quoted in Cook and Wedderburn, *op. cit.*, vol. 37, p. 199.

47. See e.g. John Ruskin, *Val d'Arno*, 1.22.

48. John Ruskin, *The Bible of Amiens*, 4.5 and n.

49. Cook and Wedderburn, *op. cit.*, vol. 36, p. 183.

50. For Hope and the theory of the 'travelling bodies', see Robert Freke Gould, *The History of Freemasonry*, vol. 1, 1883, pp. 256–61.

51. Stephen Wren, *Parentalia*, 1751, pp. 306–7.

52. *RIBA Transactions* 12, 1861–2, pp. 37–56.

53. For a succinct account of the masonic 'legends' and 'constitutions' see Douglas Knoop and E. P. Jones, *The Mediaeval Mason*, 1933, pp. 169–73; a full discussion is in Herbert Poole, *The Old Charges*, 1924, and a full bibliography in *Ars Quatuor Coronatorum* 31, p. 42.

54. *RIBA Transactions* 12, 1861–2, pp. 37–56.

55. Knoop and Jones, *op. cit.*, Chs. 1, 2 and 6.

56. *Ars Quatuor Coronatorum* 5, 1892, p. 38.

57. For Morris's historical reading see esp. Margaret R. Grennan, *William Morris, Medievalist and Revolutionary*, 1945, pp. 51–76.

58. See *Dictionary of National Biography*, sub J. E. T. Rogers. Morris and Thorold Rogers were well acquainted and once or twice shared a political platform. Morris directly cites Rogers in *Architecture and History*, 1901 (delivered 1884), pp. 15–16; he had probably consulted Rogers's *Six Centuries of Work and Wages*, 1884, rather than his longer *History of Agriculture and Prices in England*, 6 vols., 1866–87.

59. Morris's best discussions of the guilds occur in *Architecture and History*, 1901 (delivered 1884), pp. 1–33; in 'Gothic Architecture', delivered 1889, published in May Morris, *William Morris Artist Writer Socialist*, vol. 1, 1936, pp. 266–86; and in 'Art and Industry in the Fourteenth Century', written 1890, published in *Architecture, Industry and Wealth*, 1902, pp. 228–46.

60. William Morris, *The Gothic Revival II* (delivered 1884), in Eugene D. Lemire, *The Unpublished Lectures of William Morris*, 1969, p. 88.

61. *Ibid.*, p. 90.

62. *Ibid.*, pp. 91–2.

63. William Morris, *Architecture and History*, 1901, p. 27; for the decline of the guilds see also William Morris, *Architecture, Industry and Wealth*, 1902, p. 244.

64. E. S. Prior, *A History of Gothic Art in England*, 1900, p. 5.

65. *Ibid.*, pp. 7–8.

66. *Ibid.*, pp. 428–9.

67. E. S. Prior, *The Cathedral Builders in England*, 1905, p. 15.

68. *Ibid.*, p. 18.

69. *Ibid.*, p. 22.

70. W. R. Lethaby, *Mediaeval Art*, 1904, pp. 257–8.

71. W. R. Lethaby, *Westminster Abbey and the King's Craftsmen*, 1906, pp. vii–viii.

72. *Ibid.*, pp. 195–6.

73. A. Kingsley Porter, *Medieval Architecture*, 1909, pp. 189–90. These texts, from fourteenth- and fifteenth-century sermons, had been published but were not widely known before Porter translated them.

74. W. R. Lethaby in C. G. Crump and E. F. Jacob, *The Legacy of the Middle Ages*, 1926, pp. 59–60, 70.

75. For George and William Harvey, see RIBA Library, biographical files.

76. John Harvey, *Gothic England*, 1947, p. 7.

77. *Ibid.*, p. 22.

78. *Ibid.*, p. 30.

79. *Ibid.*, p. 41.

80. *Ibid.*, p. 161.

81. *Ibid.*, p. 7.

82. *Ibid.*, pp. 86ff.

83. For a balanced view of Suger as a kind of 'amateur or gentleman architect of the earlier Middle Ages' see Erwin Panofsky, *Abbot Suger on the Abbey Church of St Denis*, 1946, pp. 35–6.

84. See esp. John Harvey, *The Mediaeval Architect*, 1972, Ch. 6, and *The Perpendicular Style*, 1978, pp. 38–40.

85. G. G. Coulton, *Art and the Reformation*, 1928, Ch. 5, esp. p. 82.

86. R. E. Swartwout, *The Monastic Craftsman*, 1932, pp. 113–14.

87. See e.g. L. F. Salzman, *Building in England down to 1540*, 1952, p. 34.

88. Coulton, *op. cit.*, pp. 202–3.

89. The industrial analogy is delicately presented in Coulton, *op. cit.*, pp. 480ff.

90. See *Proceedings of the Society of Antiquaries of Scotland* 12, 1878, pp. 218–44, esp. p. 232. Ruskin refers with special affection to Rosslyn Chapel in his autobiography, *Praeterita*.

91. *The Collected Poems of Thomas Hardy*, 1919, pp. 379–86.

NOTES TO CHAPTER THREE

The evolution of the British architectural profession has been authoritatively covered by three writers, Howard Colvin in his magisterial introduction to *A Biographical Dictionary of British Architects 1660–1840*, 1978 edn., pp. 18–41; Barrington Kaye in *The Development of the Architectural Profession in Britain*, 1960; and Frank Jenkins in *Architect and Patron*, 1961. This essay attempts a more argumentative approach to the same subject, but has relied heavily on all three sources. The references are therefore mostly confined to quotations and points not covered by them. An excellent analysis of the predicament of early nineteenth-century British architects is offered by J. Mordaunt Crook, 'The Pre-Victorian Architect: Professionalism and Patronage', in *Architectural History*, 12, 1969, pp. 62–78; this differs from the present account in addressing itself especially towards stylistic dilemmas.

1. There is a modestly extensive, mainly facetious 'architectural' literature on Pecksniff. For humour, see e.g. the rather ponderous article by D. B. Wyndham Lewis in *Architectural Design and Construction*, Dec. 1932, pp. 50–3, or the preferable H. B. Creswell in *Architects' Journal*, 9 and 16 March 1921. Joseph H. Gardner's scholarly 'Pecksniff's Profession', in *The Dickensian*, 72, 1976, pp. 75–86, concerns chiefly the use made by Phiz (Hablot K. Browne) of Pugin's *Contrasts* in his depictions of Pecksniff, but also records the local Wiltshire tradition identifying Pugin the younger with Pecksniff on the grounds that both lived just outside Salisbury. This is not as far-fetched as it sounds, despite obvious differences between them. Dickens would have disapproved of the younger Pugin on political and religious grounds, and he knew little enough about architecture to imagine him a humbug. At the same time, he may also have been well informed about the Pecksniffian nature of Pugin the elder's office through Charles Mathews junior, the architect turned actor, whose memoirs were later edited by Dickens's son. There is something to be said for the hypothesis that Pecksniff conflates caricatures of Pugin the elder and the younger together with aspects of Samuel Carter Hall (editor of the *Art Journal*), who was believed to be Pecksniff during Dickens's own lifetime: see Charles C. Osborne in *The Independent Review*, 10, Sept. 1906, pp. 324–44.

2. Charles Dickens, *The Life and Adventures of Martin Chuzzlewit*, 1844, Ch. 2.

3. *Ibid.*, Ch. 2.

4. *Ibid.*, Ch. 5.

5. *Ibid.*, Ch. 6.

6. *Bentley's Miscellany*, 32, 1852, p. 25. An outline of Wightwick's career is given in Colvin.

7. *Bentley's Miscellany*, 34, 1853, p. 547.

8. *Ibid.*, p. 548.

9. Jenkins, pp. 162–4. For the original accounts, see Benjamin Ferrey, *Recollections of Pugin*, 1861, re-edited by C. and J. Wainwright, 1978; and G. G. Scott, *Personal and Professional Recollections by the late Sir George Gilbert Scott*, 1879.

10. *The Life of Charles J. Mathews*, 2 vols., edited by Charles Dickens junior, 1879, especially vol. 1, Chs. 2 and 8, and vol. 2, Chs. 2 and 5.

11. The extracts from T. W. Fletcher's memoirs are quoted from portions edited by M. H. Port in *East London Papers*, 11, 1968, pp. 20–39. Fletcher's career as a pub architect is discussed, with further extracts, by Mark Girouard, *Victorian Pubs*, 1975, pp. 104–6.

12. Port, *op. cit.*, p. 25.

13. *Ibid.*, p. 27.

14. *Ibid.*, p. 28.

15. *Ibid.*, p. 37.

16. G. G. Scott, *Personal and Professional Recollections by the late Sir George Gilbert Scott*, 1879, p. 56.

17. John Soane, *Plans, Elevations and Sections of Buildings*, 1788, p. 7. This passage is quoted by Colvin, Kaye and Jenkins alike.

18. Thomas Skaife, *A Key to Civil Architecture*, 1774 edn., p. 82.

19. Sir John Summerson, Nash's eminent biographer, revises some of his earlier strictures in *The Life and Work of John Nash*, 1980. Nash's able and decided views on building management come over powerfully in his evidence before the Select Committee on the Office of Works and Public Buildings, published in *Parliamentary Papers*, 1828, IV, fols. 44–74.

20. On the rise of the master builder, see notably the articles by E. W. Cooney in *Economic History Review*, 8, 1955, pp. 167–76, and by M. H. Port in *Economic History Review*, 20, 1967, pp. 94–110; Hermione Hobhouse, *Thomas Cubitt*, 1971, pp. 7–15; C. G. Powell, *An Economic History of the British Building Industry, 1815–1979*, pp. 27–31; F. M. L. Thompson, *Chartered Surveyors*, 1968, pp. 3–6.

21. Recent experience at the *Survey of London* suggests that perhaps more often than not, middle-class housing in Victorian London was planned in some detail by obscure architects and not just adapted by builders from previous examples, as is often assumed.

22. For architects in Thomas Cubitt's office, see Hermione Hobhouse, *Thomas Cubitt*, 1971, pp. 267–74 (not an exhaustive list). William Cubitt employed William R. Rogers to design much of his architectural work; C. J. Freake used, among others, George Edwards, William Tasker and C. H. Thomas; the William Willetts employed (successively) James Trant Smith, Harry B. Measures and Amos Faulkner.

23. Kaye, p. 80.

24. Sir Edward Cust, cited in Thomas Hopper, *A Letter to Viscount Duncannon*, 1837, p. 2. For an excellent analysis of the professional controversies surrounding the rebuilding of the Houses of Parliament, see M. H. Port, *The Houses of Parliament*, 1976, Ch. 3.

25. David Watkin, *The Life and Work of C. R. Cockerell, R.A.*, 1974, p. 222.

26. *The Newleafe Discourses* first appeared in *The Builder* between 11 July and 5 September 1846 as 'The Young Architects of England, by One of Themselves'. They were much revised for publication: see *The Builder*, 17 Oct. 1846, p. 495. As late as 1858 Kerr was still indulging in exuberant fantasies on the profession: see e.g. his sketch in the manner of *Sartor Resartus* on the hero as architect in *The Builder*, 27 Nov. 1858, pp. 794–5. Kerr's writings are discussed in Nikolaus Pevsner, *Some Architectural Writers of the Nineteenth Century*, 1972, esp. pp. 217–21, 224–6, 233–6.

27. Robert Kerr, *The Newleafe Discourses*, 1846, pp. 40–1.

28. *Ibid.*, pp. 52–3.

29. Unpublished typescript of W. W. Pocock's memoir in RIBA Library, PoFam/2/1/8(iii).

30. Christopher Christie, 'The Institute of Architects in Scotland' in Valerie Fiddes and Alistair Rowan, *David Bryce 1803–1876*, 1976 exhibition catalogue, pp. 37–41.

31. The best discussion of the themes of *Architecture a Profession or an Art* is given by Robert Macleod in *Style and Society*, 1971, pp. 123–9. See also Andrew Saint, *Richard Norman Shaw*, 1976, pp. 317–21.

32. F. M. L. Thompson, *Chartered Surveyors*, 1968, p. 316.

33. Susan Beattie, *A Revolution in London Housing*, 1980, e.g. pp. 9–13, 70.

34. For a list of early district surveyors, see C. C. Knowles and P. H. Pitt, *The History of Building Regulation in London 1189–1972*, 1972, pp. 150–3.

35. *Builders' Journal and Architectural Record*, 30 May 1900, p. 309.

36. See e.g. *Charles Canning Winmill, by his daughter*, 1946, pp. 58–9.

37. On architects and early town planning, see now Martin Hawtree, 'The Emergence of the Town Planning Profession', in *British Town Planning: The Formative Years*, ed. Anthony Sutcliffe, 1981, pp. 72–5. There are some interesting words on the lack of interest in town planning shown by English Victorian architects in Lionel Esher, *A Broken Wave*, 1981, pp. 275–6, but they lack any sense of the profession's economic impotence.

NOTES TO CHAPTER FOUR

1. *AIA Journal* 8, 1920, p. 125; Albert Farwell Bemis, *The Evolving House*, vol. 2, 1934, p. 334.

2. Talbot Hamlin, *Benjamin Henry Latrobe*, 1955, p. 149.

3. On Wight see now Sarah Bradford Landau, *P. B. Wight: Architect, Contractor and Critic, 1838–1925*, exhibition catalogue, 1981, esp. pp. 44–50.

4. Quotation from Robert D. Andrews writing in *Architectural Review* (Boston), Nov. 1917, cited by Whea-ton A. Holden in *JSAH* 32, May 1973, p. 115.

5. William Haber, *Industrial Relations in the Building Industry*, 1930, p. 531.

6. Esther McCoy, *Five California Architects*, 1975, p. 150.

7. On the George A. Fuller Company and Starrett Brothers, see especially W. A. Starrett, *Skyscrapers and the Men Who Build Them*, 1928, and Paul Starrett, *Changing the Skyline*, 1938; on the Thompson-Starrett Company: Louis J. Horowitz and Boyden Sparkes, *The Towers of New York*, 1937; on Norcross: James F. O'Gorman in *JSAH* 32, May 1973, pp. 104–13; on Todd, Robertson and Todd: Carol Krinsky, *Rockefeller Center*, 1978, and Walter H. Kilham junior, *Raymond Hood, Architect*, 1973; on Hegeman-Harris: *Design and Construction* 6, 1936–7, p. 218.

8. Asher Benjamin, *Practice of Architecture*, 1823, cited in Allen Chamberlain, *Beacon Hill*, 1925, p. 274. On Bulfinch, see especially Ellen Susan Bulfinch, *The Life and Letters of Charles Bulfinch Architect*, 1896, and Harold Kirker, *The Architecture of Charles Bulfinch*, 1969.

9. Chamberlain, *op. cit.*, pp. 58–60 and 273–5; Walter Muir Whitehill, *Boston, A Topographical History*, 1968 edition, pp. 60–6.

10. Chamberlain, *op. cit.*, pp. 273–91.

11. Walter M. Whitehill in Marvin E. Goody and Robert P. Walsh, *Boston Society of Architects, The First Hundred Years*, 1967, pp. 18–19; see also Bainbridge Bunting, *Houses of Boston's Back Bay*, 1967, pp. 160, 473.

12. Margaret Supplee Smith, 'Between City and Suburb: Architecture and Planning in Boston's South End', PhD, Brown University, 1976, Ch. 4, cites particularly the developments of Charles Kirby and Nathaniel J. Bradlee.

13. Bunting, *op. cit.*, p. 162.

14. *Ibid.*, pp. 163–4; Whitehill in Goody and Walsh, *op. cit.*, pp. 19–28.

15. Whitehill in Goody and Walsh, *op. cit.*, p. 52, citing Walter H. Kilham.

16. On the McCombs, see Agnes Addison Gilchrist in *JSAH* 28, Oct. 1969, pp. 201–10 and 31, March 1972, pp. 10–21. For the nomenclature of early builders, surveyors, housesmiths, architects etc., in New York, see the advertisements reprinted in Rita Susswein Gottesman, *The Arts and Crafts in New York*, 3 vols., 1938, 1948 and 1965.

17. *The Autobiography of James Gallier*, 1864, p. 18, cited in Jacob Landy, *The Architecture of Minard Lafever*, 1970, pp. 52–3.

18. Gallier, *op. cit.*, pp. 18–19, cited in Landy, *op. cit.*, p. 49.

19. Roger Hale Newton, *Town and Davis Architects*, 1942, pp. 91–2.

20. *Ibid.*, p. 95.

21. *Ibid.*, Chs. 2 and 3.

22. *Ibid.*, pp. 101–5; Everard M. Upjohn, *Richard Upjohn Architect and Churchman*, 1939, pp. 157–8.

23. Allan Nevins and M. H. Thomas, *The Diary of George Templeton Strong*, 1952, vol. 1, pp. 292–3.

24. Phoebe B. Stanton, *The Gothic Revival and American Church Architecture*, 1968, pp. 159–78.

25. Upjohn, *op. cit.*, Chs. 2, 3 and 7.

26. On the founding and early history of the AIA, see Upjohn, *op. cit.*, pp. 157–73; Stanton, *op. cit.*, pp. 320–4; Paul R. Baker, *Richard Morris Hunt*, 1980, pp. 108–17.

27. On Hunt, see now Baker, *op. cit.*

28. See particularly Arthur Clason Weatherhead, *The History of Collegiate Education in Architecture in the United States*, 1941; Theodore K. Rohdenburg, *A History of the School of Architecture, Columbia University*, 1954; Caroline Shillaber, *Massachusetts Institute of Technology School of Architecture and Planning 1861–1961*, 1963.

29. Baker, *op. cit.*, e.g. pp. 82–7, 210–13, 383–8.

30. Glenn Brown, *Memories 1860–1930*, 1931, p. 26.

31. Charles Moore, *The Life and Times of Charles Follen McKim*, 1929, p. 59.

32. Charles C. Baldwin, *Stanford White*, 1931, p. 362.

33. Moore, *op. cit.*, pp. 281–2.

34. John Jay Chapman, cited in Charles Moore's article on Stanford White in the *Dictionary of American Biography*.

35. Paul Starrett, *Changing the Skyline*, 1938, p. 110.

36. *Dictionary of American Biography*, *sub* Stanford White.

37. Glenn Brown, *op. cit.*, p. 203.

38. *Inland Architect and Builder* 6, Nov. 1885, p. 49; *American Architect and Building News*, 12 Feb. 1887, pp. 76–7.

39. Paul Bourget, cited by Montgomery Schuyler, *American Architecture and Other Writings*, ed. Jordy and Coe, 1961, vol. 2, p. 382.

40. Schuyler, *ibid.*, p. 407.

41. Charles Moore, *Daniel H. Burnham*, 2 vols., 1921; Thomas S. Hines, *Burnham of Chicago*, 1974. On Root, see Donald Hoffmann, *The Architecture of John Wellborn Root*, 1973.

42. Susan Beattie, *A Revolution in London Housing*, 1980, n. 110, p. 123.

43. Louis Sullivan, *The Autobiography of an Idea*, 1956 edition, p. 291.

44. Hines, *op. cit.*, p. 82, citing Harriet Monroe's biography of Root.

45. Paul Starrett, *Changing the Skyline*, 1938, p. 29.

46. Hines, *op. cit.*, p. 236.

47. Grant Carpenter Manson, *Frank Lloyd Wright to 1910*, 1958, pp. 21–34, analyses the work done by Wright for Adler and Sullivan; David Gebhard in *JSAH* 19, 1960, pp. 62–8, discusses Sullivan's relationship with Elmslie.

48. Claude Bragdon, *More Lives than One*, 1938, p. 157.

49. Frank Lloyd Wright, *An Autobiography*, 1932 edition, p. 266.

50. Bragdon, *op. cit.*, pp. 150–1.

51. On the idealist intellectual heritage of Adler and Sullivan, see Sherman Paul, *Louis Sullivan, An Architect in American Thought*, 1962, Chs. 1 and 2.

52. Wright, *op. cit.*, pp. 260–6.

53. *American Architect and Building News*, 29 Nov. 1884, pp. 255–6.

54. On early meetings of the Western Association of Architects and the Illinois State Association of Architects, see *The Inland Architect and Builder*, 1884–5, *passim*, and *American Architect and Building News*, 29 Nov. 1884, pp. 255–6.

55. *The Inland Architect and Builder* 5, Feb. 1885, p. 6.

56. *Ibid.* 6, Nov. 1885, p. 53.

57. *Ibid.* 6, Nov. 1885, esp. pp. 70–83.

58. Turpin C. Bannister, *The Architect at Mid-Century*, 1954, vol. 1, p. 356. For registration in Germany, see Herbert Ricken, *Der Architekt*, 1977.

59. *American Architect and Building News*, 7 Aug. 1897, p. 49; 18 Sept. 1897, pp. 94–6; 9 Apr. 1898, p. 11; 14 Jan. 1899, p. 10; *Inland Architect and News Record* 29, July 1897, pp. 51–2.

60. Bannister, *op. cit.*, p. 357.

61. On the preliminary steps to unification of the WAA and the ISAA, see *Inland Architect and News Record*, 1887–8, *passim*.

62. *Inland Architect and News Record* 10, Oct. 1887, p. 35.

63. Sherman Paul, *Louis Sullivan, An Architect in American Thought*, 1962, pp. 54–7; H. Allen Brooks, *The Prairie School*, 1972, pp. 37–42.

64. On the supervising architects up to 1876 see particularly the excellent articles by Lawrence Wodehouse in *JSAH* 25, Dec. 1966, pp. 268–80 (Ammi Burnham Young); 31, March 1972, pp. 22–37 (Alfred B. Mullett); 32, May 1973, pp. 175–92 (W. A. Potter).

65. *JSAH* 25, Dec. 1966, p. 279.

66. *JSAH* 31, March 1972, p. 34.

67. Glenn Brown, *Memories 1860–1930*, 1931, p. 205.

68. Lawrence Wodehouse in *JSAH* 32, May 1973, p. 180, recounts how in 1879, during the completion of a Post Office designed by Potter for Fall River, Mass., Hill allegedly 'had no ear for detail' because 'Mr Mason by the connivance of Mr Avery and the Clerk had provided a beautiful young girl for him.'

69. *AIA Proceedings* 1885, pp. 29–40, summarizes the history of measures up to that date.

70. The history of the furore over the Tarsney Act is set out most fully in Charles Moore, *Daniel H. Burnham*, 1921, vol. 1, pp. 95–116. See also Glenn Brown, *op. cit.*, pp. 206–10; Thomas S. Hines, *Burnham of Chicago*, 1974, pp. 125–33.

71. *American Architect and Building News*, 7 Apr. 1894, pp. 2–12.

72. *Inland Architect and News Record* 30, Nov. 1897, p. 36.

73. *Ibid.* 30, Nov. 1897, pp. 37–8.

74. *The American Architect*, 14 Aug. 1912, pp. 53–7.

75. William Lescaze, *On Being an Architect*, 1943, pp. 62–3.

76. *The American Architect*, 14 Aug. 1912, pp. 53–7; 28 Aug. 1912, pp. 73–7; 2 Oct. 1912, pp. 117–20; Moore, *op. cit.*, pp. 106–13.

77. *Inland Architect and News Record* 12, Nov. 1888, p. 66.

78. See notably Tom Wolfe's clever *From Bauhaus to Our House*, 1981.

NOTES TO CHAPTER FIVE

1. *The Builder* was founded by J. A. Hansom in 1842; George Godwin became editor in 1844. After this and the *Architectural Magazine*, the third but less significant pioneer of the British building press was the *Civil Engineer and Architect's Journal* (1837–67). Godwin's role in establishing the character of British architectural journalism is discussed by Anthony D. King, *Architectural History* 19, 1967, pp. 32–53; for the original, Owenite ambitions of *The Builder*, see now Michael Brooks in *Victorian Periodicals Review* 14, no. 3, 1981, pp. 87–93.

2. For the history of the early *Architectural Review*, see N. Pevsner, *AR* 138, 1965, pp. 259–64, reprinted in Alastair Service, *Edwardian Architecture and its Origins*, 1975, pp. 473–83.

3. I am greatly indebted to Creswell's daughter, Mrs Elizabeth Fish, for many details about her father's career. Besides the obituaries in *The Builder*, 15 July 1960, p. 108 and in the RIBA biography files, his reminiscences in *ABN*, 11 Aug. 1955, pp. 172–3 and in *AR* 124, 1958, pp. 403–5 (the latter reprinted in Alastair Service, *Edwardian Architecture and its Origins*, 1975, pp. 328–37) supply much valuable information.

4. *AR* 124, 1958, p. 403, reprinted in Service, *op. cit.*, pp. 329–30.

5. Creswell's most interesting pieces of early journalism are in *AR* 2, 1897, pp. 23–32 (essay on Nesfield), and *AR* 4, 1898, p. 178 ('The Duty of Vulgarity'). For his views on pubs and lavatories, see *The Builder*, 17 Nov. 1898, p. 461.

6. For Queensferry, see *The Builder*, 13 July 1901, p. 34 and 1 Dec. 1906, p. 634; also N. Pevsner in *AR* 91, 1942, p. 109.

7. *AJ*, 18 Apr. 1923, p. 699; see also Creswell in *Architectural Association Journal*, June 1940, p. 9.

8. See obituaries in n.3 and *Who's Who in Architecture*, 1923 edition.

9. The name was at first 'Karsish'. A piece on Pecksniff appeared in *AJ*, 9 and 16 March 1921, pp. 285–7 and 313–14, and the first 'causerie' in *AJ*, 16 Aug. 1922, pp. 207–8. His articles in the *Architect and Building News* were mainly written after those in the *Architects' Journal* and include some of his best pieces, e.g. 'A Dispassionate View of Regent Street' (1 July 1927), an article on architectural writing (7 Feb. 1930), and an interesting account of his visit to America (21 and 28 March 1941).

10. *AJ*, 28 March 1923, p. 555.

11. *The Honeywood File* runs from 6 March to 6 Nov. 1929; *Tribulations of Early Practice* begins on 7 July 1926 and ends on 30 March 1927.

12. *Jago v. Swillerton and Toomer* actually preceded *The Honeywood Settlement*, running from 8 Jan. to 5 March 1930. The latter, at first called *Settling-Up Honeywood*, ran from 28 May to 22 Oct. 1930.

13. Of Creswell's other novels only *Diary from a Dustbin* (1935), a sinister tale about the adventures of a late Victorian builder's bookkeeper, Mervyn Spinnerbrook, is not in some sense architectural. *Grig* (1942) collects further episodes 'extracted from the journal of John

Grigblay, Builder' which first appeared in *ABN*, 15 March 1940 to 7 Feb. 1941. It was followed by *Grig in Retirement* (1943), collected from *ABN*, 11 Apr. 1941 to 3 Apr. 1942. More vigorous but never published in book form was *Monty*, the saga of Montague Trass, O.B.E., Hon. A.R.I.B.A., an ex-architect who becomes chairman of Grierleys, an old-established brewery famous for its 'double G.G.' but now committed to 'public house betterment'. The ups and downs of Monty's pub-building programme appeared weekly in *ABN*, 7 Aug. 1942 to 10 Sept. 1943.

14. This was the last of the series in the *Architects' Journal*, published between 27 May and 28 Oct. 1931.

15. *AJ*, 25 Nov. 1931, p. 714.

16. Compare episodes in *AJ*, 3 and 10 June 1931, with *ABN*, 11 Aug. 1955, pp. 172–3 and *AR* 124, 1958, p. 403.

17. *AJ*, 17 June 1931, p. 852.

18. *AJ*, 7 Oct. 1931, p. 469.

19. *AJ*, 21 Oct. 1931, p. 531.

20. *AJ*, 28 Oct. 1931, p. 561.

21. Clough Williams-Ellis's third, posthumously published volume of memoirs is *Around the World in Ninety Years*, 1978.

22. Clough Williams-Ellis, *The Architect*, 1929, pp. 21–2, or *Architect Errant*, 1971, p. 12.

23. *The Architect*, p. 75; variant in *Architect Errant*, p. 65.

24. *The Architect*, p. 81, or *Architect Errant*, p. 69.

25. *The Architect*, p. 162.

26. *Architect Errant*, pp. 183–9.

27. *The D. I. A. Cautionary Guide to St Albans*, 1929, pp. 2–3.

28. Clough and Amabel Williams-Ellis, *The Pleasures of Architecture*, 1924, p. 99.

29. *Ibid.*, p. 235.

30. *Ibid.*, pp. 151–2.

31. *Ibid.*, pp. 174–5.

32. Clough Williams-Ellis, *The Architect*, 1929, p. 147, or *The Adventure of Building*, 1946, p. 79.

33. *The Architect*, pp. 145–6, or *The Adventure of Building*, pp. 78–9.

34. *The Adventure of Building*, p. 87.

35. *Ibid.*, p. 89.

36. Clough Williams-Ellis, *England and the Octopus*, 1930, p. 139.

37. *Ibid.*, p. 154.

38. *Ibid.*, pp. 43–4.

39. Here as elsewhere in this section I have followed Anthony Jackson's admirable *The Politics of Architecture*, 1970, esp. pp. 55–77, 161–3. See also the young John Summerson's interesting 'Bread and Butter in Architecture' in *Horizon* 6, Oct. 1942, pp. 233–43; and Peter Coe and Malcolm Reading, *Lubetkin and Tecton: Architecture and Social Commitment*, 1981, pp. 51ff., 69–74.

NOTES TO CHAPTER SIX

Wherever possible, the references in this chapter have been restricted to English language sources.

1. For The Architects Collaborative, see *The Architects*

Collaborative 1945–1965, ed. Walter Gropius *et al.*, 1966; Bernard Michael Boyle in *The Architect*, ed. Spiro Kostof, 1977, pp. 335–7.

2. See especially Walter Gropius, *Scope of Total Architecture*, 1955, and *Apollo in the Democracy*, 1968.

3. Alma Mahler Werfel, *And The Bridge is Love*, 1958, pp. 51–3, 84–91.

4. *AR* 133, 1963, p. 167.

5. Arthur Clason Weatherhead, *The History of Collegiate Education in Architecture in the United States*, 1941, pp. 59–62, 239.

6. See *The Architect at Mid-Century*, ed. Turpin C. Banister, 1954, vol. 1, pp. 106–7.

7. See e.g. Walter Gropius, *Apollo in the Democracy*, 1968, pp. 43–55, 59–67, 71–9.

8. Walter Gropius, *The New Architecture and the Bauhaus*, 1965 edition, pp. 53–4, echoed in *Apollo in the Democracy*, 1968, pp. 28ff.

9. Joan Campbell, *The German Werkbund*, 1978, pp. 9–32.

10. Marcel Franciscono, *Walter Gropius and the Creation of the Bauhaus in Weimar*, 1971, Ch. 1, esp. pp. 25–39; N. Pevsner in *AR* 133, 1963, pp. 165–8.

11. Franciscono, *op. cit.*, pp. 70–8; see also Campbell, *op. cit.*, pp. 57–81.

12. *AR* 134, 1963, p. 6, replying to Pevsner, *ibid.*, 133, 1963, pp. 165–8.

13. Translated in *AR* 130, 1961, pp. 49–51.

14. Walter Gropius, *The New Architecture and the Bauhaus*, 1965 edition, pp. 51–2, and in *AR* 134, 1963, p. 6; Hans M. Wingler, *The Bauhaus*, English edition, 1969, p. 21.

15. Alma Mahler Werfel, *And The Bridge is Love*, 1958, p. 84.

16. Sigfried Giedion, *Walter Gropius, Work and Teamwork*, 1954, p. 9.

17. Quoted by Kurt Junghanns in *Socialismo, città, architettura URSS 1917–1937*, ed. Manfredo Tafuri, 1971, pp. 277–88.

18. Quoted in Franciscono, *op. cit.*, pp. 69–70.

19. *Ibid.*, esp. Ch. 3, pp. 88–106.

20. *Ibid.*, pp. 13–25, 64–70, 127–52.

21. Walter Gropius, *The New Architecture and the Bauhaus*, 1965 edition, p. 48.

22. Franciscono, *op. cit.*, pp. 159–72; Wingler, *op. cit.*, pp. 385–8. For this period of the Bauhaus, see also Joseph Rykwert, *The Necessity of Artifice*, 1982, pp. 44–9.

23. For the garlic see Werfel, *op. cit.*, pp. 142–3; 'Inflation Saints' was a term coined by the novelist Theodore Plievier, quoted by John Willett, *Art and Politics in the Weimar Period*, 1978, p. 80.

24. Barbara Miller Lane, *Architecture and Politics in Germany, 1918–1945*, 1968, pp. 69–86.

25. *AR* 144, 1968, p. 192.

26. Wingler, *op. cit.*, pp. 66, 385–8.

27. *Ibid.*, pp. 385–8; *AR* 134, 1963, p. 6.

28. Willett, *op. cit.*, pp. 124–7; Lane, *op. cit.*, pp. 87–124; Wingler, *op. cit.*, p. 239; for May, see Justus Buekschmitt, *Ernst May*, 1963, pp. 33–57.

29. Walter Gropius, *The New Architecture and the Bauhaus*,

1965 edition, p. 96.

39. Wingler, *op. cit.*, pp. 124–5, 240–1.

31. Willett, *op. cit.*, p. 118.

32. Wingler, *op. cit.*, pp. 414–18.

33. Willett, *op. cit.*, p. 120; Claude Schnaidt, *Hannes Meyer*, 1965, introduction p. 41; Wingler, *op. cit.*, p. 427.

34. Schnaidt, *op. cit.*, gives the fullest account of Hannes Meyer's career.

35. *Ibid.*, introduction pp. 9, 19–21, text pp. 5–15.

36. *Ibid.*, introduction p. 41; the 'New World' article from *ABC* is reprinted in the main text, pp. 90–5.

37. Wingler, *op. cit.*, pp. 414–17, 493, 495; Schnaidt, *op. cit.*, pp. 38–53.

38. Wingler, *op. cit.*, pp. 136–7, 141.

39. Schnaidt, *op. cit.*, text pp. 121–3.

40. Walter Gropius, *The New Architecture and the Bauhaus*, 1965 edition, pp. 80–1.

41. Wingler, *op. cit.*, pp. 151, 159, 496, 501–3; Schnaidt, *op. cit.*, introduction pp. 43–51, text pp. 107–13.

42. Wingler, *op. cit.*, pp. 153–4; Schnaidt, *op. cit.*, text pp. 94–101.

43. Willett, *op. cit.*, p. 187.

44. Schnaidt, *op. cit.*, text pp. 103–5, and for Meyer's expulsion, introduction p. 51; the full texts of Meyer's letters are given also in Wingler, *op. cit.*, pp. 163–5.

45. Schnaidt, *op. cit.*, text p. 123.

46. John W. Cook and Heinrich Klotz, *Conversations with Architects*, 1973, p. 37.

47. Schnaidt, *op. cit.*, text p. 123.

48. Wingler, *op. cit.*, 168–9, 175–6.

49. *Ibid.*, pp. 179 ff.

50. For the German migration to Russia see now principally Christian Borngräber in *Architectural Association Quarterly* 11 (1), 1979, pp. 50–62. Hans Schmidt's accounts of the experiences of German-speaking architects in Russia may be found in his *Beiträge zur Architektur 1924–1964*, 1965, pp. 82–120; in *Wissenschaftliche Zeitschrift der Humboldt-Universität zu Berlin, Gesellschafts- und Sprachwissenschaftliche Reihe* 16, 1967, 3, pp. 383–400: and in *Socialismo, città, architettura URSS 1919–1937*, ed. M. Tafuri, 1971, pp. 257–72. For further information see Schnaidt, *op. cit.*; Tafuri, *op. cit.*; the articles appended by Ulrich Conrads to his edition of El Lissitzky's *Russia: An Architecture for World Revolution*, trans. Dluhosch, 1970, pp. 155–229; and (with caution) Rudolf Wolters, *Spezialist in Sibirien*, 1933.

51. Borngräber, *op. cit.*, pp. 53–6; Lissitzky, ed. Conrads, *op. cit.*, pp. 173–9, 188–203; *Mart Stam, Documentation of his Work, 1920–65*, RIBA Publications 1970, pp. 24–9.

52. Borngräber, *op. cit.*, pp. 55–8.

53. *Ibid.*, p. 55.

54. Tafuri, *op. cit.*, pp. 264, 296; Schnaidt, *op. cit.*, introduction p. 13; Lissitzky, ed. Conrads, *op. cit.*, pp. 12–13; Borngräber, *op. cit.*, p. 59.

55. Among Wolters's later productions were a short biography of Speer (1943) and a book published in Prague on the 'new German architecture' (1943).

56. Lissitzky, ed. Conrads, *op. cit.*, p. 183.

57. For 'urbanism' versus 'de-urbanism' in Russia see Anatole Kopp, *Town and Revolution*, 1970, Ch. 8.

58. V. Khazanova in O. A. Shvidkovsky, *Building in the USSR*, 1971, pp. 31–4; S. Frederick Starr, *Melnikov*, 1978, pp. 64–7; Kopp, *op. cit.*, p. 77; Willett, *op. cit.*, pp. 38–9.

59. On OSA and Asnova see Starr, *op. cit.*, pp. 114–17; Willett, *op. cit.*, pp. 130–1. Kopp, *op. cit.*, pp. 86–95, 126–44, is concerned to emphasize the responsibility of OSA's attitudes and perhaps unfairly denigrates VOPRA in its earliest manifestation.

60. Starr, *op. cit.*, p. 149.

61. *Ibid.*, Ch. 8, *passim*; Kopp, *op. cit.*, pp. 211–14.

62. See Schmidt in Tafuri, *op. cit.*, pp. 257–63; Kopp, *op. cit.*, p. 14; Starr, *op. cit.*, pp. 135–6, 157–60; Borngräber, *op. cit.*, pp. 50–2; Sigfried Giedion, *Walter Gropius, Work and Teamwork*, 1954, pp. 65, 153–7; Grant Hildebrand, *Designing for Industry: The Architecture of Albert Kahn*, 1974, pp. 129–32; Arnold Whittick, *Erich Mendelsohn*, 1956 edition, pp. 71, 86.

63. For Gropius's reaction to developments in Russia see *AR* 131, 1962, p. 163; for the CIAM decision and the foreigners' protest, Schmidt in Tafuri, *op. cit.*, p. 257.

64. For Taut, see Kurt Junghanns, *Bruno Taut 1880–1938*, 1970, pp. 89–92; for Lurçat, Bruno Cassetti in Tafuri, *op. cit.*, pp. 195–216.

65. Starr, *op. cit.*, pp. 220–5.

66. Borngräber, *op. cit.*, pp. 54–5; Lissitzky, ed. Conrads, *op. cit.*, pp. 184–7.

67. *Task* (Cambridge, Mass.) 3, 1942, pp. 29–30 (from Meyer's article *The Soviet Architect*); compare remarks by Hans Schmidt in *Wissenschaftliche Zeitschrift . . .* (see n. 50), p. 398.

68. Schmidt in Tafuri, *op. cit.*, pp. 270–2.

69. *Task* 3, 1942, p. 24.

70. Kurt Junghanns, *Bruno Taut 1880–1938*, 1970, pp. 92ff.; Justus Buekschmitt, *Ernst May*, 1963, pp. 79–107; *Mart Stam, Documentation of his Work 1920–1965*, RIBA Publications 1970, pp. 30–3; Hans Schmidt, *Beiträge zur Architektur 1924–1964*, 1965. For the honour in which Schmidt is held see *Deutsche Architektur*, 12, 1963, pp. 700–4 and *Architektur der DDR*, 27, 1978, pp. 762–5.

71. Schnaidt, *op. cit.*, introduction pp. 33–7.

72. Translated in *Task* 3, 1942, pp. 24–32. The original appeared in Spanish. Neither this nor the English version is easily available, but an Italian translation appears in Hannes Meyer, *Architettura o Rivoluzione: Scritti 1921–42*, 1969, pp. 191–211.

73. *Task* 3, 1942, p. 24.

74. *AR* 134, 1963, p. 6.

75. John W. Cook and Heinrich Klotz, *Conversations with Architects*, 1973, p. 38.

NOTES TO CHAPTER SEVEN

The first part of this chapter is intended to supplement Barrington Kaye's *The Development of the Architectural Profession in Britain*, 1960; the latter portion, on the United States, follows on from Turpin C. Bannister, *The Architect at Mid-Century*, 2 vols., 1954. The second half of the chapter is particularly incomplete, and is best read in conjunction with the excellent analysis of the American profession over the past thirty years by Bernard Michael Boyle in *The Architect*, ed. Spiro Kostof, 1977, pp. 309–44.

1. *RIBA Journal* 81, Dec. 1974, p. 4.

2. This account of Poulson's career draws heavily upon Martin Tomkinson and Michael Gillard, *Nothing to Declare: The Political Corruptions of John Poulson*, 1980, supplemented by the following sources: *Private Eye*, 24 Apr., 8 and 22 May 1970; 30 June, 8 and 22 Sep., 6 Oct. 1972; 9 and 23 Feb., 27 July 1973; *The Times*, 30 Jan. 1973; 12 Feb., 15 and 16 March 1974; *RIBA Journal* 80, Feb. 1973, pp. 63–5; *Building*, 15 Feb. 1974, pp. 56–7.

3. Tomkinson and Gillard, *op. cit.*, pp. 4–5.

4. *Ibid.*, pp. 8–16, 43–6, 96ff.

5. *Ibid.*, p. 12.

6. *Ibid.*, pp. 16–17, 96–8.

7. *Ibid.*, *passim*, esp. pp. 102–10, 199–213.

8. *Ibid.*, pp. 120–4 (Mocamedes), pp. 150–3 (bankruptcy).

9. *Ibid.*, p. 29.

10. *Ibid.*, p. 153; see also pp. 29–42.

11. *RIBA Journal* 80, Feb. 1973, p. 65.

12. *Ibid.* 81, Dec. 1974, p. 4.

13. *Ibid.* 82, March 1975, p. 24.

14. *The Architect and His Office*, 1962, sec. 2, pp. 27–65, esp. pp. 27, 29.

15. *Ibid.*, sec. 4, summary of findings, p. 101.

16. *Ibid.*, pp. 45ff., esp. diagram, p. 47.

17. *Ibid.*, sec. 2.127–8, pp. 49–50.

18. *Ibid.*, summary of secs. 2–6.

19. Oliver Marriott, *The Property Boom*, 1967, p. 27.

20. *Evening Standard*, 22 June 1965.

21. *Sunday Times Magazine*, 13 Feb. 1972, p. 21.

22. Marriott, *op. cit.*, pp. 110–18.

23. *Time Out*, 6–12 July 1973.

24. *Building*, 10 Feb. 1967, pp. 94–6.

25. *Sunday Times Magazine*, 13 Feb. 1972, p. 21.

26. *Building*, 21 Feb. 1975, pp. 74–6.

27. *Ibid.*, 10 Feb. 1967, pp. 94–6.

28. Brunton, Baden Hellyard and Boobyer, *Management Applied to Architectural Practice*, 1964, p. 100.

29. *RIBA Journal* 67, May 1960, pp. 251–64, esp. pp. 256, 261.

30. *Ibid.* 75, Oct. 1968, p. 450.

31. Monopolies and Mergers Commission, *Architects' Services*, 1977, para. 30 and table 10.

32. On architects' earnings and fees, see e.g. *RIBA Journal* 66, Apr. 1960, pp. 195ff.; *Earnings of Architects and their Support Staff*, RIBA Survey, 1970, 9.1–4 and 10.2; Monopolies and Mergers' Commission, *op. cit.*, paras. 34–60.

Monopolies and Mergers Commission, *op. cit.*, paras. *passim*, and paras. 271–2, 282.

34. See e.g. *Building*, 24 Oct. 1975, p. 43 and 13 Feb, 1976, pp. 62–3.

35. *RIBA Journal* 82, June 1975, pp. 10–12.

36. Earlier groups representing salaried staff included the Architects and Technicians Organization and the Association of Architects, Surveyors and Technical Assistants (later the Association of Building Technicians). See esp. Anthony Jackson, *The Politics of Architecture*, 1970, pp. 68–71, 76, 161.

37. *RIBA Journal* 79, May 1972, p. 199.

38. *Ibid.* 80, Sep. 1973, pp. 395–403; on local authority departments, see further George Oldham, *ibid.* 80, May 1973, pp. 232–4 and Gordon Wigglesworth in *AJ*, 21 Feb. 1973, pp. 430–1.

39. On recent developments, see e.g. *The Guardian*, 8 Aug. 1980.

40. Malcolm MacEwen, *Crisis in Architecture*, 1974, *passim*; his revised views of 1977 were presented in *Building*, 14 Oct. 1977, pp. 109–10.

41. New Architecture Movement, *Do Not Pass Go . . . Do Not Collect 6%*, 1977, p. 19.

42. For the history of ARCUK, see Barrington Kaye, *The Development of the Architectural Profession in Britain*, 1960, pp. 151–6; New Architecture Movement, *Way Ahead – A New Fee System for Architects*, 1978, Appendix 5.

43. New Architecture Movement, *Handbook 1978–9; Do Not Pass Go . . .* (see n. 41), 1977, Appendix.

44. For Portman's career see John Portman and Jonathan Barnett, *The Architect as Developer*, 1976, pp. 23ff.; James Starbuck, *John Portman: An Introduction and Bibliography*, 1974.

45. Portman and Barnett, *op. cit.*, pp. 22–43.

46. *Ibid.*, pp. 43–52; for the 'Great Park', I am grateful for information from Robert Thorne.

47. Portman and Barnett, *op. cit.*, pp. 22–52.

48. *Ibid.*, p. 135.

49. *Ibid.*, p. 136.

50. *Fortune Magazine*, Nov. 1971.

51. William Wayne Caudill, *Architecture by Team*, 1971, p. 63; Thomas Obermeyer, *Architectural Technology*, 1976, p. 5.

52. Bernard Michael Boyle in *The Architect*, ed. Spiro Kostof, 1977, p. 318; see also G. Brino, *La professione dell'architetto in USA*, 1968, Ch. 4.

53. Brino, *op. cit.*, Ch. 5, pp. 54–62.

54. John W. Cook and Heinrich W. Klotz, *Conversations with Architects*, 1973, p. 23.

55. August E. Komendant, *18 Years with Architect Louis I. Kahn*, 1975, pp. 130–1, 185.

56. Robert Goodman, *After the Planners*, 1971, p. 113.

57. *Ibid.*, p. 118.

58. Royal Barry Wills, *This Business of Architecture*, 1941, Ch. 3 ('Stalking and Capture of Clients').

59. Morris Lapidus, *Architecture: A Profession and a Business*, 1967, esp. pp. 12–16, 53–64.

60. Wendell E. Rossmann, *The Effective Architect*, 1972, pp. 36–47, 122–32.

61. *Ibid.*, p. 135.

62. *Ibid.*, p. 123.

63. William Wayne Caudill, *Architecture by Team*, 1971, esp. pp. 10–20, 137ff., 296, 298.

64. *Ibid.*, pp. 31–3.

65. Weld Coxe, *Marketing Architectural and Engineering Services*, 1971, *passim*, esp. pp. 26, 73–9; Gerre L. Jones, *How to Market Professional Design Services*, 1973, *passim*, esp. pp. 200–4.

66. Jones, *op. cit.*, pp. 101, 165–90.

67. *AIA Journal* 65, Jan. 1976, pp. 46–7.

68. Brino, *op. cit.*, Chs. 6 and 7.

69. On the development of the AIA code see Coxe, *op. cit.*, pp. 11–18 and *AIA Journal* 67, Dec. 1978, pp. 55–7.

70. *Building, U.S.A.*, Architectural Forum ed., 1957, pp. 131, 141.

71. Brino, *op. cit.*, Ch. 7; C. W. Griffin, *Development Building: The Team Approach*, 1972, p. 102.

72. *AIA Journal* 63, June 1974, p. 37.

73. *RIBA Journal* 84, Sept. 1977, p. 395.

74. *Architectural Record* 164, July 1978, pp. 55–7; *AIA Journal* 68, May 1979, pp. 48–55.

75. Coxe, *op. cit.*, pp. 10–11. The implications of *Goldfarb v. Virginia State Bar* (1975) are examined in *Progressive Architecture* 58, March 1977, p. 84; and of *Bates et al. v. State Bar of Arizona* (1977) in *Architectural Record* 163, Jan. 1978, pp. 55–7. A further Supreme Court decision of 1978 relating to engineers put yet more pressure on architects.

76. *AIA Journal* 66, Sept. 1977, p. 8.

77. *Ibid.* 68, Aug. 1979, p. 21.

78. Bernard Michael Boyle in *The Architect*, ed. Spiro Kostof, 1977, p. 330.

79. *Ibid.*, p. 328.

INDEX

Note: numbers in italics refer to illustrations or captions, by page number.